THE CHALLENGE OF TED HUGHES

The Challenge of
Ted Hughes

Edited by

Keith Sagar
Reader in English Literature
University of Manchester

St. Martin's Press

First published in Great Britain 1994 by
THE MACMILLAN PRESS LTD
Houndmills, Basingstoke, Hampshire RG21 2XS
and London
Companies and representatives
throughout the world

A catalogue record for this book is available
from the British Library.

ISBN 0–333–61063–6

Printed in Great Britain by
Ipswich Book Co Ltd
Ipswich, Suffolk

First published in the United States of America 1994 by
Scholarly and Reference Division,
ST. MARTIN'S PRESS, INC.,
175 Fifth Avenue,
New York, N.Y. 10010

ISBN 0–312–12054–0

Library of Congress Cataloging-in-Publication Data
The Challenge of Ted Hughes / edited by Keith Sagar.
p. cm.
Includes bibliographical references and index.
ISBN 0–312–12054–0
1. Hughes, Ted, 1930– —Criticism and interpretation.
I. Sagar, Keith M.
PR6058.U37Z633 1994
821'.914—dc20   93–39883
                                                          CIP

One of the great problems that poetry works at is to renew life, renew the poet's own life, and, by implication, renew the life of the people, if they respond to the way he has done it for himself.

(Ted Hughes in an interview with Amzed Hossein, 1989)

Contents

Acknowledgements

The editor, contributors and publishers are grateful to the following for permission to use copyright material: Faber & Faber Ltd for quotations from the works of Ted Hughes published by them – *The Hawk in the Rain* ©1957; *Luperal* ©1960; *Wodwo* ©1967; *Crow* ©1970; *Gaudete* ©1977; *Cave Birds* ©1978; *Remains of Elmet* ©1979; *Moortown* ©1979; *River* ©1983; *Wolfwatching* ©1989; Harper & Row Publishers, Inc. for quotations from the works of Ted Hughes published by them in the USA – *The Hawk in the Rain* ©1957; *Lupercal* ©1960; *Wodwo* ©1967; *Crow* ©1970; *Gaudete* ©1977; *Remains of Elmet* ©1979; *Moortown* ©1979; *River* ©1983; *Wolfwatching* ©1990; Viking Press for the US edition of *Cave Birds* ©1978; Olwyn Hughes for all previously unpublished or uncollected material by Ted Hughes; Macmillan Inc. for quotations from *The Collected Letters of Dylan Thomas* ©1985.

An early version of Chapter 6 appeared as 'Ted Hughes and Women' in *British Poetry since 1960*, O'Gorman and Orr (eds) (Penkevill, 1991).

Notes on the Contributors

Nathalie Anderson teaches at Swarthmore College, Pennsylvania. Her PhD was on the use of myth in Hughes and Heaney.

Nicholas Bishop is the author of the recently published *Remaking Poetry: Ted Hughes and a New Critical Psychology*, his first book.

Rand Brandes is Associate Professor of English, Lenoir-Rhyne College; he is the author of *Behind the Bestiaries: The Poetry of D. H. Lawrence and Ted Hughes*; and co-author of *Seamus Heaney: An Annotated Bibliography*.

Alexander Davis is Lecturer in English at University College, Cork; at present he is working on a study of Ted Hughes.

Roger Elkin is Section Head of Continuing Education at Leek College; he was formerly the Editor of *Prospice*, and has been the recipient of several awards for poetry, including his first collection, *Pricking Out*.

Terry Gifford teaches at Bretton Hall College of Further Education; he is co-author of *Ted Hughes: A Critical Study*, and a poet and mountaineer.

Neil Roberts is Senior Lecturer in English Literature at the University of Sheffield. He is co-author of *Ted Hughes: A Critical Study* and author of *George Eliot: Her beliefs and her art*, and of a forthcoming study of Peter Redgrove. He is currently working on the novels of Meredith and the poetry of D. H. Lawrence.

Keith Sagar is Reader in English Literature at the University of Manchester. He is the author of *The Art of Ted Hughes*, co-author of *Ted Hughes: A Bibliography* and editor of *The Achievement of Ted Hughes*. He is the author and editor of several books on D. H. Lawrence, and recently completed *Literature and the Crime against Nature*.

Leonard M. Scigaj is Associate Professor of English at Virginia Tech. He is the author of *The Poetry of Ted Hughes*, and *Ted Hughes* in the Twayne Authors Series, and editor of *Critical Essays on Ted Hughes*.

Ann Skea is a Londoner now working as a freelance writer and teacher in Sydney. She is the author of a study of Hughes and alchemy.

All the contributors would like to acknowledge their debt to the other participants in the conference on *The Challenge of Ted Hughes* which Keith Sagar directed at Holly Royde College, Manchester, in July 1990. They were: Izabel Brandao, A. J. Head, M. A. Hill, Mark Hinchliffe, Nancy Holden, Fred Rue Jacobs, O. C. Johnson, David Kuhrt, D. E. Macaulay, John Mallows, Joanny Moulin, Marjorie Partridge, J. C. Pike, Nancy Simmons and Sahar El-Mougy.

Introduction

The poetry of Ted Hughes challenges the reader in many different ways. One problem is that Hughes, when his imagination is at full stretch, tends towards works of almost epic scale. These are rarely completed according to the original conception, but end up concentrated into sequences of poems which relate closely to each other, clarify, support and enrich each other, develop out of each other, or fight each other to the death. The work in its published form is often merely the tip of an iceberg. The narrative or dramatic or thematic context has to be inferred. And each sequence is in turn part of a dramatically developing *oeuvre*, a poetic quest. Thus, though the anthology poems reveal a gifted and powerful poet, only the reader who has read the complete works in order is really in a position to recognise the magnitude of the achievement.

There is often the kind of difficulty we anticipate from modern poetry, with its complex symbolism and its lack of a rational or grammatical structure. But there is also, and increasingly with the later poems, a less familiar difficulty which arises from an extreme linguistic simplicity, an absence of what we have come to expect from almost all poetry, and yet the charge is clearly there, all the stronger for the lack of those verbal tricks the critic is trained to put his finger on. These poems are sources of great psychic or spiritual power if we can tap them; but our standard critical equipment seems obsolete. Perhaps part of the difficulty is that we bring inappropriate expectations to the poems, expecting lyrical beauty, crafted shapeliness or kinds of rational, paraphrasable meaning that the poems do not in fact offer. We tend to demand a continuance of the rich verbal surface and strong stylistic signature which got so many of the early poems into the anthologies, poems which are all many readers know of Hughes.

There is a real continuity from the Romantic poets through Hopkins and Yeats and Dylan Thomas to Hughes. But there is also discontinuity there which cannot be accounted for by the influence of the freer verse of Whitman and Lawrence and Eliot. Given the nature of Hughes's undertaking (which will be described in several of the following essays) the English poetic tradition was, for him, because of its very richness, a sort of 'material octopus' from which he had to try to extricate himself. The high degree of formalism in English verse accounts, of course, for many of its glories. But there is a boundary beyond which, by its very nature, self-consciously imposed form cannot often go. This boundary is virtually co-extensive with that of the ego. The writing of self-consciously crafted poems is itself, in varying degrees, a self-worshipping act. Beyond this boundary lies the very territory which Hughes wishes to explore. Formalism implies the superiority of Art to Nature, that the very purpose of Art is to process chaotic Nature in order to bring it under control, to make it yield to human modes of understanding and value systems. There is, however, a quite opposite view of Art, or rather of imagination, which regards it as our one means of escaping in some degree from the tyranny of the self-conscious ego and from the conditioned reflexes of our anthropocentric culture, as a means of trying to discover what Nature herself, buried deep within us, is trying to say.

We must therefore look beyond our familiar parochial English tradition and take in, for example, the very different kind of poetry which has been written in Eastern Europe since the Second World War. But whereas the stark nature of that poetry has been historically and politically determined, as a response to the war and to repressive postwar experience in those countries, Hughes has learned from them as part of an enterprise which is simultaneously more personal and more universal, an enterprise within which the influence from Eastern Europe is subsumed together with that of other simplifying poets – Keith Douglas, Stephen Crane, Emily Dickinson, with Ramanujan's translations of the medieval Indian *vacanas*, with shamanic poetry such as that collected by Joan Halifax in *Shamanic Voices*, and with the simplifications of all the world's folk poetry.

The strongest influence of all is always Shakespeare, for Shakespeare too was wrestling with the task of converting his own deeply personal sexual/religious problems into generally applicable wisdom, and, in the process, stripping away his own superb rhetoric to get down to the bedrock, to the ultimate styleless simplicity of 'Never, never, never, never, never'.

But the challenge to the reader is far greater than that of simply perceiving the relevant literary antecedents and influences. We are also challenged to redefine what the vocation of the poet is, and therefore what poetry is. Replying to Ekbert Faas's question about shamanism, Hughes said: 'Poets usually refuse the call. How are they to accept it? How can a poet become a medicine man and fly to the source and come back and heal or pronounce oracles? Everything among us is against it.' (Faas, p. 206.) Hughes is doing no less than this, on behalf of the race in its perhaps terminal sickness. Hughes himself is, of course, by no means exempt from that sickness. The poet-shaman is also scapegoat, seeking to locate in himself, as actual or potential, the crimes of his sex, race and species. He accuses himself through his protagonists – Crow, Prometheus, Adam, the nameless protagonist of *Cave Birds*, Nicholas Lumb – of criminal complicity, of being himself the sickness in some of its most virulent forms. The poems of the middle period (the later 1960s and earlier 1970s) are his painful efforts to correct himself, and serve also, if we are open to them, to correct the reader, to strip away all those things which are against our openness to spirit, and therefore to our own healing.

Here is another challenge. Everything among us is so against spirit that we are embarrassed by the very word; even more so 'sacredness' or 'miracle'. Hughes breaks down this resistance by grounding spiritual experience in the material world that every reader must recognise as tangible and real. If Hughes is a priest, he is a priest of a religion totally without transcendence, anti-metaphysical. His god is to be looked for under our boot-soles.

Poetry of this kind has, perhaps, more in common with other non-literary forms of truth-seeking than it has with literature as we have come to view it: with mythology and anthropology, psychology and philosophy, theology and the hermetic sciences, with feminism and with deep ecology. We respond to everything we read in terms of a set of coordinates. These are usually provided for us, unconsciously, by our culture. Poets such as Hughes cannot be measured against such coordinates. They are on a different scale entirely. Even the coordinates provided by an enlightened literary education are inadequate, and may be even worse, since they pretend to be on the same scale. Hence the failure of so many of our most respected Establishment critics to respond adequately to Hughes. They want to keep the poems manageably on the page. But a living poem is quickly off the page and into the psyche. It explodes, and the reverberations cannot be contained within the compartment labelled 'poetry'. Or, working more subtly, it sends tendrils out into every compartment, undermining the partitions between them. We must seek out new coordinates, and these might take us into very unfamiliar territory for the average reader or literary critic. We might find ourselves reading Schopenhauer, Nietzsche and Heidegger; Frazer, Graves's *White Goddess* and Joseph Campbell; Jung, Gurdjieff and Simone Weil; Lorca's 'Theory and Function of the Duende'; Castaneda; perhaps even alchemical texts (to which a painless introduction would be Lindsay Clarke's recent novel *The Chymical Wedding*); and the growing list of classic texts in deep ecology, beginning with Max Nicholson's *The Environmental Revolution*.

Such new coordinates, and such an upgrading of the status and function of the poet would, of course, have implications far beyond Hughes studies. As Eliot claimed, every new great writer who is added to the tradition changes the tradition, forces us to revalue all that has gone before in the light of his work. This has never been truer than it is of Hughes. The new coordinates we have to find for Hughes, for example, might well prove revelatory when applied to, say, Shakespeare. And Hughes himself has shown how criticism can escape from its present sink and become a source – itself an imaginative act. His own study of Shakespeare reveals how history works through the traumas and obsessions of the personal life of the imaginative writer to produce that particular organisation of revelatory language which is a work of literary art.

The challenge of Ted Hughes is, ultimately, no different from the challenge of all great literature. It is not a matter of passing judgement upon it (however favourable), but of allowing it to pass judgement on us and to contribute to the process of regeneration. It can burn away complacency, sentimentality, inauthenticity. It can fertilise the imagination, cleansing the doors of perception. It can heal the dualistic split. It can help to resacralise the world. The great gifts are all there waiting. The function of the critic is to open some of them, and to help others to open them.

1

Ted Hughes and the Death of Poetry

Nick Bishop

The title of this chapter must seem, at first sight, puzzling. How can one of the foremost exponents of poetry be associated with its 'death'? I hope to answer that question: to illuminate not a hopeless contradiction but a necessary and desirable paradox in our under-standing of Hughes's poetic development. The idea of what exactly constitutes poetic development filters directly into the central issue. Does 'development' for the poet mean primarily a certain evolution or refinement of linguistic procedures, or does it mean *self-development*, the evolution of a living human being occurring secondarily – almost accidentally – *through language*? The idea of poetic development may have either an aesthetic or a psychological (I would like to use the word 'moral') core, and it appears to me that what occurs in Hughes's work is really a gradual transition from the first to the second core, from one understanding of poetic develop-ment to the other.

A great deal of Hughes's early poetry is based on the self-contained, even 'outright-masculine' impulse to assert a kind of authority through the strenuous use of language (*The Hawk in the Rain*), or through the carefully-styled perfection of the verbal artefact (*Lupercal*); but whether Hughes is wielding language as a broadsword, or painting with the delicacy of an artist (in poems as diverse as 'Egg-head' and 'To Paint a Water Lily'), the common denominator is an obsessive preoccupation with words-as-words, with the expressive resources of language – language almost as world-unto-itself. It is no wonder that the 'feminine' desire to expand and complete the self, subordinating language to a tool or instrument of the psychological process, struggles to survive in a handful of poems – in these volumes. The psychological core of poetic development could be said to dominate only two of

1

Hughes' first sixty or so poems, 'The Thought-Fox' and 'Hawk Roosting'.

What I am saying is that Hughes's obsession with language has a psychological root that must be severed for the poet to make real progress, and the feminine element to be given a full voice within the conscious individual. It is no accident that the reader often feels in Hughes's early work that he/she is being overpowered by the torrential downpour of words or the self-conscious opulence of the 'beautiful poem', because the huge downward pressure exerted by the poet on the reader – as it were, forcing the head down into submission – is the same as that exerted by the poet on his greater, invisible self. Hughes's over-masculinist, over-literary ego-personality has to 'die', along with its dependence on the purely linguistic creation, in order that the real poetry of the psychological process can be allowed to take place, to express itself.

My description of the 'aesthetic' impulse to achieve what Janos Pilinszky[1] calls the 'certainty of stylistic appearances' as masculine, and the psychological urge towards self-expansion/completion as feminine may seem deliberately provocative, but it does have a concrete point: poems such as 'The Thought-Fox' are produced by a conscious attitude significantly more passive, humble and attentive to the 'other' than those where an authoritarian 'I' tries to dominate his material by the strength of his style. As in 'Pike', the poetic persona waits, listening, for 'what eye might move…', de-emphasising the masculine drive to impose himself on the imaginative environment of the poem. And Jung indicates, in his many writings on the subject, that the 'other' always crystallises – for the male poet – as a woman, first as 'shadow', then finally as 'anima'. So in Hughes's own mythologies the primary task is always to locate and liberate some aspect of the female principle – Moa in *Orghast*, the baboon-woman in *Gaudete*, the ogress to be transformed into a beautiful maiden in the *Crow* skeleton-narrative.

Jung's terminology is only one aid in the effort to recover the fundamental psychological pattern of literary development to which the poet owes primary allegiance. Hughes, both in his own critical prose and in his poetic mythology, unearths with remarkable consistency the overweening need for 'death and rebirth', whether it is in the shamanic form of ritual dismemberment, stripping-to-the-bones and subsequent clairvoyant return, or the Sufic annihilation of self in the 'living body of Allah'[2] or the mythic narratives that so clearly underpin *Gaudete* and *Cave Birds*. Even in his first wife,

Sylvia Plath, Hughes observed 'the central experience of a shattering of the self, and the labour of fitting it together again or finding a
new one'.

Without delving too deeply into esoteric background, I find the
clearest summary of the necessary pattern of poetic development in
Maurice Nicholl's commentary on the teachings of G. I. Gurdjieff.
Here he is inverting Plato's parable of a man trying to drive a horse
and carriage as an analogy for the individual's struggle to re-inhabit
or repossess his own whole psyche:

> To drive he must ascend above the level of the ground. But before
> this can happen, he must say 'I will drive'. That is a decision and
> it is followed by having to go *up*. Now here is something very
> strange, because actually he has to go *down*. He cannot drive
> from… False Personality, from anything in him which *thinks it can
> do*. He will never be able to drive from pride or vanity, but only
> from what is lowest in him in this respect – from what is most
> simple and humble and genuine and sincere. *So to go up he must go
> down*. When he says 'I will drive', if he thinks he can do it himself
> and for himself, he will break reins, smash wheels and fall off.
> This decision 'I will drive' must be said with a delicacy of under-
> standing that implies the existence of something else being
> necessary. *To do* in the work-sense ultimately means *to obey* the
> Master who may suddenly appear in the carriage.[3]

Within this frame of reference, Hughes will have to abandon his
aesthetic False Personality, and its super-confidence in the controlling or organising powers of language, to 'go down' into the apparently lowest elements of the psyche, to find, as in 'The Thought-
Fox', that 'Something else is alive/Beside the clock's loneliness/
And this blank page where my fingers move' and that the 'Master'
may appear, if passively invited: 'With a sudden sharp hot stink of
fox/It enters the dark hole of the head'.

To shift from the general to the particular, I will examine now
three poems from very different phases of Hughes's development.
First, the title-poem of Hughes's first published volume *The Hawk in
the Rain*. The poem witnesses the dramatic collision of those two
contradictory impulses within the self, to *ascend* or to *descend*, as a
crisis of attitude towards, and usage of, poetic language. I mean that
the psychological crisis is really manifesting itself as a linguistic
crisis. In the first stanza, for example, the consonantal grip – the

clenched fist of the old Anglo-Saxon line in contemporary free verse – tightens in direct response to the 'I''s psychological need to keep clear of the *matter* 'lowest down' which seems to menace its authority:

> I drown in the drumming ploughland, I drag up
> Heel after heel from the swallowing of the earth's mouth,
> From clay that clutches my each step to the ankle
> With the habit of the dogged grave....

The lines are formally complete, they represent Pilinszky's 'stylistic certainty', the headlong flight into poetry's aesthetic centre as a way of avoiding confrontation with one's own psychological depths. Style is trying to resist the consuming pressure of internal reality, and so it is no wonder that the poem's 'aesthetic I' accepts the impulse to *ascend*, thinking to 'go up' and 'drive the carriage immediately': '... but the hawk/Effortlessly at height hangs his still eye'. It is, of course, possible to appreciate the felicity of the aesthetic manoeuvre whereby the word 'hangs' seems to suspend itself in the exact centre of the line much as the hawk itself is supposed to hover, timelessly, above the chaos below, and to appreciate the witty conflation of 'eye' and 'I', suggesting that the point-of-orientation *above* that chaos is within both poet's and reader's grasp. In this, and the alliterative symmetry of the following two lines, the poet does indeed seem to have gained a mastery over his environment, a mastery the reader is encouraged not only to share, but also to admire critically for the aesthetic control upon which that dominance is built. In short, we consent to the illusion that a certain formal control of language naturally implies conscious control and harmonisation of the whole psyche, provides a trustworthy orientation within the chaos, 'pole-stars/The sea drowner's endurance'.

On the other hand, if we remember 'The Windhover', and the opening of Dylan Thomas's 'Over Sir John's Hill' – 'Over Sir John's hill,/The hawk on fire hangs still' – we might begin to suspect that Hughes's linguistic resolution is not fully his own. That suspicion is confirmed in lines 8–10, where the violence inflicted on the poem's 'I' appears almost as a necessary swingeing counter-reaction to, or compensation for, the poet's premature identification with the hawk-image, his attempt to 'drive the carriage' by the formal manipulation of language.

Moreover, Hughes's two further efforts to resuscitate the aesthetic image only worsen the situation. Not only do these formulations (lines 10–12 and 14–15) lack the compactness of the initial version, they provoke ever more brutal compensations. After the first re-assertion, the 'I' ironically dissolves to the 'lowest' linguistic level of the entire poem, as a 'Bloodily grabbed dazed last-moment-counting/Morsel in the earth's mouth'. And the final, straining attempt to 'go up' directly 'towards the master-/Fulcrum of violence where the hawk hangs still' results in nothing less than the total destruction of the image:

That maybe in his own time meets the weather

Coming the wrong way, suffers the air, hurled upside down,
Fall from his eye, the ponderous shires crash on him,
The horizon trap him; the round angelic eye
Smashed, mix his heart's blood with the mire of the land.

This moment-to-moment staccato improvisation is a parody of the verbal control exhibited in the first five lines. But it is just this 'death' of the image and of the 'aesthetic' language clustered around it, that is alone desirable in psychological terms. If the reader refuses to 'go down' with the poet – by elevating the aesthetic qualities of line 5 and rejecting the 'ugly' diction of lines 13–14 – he demonstrates his ignorance of a truly psychological vocabulary, committing a divisive and dualistic act in his reading of the poem.

I hope this summary begins to explain the necessity for the transition from an 'aesthetic' to a 'psychological' understanding of poetic development. After all, the brutalised residue of the aesthetic image in 'The Hawk in the Rain' actually gestures in the last stanza, albeit primitively, towards the throwaway provisional language which became Hughes's ideal, and, in lines 13–14, to the super-simple, super-ugly language of *Crow*.

Crow in fact provides my next example of the 'death of poetry' at a more advanced stage of development. Where 'The Hawk in the Rain' witnessed the collapse of the authoritarian/aesthetic False Personality *unconsciously* (the poem's 'I' swinging wildly between efforts to sustain and destroy it), 'Crow and the Birds' makes a ritual of destroying its power *deliberately*, in full consciousness. It is as if Hughes wishes systematically to identify the exact moment at which language ceases to be transparent instrument and becomes reflexive world-unto-itself, producing not 'instances of reality' but 'instances of (pure) discourse', to adapt Barthes' words. The moment of the aesthetic transition is located, then purged ruthlessly in the last line of the poem. There the cluttered surface of language is wiped clean, and its obligation to matter 'lowest down' renewed.

When the eagle soared clear through a dawn distilling of emerald
When the curlew trawled in seadusk through a chime of
                                                    wineglasses
When the swallow swooped through a woman's song in a cavern
And the swift flicked through the breath of a violet

When the owl sailed clear of tomorrow's conscience
And the sparrow preened himself of yesterday's promise
And the heron laboured clear of the Bessemer upglare
And the bluetit zipped clear of lace panties
And the woodpecker drummed clear of the rotovator and the
                                                    rose-farm
And the peewit tumbled clear of the laundromat

While the bullfinch plumped in the apple bud
And the goldfinch bulbed in the sun
And the wryneck crooked in the moon
And the dipper peered from the dewball

Crow spraddled head-down in the beach-garbage, guzzling a
                                              dropped ice-cream.

Both poet and reader start the poem gazing upward, at birds in flight, 'above'; and yet, in that first stanza, just at the point where the verbs in each line encourage us to focus in on their subject-'matter', the lens of the clear expectation is hopelessly diffused by the sentimental aesthetic additions which complete the line. The reader receives a mid-line shock which can only force him/her to feel the superfluousness of poetic or beautiful language unrelated to the pressure of circumstances. There is no development in the first four lines of the poem; all the birds are imprisoned within what Jung calls the 'false glamour of aestheticism'. 'Craftsmanship', in Zbigniew Herbert's phrase, has been released from its obligation 'to probe to the bottom of cruelty', the dark chaos of the psyche, and we observe this abdication at the centre of each line.

The next six lines catalogue the imprisonment of the natural by human interpretive grids other than language, ritualistically 'liberating' each bird in turn, while lines 11–14 are little more than a compressed reprise of the first stanza. The whole poem is then ferociously undermined by the last line: 'Crow spraddled head-down in the beach-garbage, guzzling a dropped ice-cream'. Crow is the only bird from 'below' – clearly at root-level – in the entire poem, and the language, while consciously abandoning all poetic properties, focuses him unflinchingly throughout the full long line. The line follows not from the principle of ascension, but from the principle of descent. The conclusion of the act demonstrates Hughes's separation from the False Personality which dominated 'The Hawk in the Rain'; and language, as a result, has fallen into its proper place as a transparent medium to *matter*, even at its grossest level. It has been reduced, as Hughes says of Keith Douglas (1987), to 'a functional minimum'. It no longer seeks to escape its status as machine. The preponderance of repetitive, formulaic poems in *Crow* as a whole is a symptom of this acknowledgement, as are those poems which specifically attack the hypnotic qualities of language ('A Disaster', 'Crow Goes Hunting', 'The Battle of Osfrontalis' and so on). If this is a 'death' of poetry, it is death 'consummately to be wished', because it opens the psychological or moral *origin* of poetry, its true nature and purpose *ab initio*.

The happy flexibility and breadth of poetic grasp which can literally pick up language from anywhere for its immediate purpose ('spraddled', 'beach-garbage', 'guzzling'), and which descends regularly into the psychological 'depths', finds one of its purest and most homogeneous expressions in *River*. Once again it is the psychological change which comes first, which language follows. Language is more transparent because Personality is less egoistic, more open, receptive and 'feminine'. The clearest example is, perhaps, 'Go Fishing':

Join water, wade in underbeing
Let brain mist into moist earth
Ghost loosen away downstream
Gulp river and gravity

Lose words
Cease

Let the world come back, like a white hospital
Busy with urgency words

> Try to speak and nearly succeed
> Heal into time and other people.

The False Personality, which was so strongly attached to the manipulative use of poetic language, no longer seeks to 'telepathically overpower' its victims. The hunter/fisherman/poet of 'A Cormorant' voluntarily allows something else to 'appear suddenly in the carriage' and do the driving for him. The personality itself becomes an object of observation:

> The cormorant eyes me, beak uptilted,
> Body-snake low – sea-serpentish.
>
> He's thinking: 'Will that stump
> Stay a stump just while I dive?' He dives.
>
> He sheds everything from his tail end
> Except fish-action, becomes fish,
>
> Disappears from bird,
> Dissolving himself
>
> Into fish, so dissolving fish naturally
> Into himself. Re-emerges, gorged,
>
> Himself as he was, and escapes me.
> Leaves me high and dry in my space-armour,
>
> A deep-sea diver in two inches of water.

The poem's 'I' has dissolved itself willingly, and cannot be afraid of its comically awkward posture in the last two lines. The poet's real fish has already been caught, paradoxically, by his own conscious renunciation of power. Something similar occurs in 'Strangers' where the poet sees

> The sea-trout, upstaring, in trance,
> Absorb everything and forget it
> Into a blank of bliss.

And this is the real samadhi – wordless, levitated.
Till, bulging, a man-shape
Wobbles their firmament.

                                     Now see the holy ones
Shrink their auras, slim, sink, focus, prepare
To scram like trout.

As soon as the Personality casts its shadow over the vision, it vanishes – but the poet has no desire to continue the poem on his own terms, or create some sort of permanent aesthetic shrine to the experience. He simply lets it go, keeps space open for the 'other' to return in its own time.

That temptation is stronger in 'That Morning', where Hughes finds himself amongst a solid mass of salmon,

> …their formations
> Lifting us toward some dazzle of blessing
>
> One wrong thought might darken. As if the fallen
> World and salmon were over. As if these
> Were the imperishable fish
>
> That had let the world pass away –
>
> There in a mauve light of drifted lupins
> They hung in the cupped hands of mountains
>
> Made of tingling atoms. It had happened.

The possibility of lyrical or aesthetic afflatus is pronounced, but it is simply cut off by the deeper responsibility to the apparently 'dark' whole of the experience:

> Then for a sign that we were where we were
> Two gold bears came down and swam like men
>
> Beside us. And dived like children.
> And stood in deep water as on a throne
> Eating pierced salmon off their talons.

So we found the end of our journey.

So we stood, alive in the river of light
Among the creatures of light, creatures of light.

Hughes 'goes down' into the violence of the event and returns finding it included in Nature's celebration of itself. Aestheticism had to
die when it was a property of a limited, inflexible conscious attitude,
but here it can be transformed into a productive instrument of that
celebration because it is in the hands of an expanded, expansive
psychology. Everything dissolves into light and its original unity at
the end of the poem as the Personality no longer obtrudes, with its
false attitudes, on the 'Matter' of the experience. There is no longer
an arbitrary division between serenity and beauty above, and
violence and beastliness below, as there is no longer the need for
Hughes to cry out, in the same breath as the Polish poet M.B.: 'Strike
me,/Construction of my world!'

Notes

1.   Pilinszky, Janos, '"Creative Imagination" in our Time', in *Ocean at the
      Window: Hungarian Prose and Poetry since 1945* (University of Minne-
      sota Press, Minneapolis, 1980), p. 144.
2.   Hughes, Ted, 'Secret Ecstasies' (Hughes's review of Idries Shah's *The
      Sufis* and Mircea Eliade's *Shamanism*) in *The Listener*, 29 October 1964.
3.   Nicoll, Maurice, *Psychological Commentaries on the Teachings of Gurdjieff
      and Ouspensky* (Shambhala Press, USA, 1985), III, p. 826.

2

Neglected Auguries in
Recklings
Roger Elkin

Given Hughes's standing in contemporary world literature, it seems incomprehensible that *Recklings* (published in a limited edition of 150 copies in 1966) has received only scant critical appraisal. For, although there are several full-length studies of Hughes's output, discussion of the *Recklings* collection is limited to, at most, three pages. Such a cursory examination is regrettable, for *Recklings* contains in collected form the only corpus of poetry for adults which Hughes published between *Lupercal* (1960) and *Wodwo* (1967). As such, the volume stands at the stylistic and thematic crossroads of his poetic development. What makes a fuller assessment of its contents compulsory is the fact that, unlike most of Hughes's other limited editions, *Recklings* has not been subsequently published in a trade edition. Furthermore, while it has become almost critical literary staple to suggest that each Hughes volume initiates stylistic and thematic ground, no period in his output has marked such redirections in subject-matter and experimental handling of structures, expression, symbol and theme as the seven-year interstice between *Lupercal* and *Wodwo*. Such were the advances that critics and commentators were baffled and disturbed by the originality and unexpected experimentations of *Wodwo*; and some considered that Hughes had lost his poetic direction. Had *Recklings* been released commercially, readers might have been prepared to receive the bleaker world of *Wodwo* in much the same manner that that volume anticipates the nihilism and sardonic humour of *Crow*, which in turn spawned the subsequent mythic worlds of *Prometheus on His Crag*, *Cave Birds* and *Gaudete*.

However, a quarter of a century after its initial publication, *Recklings* still presents the reader with a challenge, mainly because the wide provenance of its thirty-two poems (drawn from Hughes's output between 1956 and 1966), and the consequent varied stylistic expression and thematic concerns, give the impression of opacity of meaning, and the suggestion of experimentation. The absence of a title-poem that either illustrates the general stylistic feature of the volume or exists as a statement of its thematic preoccupations (cf. 'The Hawk in the Rain', 'Lupercalia' and 'Wodwo' with reference to Hughes's poetic strategy or thinking as explored in their respective volumes) means that the reader has no immediate focus from which to appraise the entire collection. This absence of viewpoint is compounded by the fact that *Recklings* does not follow any pattern of chronology (it *concludes* with one of the earliest poems, 'Bawdry Embraced', written in 1956) or schematic unity (the poems 'A Match', 'On the Slope', 'To be a Girl's Diary' which became the three parts of 'Root, Stem, Leaf', in *The Selected Poems* are located on pp. 27, 7 and 30 respectively). Similarly, there is an element of inconsistency or even idiosyncrasy in the selection: of the four poems that constitute the uncollected cycle 'Dully Gumption's College Courses' only one poem, 'Humanities', features in *Recklings* (p. 35); while the sole reference to 'Dully' appears in the quasi-autobiographical 'Dully Gumption's Addendum' (pp. 10–11). Furthermore, the reader may be dissuaded from serious consideration of the poems by the suggestion implicit within the volume's title that Hughes had some reservations about the contents ('recklings' are the weakest of a litter, runts, those least able to survive). Thus, Hughes must share some responsibility for the dismissive stance that critics have taken: the poems are seen as 'fumblings' (Derwent May); 'throwouts and failed experiments' (Keith Sagar); 'fugitive pieces' (Dennis Walder); and 'scrappy leftovers from stylistic experiments' (Ekbert Fass).[1] Faced with such unanimity of critical response, the reader is hardly encouraged to embark on an exploration of the wealths that *Recklings* contains. However, where the critics have erred is in the tendency to view *Recklings* in the context of the three early trade volumes, rather than measuring it against his entire output. Thus, though several poems ('Bawdry Embraced', Unknown Soldier') cast a retrospective look stylistically at *The Hawk in the Rain* and *Lupercal*, the majority anticipate Hughes's subsequent poetic direction: some ('Memory', 'Flanders', 'Water') share similarity of form and expression with poems from *Wodwo*; while several ('Humanities', 'Fallen Eve', 'Small Events', 'Thaw', 'The Toughest'), in their theological questioning and examination of the anaesthetisation of contemporary sensibility, point towards *Crow*; and others ('Trees', 'Plum-

Blossom'), in their epigrammatic structure and opaque symbolism, anticipate *Cave Birds* and the *Gaudete* Epilogue poems.

This crucial role that *Recklings* performs in forging the links between the various volumes serves to emphasise the interrelationship of the poetry as part of 'the single adventure' that informs Hughes's output. This is evident, for example, in the way in which one of the more readily accessible *Recklings* poems, 'Stealing Trout on a May Morning' (pp. 31–4, *Selected Poems*, pp. 88–91), via the utilisation of Jungian archetypes in which water and fishing are used symbolically as vehicles for the exploration of the unconscious and the creative/poetic process, both develops ideas from the volumes preceding *Recklings* and anticipates his later thematic concerns. In the *Recklings* poem Hughes becomes completely identified with the river in a hurried moment that is almost animal in its intensity:

> My mind sinks, rising and sinking...
> My boot dangles down, till a thing black and sudden
> Savages it, and the river is heaping under,
> Alive and malevolent...
> Soon I deepen. And now I meet the piling mob
> Of voices and hurriers coming towards me
> And tumbling past me...
> They drag the flag off my head, a dark insistence
> Fearing the splints from my mind's edge.

To regain safety from the swirling river he needs to be dragged out of it – by a fish. He has become the quarry; and the fish the symbol of the magical healing powers existing in the storehouse of the unconscious:

> To yank me clear takes the sudden, strong spine
> Of one of the river's real members –
> Thoroughly made of dew, lightning and granite
> Very slowly over three years. A trout a foot long,
> Lifting its head in a shawl of water,
> Fins banked stiff like a schooner
> It forces the final curve wide, getting
> A long look at me.
>   So much for the horror:
> It has changed places.

The transference of horror from man to fish is reminiscent of 'Pike', which 'rose slowly towards me, watching' in a similar manner to the trout taking 'A long look'. The therapeutic nature of this moment of transcendence from fear to ecstasy and calm is emphasised in the poem's concluding lines. Instead of seeing himself as an unwanted poacher in alien surroundings he is now so possessed by fish and river that he has become an image of previous times. Like the 'Retired Colonel' he is 'mounted', though not in rhymes, but in an imaginary painting:

> Now I am a man in a painting
> (Under the mangy stuffed head of a fox)
> Painted about 1905
> Where the river steams and the frost relaxes
> From the pear-blossoms. The brassy wood-pigeons
> Bubble their colourful voices, and the sun
> Rises upon a world well-tried and old.

The line in parenthesis not only serves to reinforce the idea of former decades of comparative harmony, but also, via such poems as 'The Thought-Fox', makes an oblique reference to Hughes's idea of writing poetry as akin to hunting animals. In recording an experience of poaching, Hughes has fished into his own mind and the poem is the net in which he himself has been poached.

What is of importance is the way in which (as with the relationship between 'The Jaguar' and 'Second Glance at a Jaguar') the *Recklings* poem is a preparatory act of creation for Hughes's subsequent poems. Of particular note is the Lawrentian celebration of his first sighting of a trout as described in 'The Long Tunnel Ceiling' from *Remains of Elmet* (1979):

> An ingot!
> Holy of holies! A treasure!
> A trout
> Nearly as long as my arm, solid
> Molten pig of many a bronze loach!
> There he lay – lazy – a free lord,
> Ignoring me.
>
> A seed
> Of the wild god now flowering for me

Such a tigerish, dark, breathing lily.

Nearer in content and skill in transmitting the creative energy cap-
tured in 'Stealing Trout on a May Morning' is 'Earth-Numb' from
Moortown (1979) which, apart from the fact that the ostensible
quarry is salmon not trout, records an identical experience. The
note-like nature of the lines (an extension of the predominant stylistic device of the *Moortown* poems) gives the impression of a series
of immediate visual and aural incidents carefully and sensitively
apprehended. Though Hughes is searching and fishing for salmon,
he is soon aware that he is

> hunted
> And haunted by apparitions from tombs
> Under the smoothing tons of dead element
> In the river's black canyons...
>
> And bang! the river grabs at me
>
> A mouth-flash, an electrocuting malice
> Like a trap, trying to rip life off me –
> And the river stiffens alive,
> The black hole thumps, the whole river hauls
> And I have one.

As in 'Pike' and 'Stealing Trout on a May Morning', the instant of
contact with the fish is an act of revelation, a glimmer into the darkness of self, an exposure of the hidden fears and anxieties in the
unconscious, and an awareness of life-and-death forces at work. At
that moment Hughes becomes part river and part fish. Like the
thoughts rising out of the collective memory of the race (or the
'Thought-Fox' coming into poetic consciousness), the salmon
emerges, takes form, and finally clears into solid shape; the fish is
the poem:

> A piling voltage hums, jamming me stiff –
> Something terrified and terrifying
> Gleam-surges to and fro through me
> From the river to the sky, from the sky into the river
> Uprooting dark bedrock, shatters it in air,
> Cartwheels across me, slices thudding through me

As if I were the current –

Till the fright flows all one way down the line

And a ghost grows solid, a hoverer,
A lizard green slither, banner heavy –

Then the wagging stone pebble head

As with the earlier poems, 'Earth-Numb' captures the creative thrill of both fishing and writing. In plumbing the depths, Hughes's mind is also plumbed, and his fears, of the instant and of the racial memory, are resolved in the process of creative will. Invoking the fish, Hughes creates a poem.

The culmination of this particular aspect of Hughes's poetic development is presented in *River* (1983). By far the most significant poem in terms of the therapeutic nature of fishing/poetic creativity is 'Go Fishing' in which Hughes exhorts:

Join water, wade in underbeing
Let brain mist into moist earth
Ghost loosen away downstream
Gulp river and gravity…

Become translucent – one untangling drift
Of water-mesh, and a weight of earth-taste light
Mangled by wing-shadows
Everything circling and flowing and hover-still

Crawl out over roots, new and nameless
Search for face, harden into limbs

Let the world come back, like a white hospital
Busy with urgency words

Try to speak and nearly succeed
Heal into time and other people

While the obvious antecedents for these ideas are seeded in 'Stealing Trout on a May Morning', the more muted tone and sensitive phrasing inhabit a similar 'feminine' world to that of the *Gaudete*

Epilogue poems, in which Hughes explores the psychological and spiritual catharses that are to be gained from a total submission to and immersion in the forces of Nature as a stage in the recreation of harmony between inner and outer worlds, self and others.

An examination of the *Recklings* opening and closing poems (always crucial positions in Hughes's collections) rehearses similar ground stylistically while simultaneously demonstrating the way in which these two particular poems also anticipate much later works. The concluding poem, 'Bawdry Embraced', is the earlier and much more poetically derivative. Composed shortly after Hughes met Plath in February 1965 (see *Letters Home*, pp. 259 and 270), the poem celebrates their relationship in a manner resembling an imitation Jonsonian Epigram. Typical of the flavour of the poem are the last five stanzas (13–17), the conclusion of the Tailfever narrative which records the climax of an urgent sexual passion in which the practitioners are elevated to almost mythical proportions:

> They caught each other by the body
>   And fell in a heap:
> A cockerel there struck up a tread
>   Like a cabman's whip.
>
> And so they knit, knotted and wrought,
>   Braiding their ends in;
> So fed their radiance to themselves
>   They could not be seen.
>
> And thereupon – a miracle!
>   Each became a lens
> So focussing creation's heat
>   The other burst in flames.
>
> Bawdry! Bawdry! Steadfastly
>   Thy great protagonists
> Died face to face, with bellies full,
>   In the solar waste
>
> Where there is neither skirt nor coat,
>   And every ogling eye
> Is a cold star to measure
>   Their solitude by.

Despite the fact that 'Bawdry Embraced' inhabits a vastly different philosophic and stylistic world, it foreshadows in quite significant ways the later *Cave Birds* marriage poems (1978). Jung's analysis of the alchemical process (a parallel for his psychological theory of individuation) forms the skeleton outline for the two works:

> The *nigredo* or blackness is the initial state…then a union of opposites is performed in the likeness of a union of male and female…followed by the death of the product of the union…and a corresponding *nigredo*. From this the washing either leads to the whitening (*albedo*), or else the soul…released at the 'death' is reunited with the dead body and brings about its resurrection…. The *nubedo* then follows direct from the *albedo* as the result of raising the heat of the fire to its highest intensity.[2]

The relationship between Tailfever and Sweety Undercut encompasses these colour changes – the *nigredo* of 'the dark' of stanza 8; the *rubedo* of their ignited, fiery passion; and the *albedo* of their union in the whiteness of 'solar' 'radiance'. It is possible that the two protagonists with their cosmic proportions and fiery and quicksilver characteristics exist as analogues for the male and female elements in the alchemical process, the *sponsum* and *sponsa*, 'Mercury' and 'Sulphur'. Jung states that in alchemy these opposites were often described as 'cock and hen' which the alchemist combined in a 'mystic marriage'.[3] Significantly, prior to their union, Tailfever is described as a 'cockerel' who 'treads' the hen of Sweety Undercut; and in *Cave Birds* Hughes's main protagonist is a humanist Socratic cockerel who, though having little knowledge of self or the world, proclaims himself 'lord of middens' (p. 24).

To turn to the opening poem, 'On the Slope', is to chart Hughes's movement from mimicry of Metaphysical style to an exploration and apprehension of metaphysical issues; simultaneously it highlights what is probably the most immediate feature of the majority of the *Recklings* poems differentiating them from the early Hughes style – their visual presentation. Generally speaking, the tightly-structured quatrain has been abandoned in favour of a freer verse-patterning with lines made from a single phrase, or even word, followed by a line accommodating the width of the page and spilling on to the next. The verbal violence, tortuous syntax and period diction have been replaced by colloquial but precise phraseology; while parallelism and anaphora have displaced regular metrical pattern and rhyme. The poems explore the extra-semantic meanings that spatially-isolated lines can add to the argument, and many of the lines, or even whole poems, are unstopped or not punctuated grammatically. Collectively, these features identify Hughes's adoption of the natural folk-line, which with several refinements has become the predominant voice of his later work. The position of 'On the Slope' as the *Recklings* opening poem is a clear acknowledgement of the significance of this stylistic development:

> Having taken her slowly by surprise
> For eighty years
> The hills have won, their ring is closed.
>
> The field-walls float their pattern
> Over her eye
> Whether she looks outward or inward.
>
> Nothing added, nothing taken away.
> Year after year the trout in the pools
> Grow heavy and vanish without ever emerging.
>
> Foxglove and harebell neither protest nor hope
> By the steep slope where she climbs.
> Out of nothing she grew here simply
>
> Also suffering to be merely flowerlike
> But with the stone agony growing in her joints
> And eyes dimming with losses, widening for losses.

One of the few *Recklings* poems to have 'survived' (as Part II of 'Root, Stem, Leaf' in the *Selected Poems*), 'On the Slope' is in many ways a reworking of Hughes's description of the moorlines from his autobiographical piece, 'The Rock' (1964):

> They did not impose themselves. They simply surrounded and waited.... They hung over you at all times. They were simply a part of everything you saw.... The earth was held down by that fine line of moor, mostly a gentle female watery line.... The visible horizon was the magic circle, excluding and enclosing.[4]

In the poem's opening lines the rather sinister omnipresence of the moors is communicated by the use of animism, so that their haunting existence becomes a concerted ambush in which, at this single instance in her eighty years' knowledge of them, the woman has been caught in her slow upward climb. Out of breath (the poem was originally published as 'A Pause For Breath'),[5] she is defeated by the hills' continuance and immovability: all they have had to do is wait until they can possess her. The stone-like effect of her progress and her arthritic condition, 'the stone agony growing in her joints', completes the 'ring' of the horizon in terms suggestive of both encirclement and union. The suddenness and immediacy of her apprehension that she is becoming part of something which she has always considered a separate reality is concealed in the use of the transferred epithets: it is she that moves 'slowly', she that is taken 'by surprise'.

In the remainder of the poem there is little forward movement, almost as if, because the old woman has discovered the significance of this revelation and her relationship with the environment, the brevity of her life and her position in the natural order, all form of progress is denied. The poem opens inwards in an almost self-exploratory manner that replicates the woman's newly-formed self-knowledge. Such is the union between woman and Nature that the dividing lines between them become blurred and merged and, in consequence, the imagery is freely associative rather then being part of a unified scheme. Just as the visual image of the field-walls is mirrored in her eyes, deep in her mind there is forming the realisation of her physical position as a victim of time. She will not emerge from the landscape, as the trout never leave their pools: like them she grows 'heavy'; it is as a fish *in water* that she will vanish. Nothing will be 'taken away' because her death will be an extension of the process of the total identification with locality; nothing will be 'added' because she has always been there. The concept of rootedness extends to embrace the vegetable world. Hughes suggests that the apparently patient, delicate and frail (foxglove and harebell, and by association the woman) should not be despised for their lack of outward 'protest' or 'hope'. Consequently, there is no ridicule in the fact that the woman 'grew here simply...suffering to be merely flowerlike'. Hughes honours her stoical persistence for nothing more than existence; for though her horizons may diminish visually and personally, they simultaneously widen to include a realisation that her losses of vitality, of faculty, of identity are the very things that define her position in the environment, in time, in the natural design, and in self.

Stylistically, 'On the Slope' is controlled by the adoption of a restricted and muted sound pattern. There is limited use of the rich heavy sounds of the early Hughes style (e.g. the plosive 'b', or the harsh, incisive 'k'), and none of its insistence on metrical tread and external rhyme. Instead he employs a more colloquially-based fluency, the sounds and rhythms of which echo and ring throughout the lines. This conditions the phraseology and general syntactical expression: the sentences flow simply, without tortuous qualifying subordinate phrases and clauses, so that a sentence is contained within a few lines. The absence of descriptive passages means that the weight of the poetic idea is carried by practically every word, so that there is little room for virtuoso self-indulgent sound-patterning at odds with the sonic mood. Similarly, only three nouns are qualified by adjectives – 'eighty', 'steep', 'stone' – which are used to convey the poem's major concern rather than as 'decoration' or devices to satisfy the resolution of metre, for the stress-pattern falls naturally on the rhythms of the human voice. Consequently the structure seems casual, almost prosaic, in expression; and the sound-pattern emerges as integral to the poem's mood. This sound-pattern is controlled by balanced lines; by line enjambment which, falling against the units of usual grammatical continuity, adds a note of hesitancy and wondering; and by the carefully discreet use of punctuation and line-ending, which lead and nudge the voice and eye in a series of exploratory statements. A further feature is the use of repetition, either in words ('dimming with losses, widening for losses'; 'nothing added, nothing taken away'; 'year after year') or in balancing phrases ('outward or inward'; 'neither protest nor hope'; 'heavy and vanish'; 'foxglove and harebell'). Stylistically, this anaphoric structuring anticipates the *Gaudete* Epilogue poems; while in matters of content 'On the Slope' would not be out of place in *Remains of Elmet*, the contents of which record more fully Hughes's response to the landscape of moorline and field-walls. Moreover, the reference to 'the ring of horizons' in 'Climbing into Heptonstall' (*Wolfwatching*, 1989) not only confirms the significant hold that the landscape of Hughes's youth exercises over his poetic vision, but also demonstrates the way in which the earlier poetry provides a grounding for his subsequent explorations.

Hughes's handling of this natural folk-line is modified substantially in the other *Recklings* poems, the primary concern being to adjust the total mood and delivery of the poem in keeping with the argument. For example, in 'The Toughest' he carefully deploys the verse-patterning to point the argument as the poem mimes out structurally the particular moods – order, dissipation, chaos, renegotiation, quest – he wishes to convey. Such an approach reinforces Hughes's preoccupation with the need to channel the energies of the inner world which man has systematically denied and thus restore the balance and harmony with the agencies of the outer world. In keeping with Hughes's movement towards myth and the adaptation of shamanistic example, the poem takes a surrealistic turn, with parts of the body functioning independently and severed from their physical bond with the complete human shape. Hughes's experiences are handled in a detached manner, and the personal, almost confessional, nature of the poem (suggested by the homonym 'eye/I' and the use of phrases coded by the initials of the words) is obscured by his resort to fable and myth. In several ways 'The Toughest' anticipates the poetic statements of *Crow* and the *Gaudete* Epilogue poems, and his expository essays such as 'Myth and Education'.

Part I of the poem is the easier to follow. The opening lines, compact and organised in grammatical and syntactical sense, present the world of scientific observation and man's solution of his attempt to come to terms with primal, natural and animal forces. In lines redolent of the arrogant attitudes of 'Egg-Head' the eye, as chief receptor of image, is presented as a controlling equestrian riding roughshod, aggressively over a nervous earth, recoiling, but waiting, beneath its prints. Paradoxically, Hughes indicates, this very vision is blind, because its parameters are limited by its too-narrow rationalising and objectivity:

> The eye was a masterful horseman
> Hardened, proud and fierce.
> He reined in the listening tremors of the earth,
> He spurred its humped blindness.

The presentation of the lines in a quatrain is an oblique reference to the stylistic and thematic preoccupations that pervade the two early volumes. This suggests that the preponderance, particularly in *Lupercal*, of the distanced, objective and anecdotal is not in itself sufficient to redress the misunderstanding and violence caused by man's division from the world of Nature and the rejection of the inner self. Only some cataclysmic and external event taking shape outside the control of such objectivity is sufficient to drive the eye into the inner recesses of the mind to come to terms with primal fears and anxieties. Such an event may be a cosmic catastrophe, 'the sky-collapse of lightning', or a personal happening such as Hughes witnessed in Plath's 'central experience of a shattering of the self, and the labour of fitting it together or finding a new one':[6] 'But the sky-collapse of lightning/The earth flopping in violet like a fish jerked from its element/Drove the eye squirming into the skull – '. The physical shock to the eye is reminiscent of the fishing images in 'Stealing Trout on a May Morning' and the *Moortown* 'Earth-Numb' as Hughes, experiencing the horror of trout and salmon being dragged suddenly out of their element, is brought face to face in a therapeutic link with inner, primal forces. Driven by necessity to survive via an exploration of self and mind, the eye has access 'to the world under the world' ('Crag Jack's Apostasy') and thus the inner world, continues in existence, while a 'church-tower', symbol of organised religion, particularly Christianity, has failed. The lineation, use of end space and line space, and direct statement, factual rather than descriptive, mime the action, and thus reinforce the idea: 'It survived/Where a church-tower did not./The eye reappeared, close to orange lichens'. In opposition to the aspiring church-tower, the eye is reduced to the physical and natural level of the lichens, one of the oldest and most primitive forms of vegetable life, and symbolic of the therapeutic value of primordial life. Instead of its former 'proud and fierce' spurring, the eye is rooted close to lowly life-forms: like the Wodwo's closest experience of self-identity, poetic consciousness is at ground level. In contrast, the ears, receptors of aural rationalising and traditional theology, and incapable of making so distinctly fine a choice of what to receive, are allowed to wander, free agents in some great outer void:

> While the ears ranged far off
> Where the laughter of great outer darkness threatened to close
> its teeth on the skull
> And the mouth chewed lumps of sun that were melting the
> brains.

The suggestion is that this 'great outer darkness' ('god' by initials), as representative of objective rationalising, threatens to annihilate by ridicule this inner world. Similarly, the mouth is lost to Christ, the light of the world (the sun), as it is preoccupied with an act of communion that, because it is illogical, is undermining all rational thought. The poem's idea-system and verbal texture anticipate such poems as 'Crow Tyrannosaurus': Crow's quest to 'try to become the light' brings selective self-illumination via the suffering consequent on the very thing he seeks to deny – his instinctual eating:

> Weeping he walked and stabbed
> Thus came the eye's
>   roundness
>   the ear's
>   deafness.

Part II of 'The Toughest' takes as its form an extension of the open-ended structure of the *Recklings* 'To be a Girl's Diary', with which it shares the positing of an ideal state. The argument is opaque and obscure; but as in Part I, the insistence is on the necessity of the existence of the inner eye as gateway to understanding. Even after world-shattering events, the 'vanishing of islands', and great personal loss, 'huge weepings', the eye must maintain its quest in single-minded fashion:

> To watch
> Because nothing else can watch
>
> Leading
> A ghost
> Of query, alone, to a
>
> Doubtful haunting –

The guiding lights of the sky, the stars, as in 'To be a Girl's Diary', offer no external aid. Science has reduced outer Nature to an 'empty chart'. In contrast, Hughes links 'the Great Outer Darkness' ('GOD') with the 'lucid moon', manifestation of the pre-Christian deity in her role as fount of poetic creativity. The personal significance to Hughes of the White Goddess is emphasised by the capital letters. In the lines, 'The lucid moon, and the Great Outer Darkness/Which is the same as the small inner darkness', Hughes suggests the bond of identity between the older pre-Christian religion, 'the world of the little pagan religions and cults, the primitive religions from which of course Christianity itself grew[7] and the inner world of the consciousness, the 'inner darkness' (the id). It is 'small' because, although representative of the residues of the racial unconscious, it is subjective and individualised. The way forward is a closer communion with the natural world, here as in Part I represented by vegetable forces, 'the hopeful light of the leaf'. The leaf symbolises potential life, a bud of hope from which new forms can grow as it, like the inner eye, nudges into understanding against the darkness of ignorance. The unpunctuated last lines not only indicate the continuing quest and the growing of the leaf, but also link with Hughes's stylistic strategy in poems of the period such as 'Wodwo' and 'To be a Girl's Diary'.

The shortcomings of scientific objectivity are also important in punctuating the argument of the *Recklings* poem 'Thaw', which is written in more prosaic style. 'Thaw', like the *Recklings* poems 'Logos' and 'Fishing at Dawn', presents God as a well-intentioned but incompetent, bungling figure in comparison with the creative-destructive forces of the material-maternal deity of the under-civilised world, the White Goddess. The opening verse mirrors the questioning techniques of *Crow*, and suggests that the God of Logos, the product of the rational mind, cannot provide answers to the inner wonders, both life-confirming and death-enforcing, of Nature: 'Who'll read off the pulsings of thaw? Who'll calibrate/Combustion of the maniac's nerve? Or appraise/The damp straw's prayer to the sunrise?' Thus, while the newborn lambs 'totter out' with their perfections, God, the product of man's incomprehension of such wonders, has shrunk to insignificance:

> The Universe thickens to numbness, fumbled
> By the huge lips of a phantom.
>
> But already lambs totter out, and are apt.
> And the Almighty's crept into snowdrops, where He'll be
>   believed.

In comparison with the mysteries of Nature, the calculations of the rational mind are depicted as the spilt beads of mercury from God's broken barometer. This metaphor is further compounded to suggest the limitations of man's knowledge (in quantitative and calculable terms) of the extent of the outer void of the cosmos. The description, cold, brittle and dead, is so fitting. 'The star-litter is all that's left/Of his broken barometer'. While man seeks such impossible truths, the substance of Nature, and its knowledge of the process of creation and destruction ('pulsings', 'combustion', 'prayer'), remains earth-bound, lost in its own anguished, full swell of self-praise: 'The swollen statistics of anguish/Are jumbled and lost in the voices of water'.

'Small Events' similarly presents the God of Logos as possessing only limited power. The opening verse-paragraphs sensitively and compassionately describe an old man's dying hours:

> The old man's blood had spoken the word: 'Enough'.
> Now nobody had the heart to see him go on.
> His photographs were a cold mercy, there on the mantel.
> So his mouth became a buttonhole and his limbs became
>   wrapped iron.
>
> Towards dying his eyes looked just above the things he looked at.
> They were the poor rearguard on the beach
> And turned, watering, with all his hope, from the smoke
> To the sea for the Saviour
>
> Who is useful only in life.

The imagery, with its emphasis on coldness and iron, captures the inevitability of death and the reduction of a living being into something insignificant as 'his mouth became a buttonhole'. Hughes's suggestion that for man the Christian God 'is useful only in life' is continued in the remaining verse-paragraphs which, similarly sensitive in detail, forge a link between man, a tree-creeper, a mouse, and a swift's embryo.

> So, under a tree a tree-creeper, on dead grass sleeping –
> It was blind, its eyes matte as blood-lice
> Feeding on a raw face of disease.
> I set it on dry grass, and its head fell forward, it died
>
> Into what must have cupped it kindly.
>
> And a grey, aged mouse, humped, shivering
> On the bare path, under November drizzle –

A frail parcel, delivered in damaging mail and still unclaimed,
Its contents no longer of use to anybody.

I picked it up. It was looking neither outward nor inward.
The tremendous music of its atoms
Trembled it on my fingers. As I watched it, it died.
A grey, mangy mouse, and seamed with ancient scars,

Whose blood had said: 'Sleep'.

So this year a swift's embryo, cracked too early from its fallen
   egg –
There, among mineral fragments,
The blind blood stirred,
Freed,

And, mystified, sank into hopeful sleep.

Like man they are insignificant creatures, small or old, 'blind' and
'no longer of use to anybody'. Like man their blood has freed them
not into everlasting life but into death, which is seen as a release
from a living which has diseased, scarred and mystified them.
Death is 'what must have cupped it kindly', a 'hopeful sleep'.
Hughes suggests that, at the last resort, man is little different from
his animal 'inferiors'; his Saviour is useless, except as a release.
Death is not Christian, but a part of a natural cycle. This is further
reinforced in the description of the mouse's eyes 'looking neither
outward nor inward', which recalls the description of the aged
woman in the volume's opening poem, 'On the Slope'.

Stylistically 'Small Events' is important. Its semi-narrative
approach, almost colloquial in phrasing, is part of the search for a
poetic voice free from ornateness and posturing. The poem is, by
and large, precise in description and intimate in tone; the content is
presented in varied phrase-lengths which emphasise the emotional
rise and fall, the breathing-pattern, of the argument. Such features
were to be perfected in the *Crow* poems, either in the 'Just-So'
narrative devices of 'There was this man...', or in those poems
where the phraseology is so tailored that the absence of orthodox
punctuation intensifies, rather than weakens, the sense.

In thematic and stylistic terms the *Recklings* poem which most
clearly demonstrates Hughes's development towards *Crow* is

'Fallen Eve'. The poem's exploration of the Genesis Creation myth shares similar concerns with 'Logos'. Graves's *The White Goddess* provides a partial gloss:

> In the Genesis story of Adam and Eve the iconotropic distortion is ...very thorough. Clearly, Jehovah did not figure in the original myth. It is the Mother of all Living, conversing in triad, who casts Adam out of her fertile riverine dominions because he has usurped some prerogative of hers.... He is sent off to till the soil in some less bountiful region.... The curse in Genesis on the woman, that she should be at emnity with the serpent, is obviously mis-placed: it must refer to the ancient rivalry decreed between the sacred king Adam and the Serpent for the favours of the Goddess; Adam is fated to bruise the Serpent's head, but the Serpent will sting Adam's sacred heel, each in turn bringing the other to his annual death.[8]

Moreover, 'Fallen Eve' is Hughes's reworking of Graves's explana-tion of the philosophical and theological dichotomy occasioned by the enthronement of the God of Logos:

> The new God claimed to be dominant as Alpha and Omega, the Beginning and the End, pure Holiness, pure Good, pure Logic, able to exist without the aid of woman; but it was natural to iden-tify him with one of the original rivals of the Theme and to ally the woman and the other rival permanently against him.[9]

Hughes develops this conflict by forging a link between Eve, the biblical maternal progenitor, and the White Goddess, Mother of All Living, who, in 'Logos', spat out the nightmare of God. In 'Fallen Eve' the loss of innocence is described solely as man's loss: Eve rel-ishes her revenge on a masculine God reduced to despair. The force of awakened sexuality and the blood-pulse of the lust within keep man ensnared to fleshly delights against which love in a spiritual sense, the love of Logos, is defenceless. The cyclical process of cre-ation, an act both of desire and love, is as magnetic and repetitive as a 'gruelling drum-beat'. Furthermore 'Fallen Eve' suggests that love, particularly sexual love, is a compound of creative hope and destructive desolation. As a consequence, Eve's song of creativity is, simultaneously, one of loss. Man may aspire to renew himself (in spiritual, regenerative and sexual senses), but Eve is both author of

life and the grave of death. Man is kept earth-bound through possession of the phallic serpent, which 'rooting in crevices', is instrument of his own death. April, Eliot's 'cruellest month', is the only
time when Eve suffers remorse. It is not only the period of natural
creativity, but also, in the church calendar, the period of Christian
reaffirmation in reference to Christ's suffering and resurrection. Eve
is reminded of her action and her loss, for her disobedience
necessitated the existence of Christ, the only force able to challenge
her control, as witnessed in the usurpation of the Mother Goddess
by the God of Logos. Like Christ, Eve capitalises on flesh: not as
instrument of spiritual rebirth, but as vehicle for man's spiritual loss
by binding him more firmly to dependence on material/sexual
pleasures. As a consequence, Eve must suffer the nightmare reality,
shared by mankind, that her experience and the world include
sexual awareness and death, the very things which the God of
Logos, via the immaculate conception, the Virgin Birth, and the
Resurrection, denies:

> My mouth is the despair of God
> Formed only for men.
>
> The serpent remains earthen, brutishly-veined,
> Rooted in crevices, living on flies and men -
>
> The serpent that should have strangled me
> And then eaten itself.
>
> I sing, stamping the gruelling drum-beat
> To renew fallen men.
>
> Love is weak to protect as webs.
>
> In April my body begins to frighten me
> And my sleep fills with weeping -
>
> Again and again the forced grave of men.

Although not confirmed as such by Hughes, it seems probable
that 'Fallen Eve' was 'part of a sequence...round the theme of
Adam and Eve...which [he] didn't keep'.[10] The two most important poems which he retained from the sequence – 'Theology' and

'Reveille' – have prominent positions in *Wodwo*, and like several of the *Recklings* poems, are further evidence of Hughes's developments of a mythic framework which was to lead eventually to *Crow*.

At face value, 'Plum-Blossom' seems an exercise in gratuitous and self-indulgent poeticising. This is mainly because its three apparently unconnected sections obscure even an immediate level of understanding. However, an investigation of its symbolism indicates the central position the poem has in Hughes's thematic and stylistic development. An earlier, lengthier version of Part I (the *Recklings* version is reduced to lines 5–12) is crucial in providing the key to Hughes's intention. What Hughes is concerned with is the paradox between the delicacy and apparent frailty of the plum-blossom and its passionate urge for survival and continuance. Hughes insists on the tree's restless, violent (almost militant) surging into life:

> Not the snail's river of itself
> Nor a man's mental den of no departure
> But all night
> The shadow of these riders trampling the street-lamps.
>
> The plum tree has battled the whole way
> Up the hard road of the roots, its mouth full of stones.
> The buds of the plum tree are scarred veterans.
> Full of last words, the old saws of zero.
>
> But the plum-blossoms open
> Volcanoes of frailty -
> Mouths without hunger but to utter
> Love, love to each other.
>
> Neither the granite, hewn, bag-breasted Sheilas,
> With their knees hauled back,
> Pulling themselves, big-fingered wide-open,
> Presenting the voice in their bellies
>
> Or the dog-heads of infernal darkness
> Gripped into grinning gargoyle stone
> Shall protect the time-blackened Cathedrals
> From the plum-blossom.

Past, present, future –
Luckless snow-crystals
In the silent laughter
Of these raw barbarians, these burning hairy mouths.[11]

The images referring to the plum-blossom's determination to survive link the poem directly with Hughes's 'flower' poems from
Lupercal, *Recklings* and *Wodwo*, such as the snowdrop who 'pursues
her ends,/Brutal as the stars of this month', the thistles 'stiff with
weapons' and the fern, 'plume/Of a warrior returning'. As in 'The
Green Wolf' (*Wodwo*, p. 40) the link between man and vegetative
life-forces is important. In 'The Green Wolf' a description of a man
paralysed by a stroke develops into a metaphysical comment on
man's relationship with other forces which move towards death, so
that – as the conclusion of 'To be a Girl's Dairy' suggests – 'Everything is inheriting everything'. This insistence on vegetative forces
as part of man's unmaking and remaking is paralleled in the *Recklings* poem, in the idea that the plum-blossom's single purpose of
'Mouths without hunger but to utter/Love, love to each other' as
process of fertilisation, fruition and self-regeneration, will transcend
man's material attempts at self-protection and self-extension in
after-life by erecting religious edifices. For these 'time-blackened
Cathedrals' of 'Past, present, future' will be as 'Luckless snow-
crystals' in comparison with 'raw barbarians' of plum-blossom with
'burning hairy mouths'. Furthermore, the use in 'The Green Wolf' of
hawthorn and beanflower, both sacred to the White Goddess as part
of the process of death-and-life agencies, is echoed in 'Plum-
Blossom': for, according to Friend, not only hawthorn, but also
'boughs of the Plum-Tree are placed over windows and doors, to
keep away witches'.[12] This idea is connected with Hughes's reference to the limited function of cathedral gargoyles in preserving the
Church from the forces of evil, for they in time will become victims
of the forces of natural regeneration. Hughes's claim that 'When
Christianity kicked the devil out of Job what they actually kicked
out was Nature…and Nature became the devil'[13] is worked into the
following lines:

Neither the granite, hewn, bag-breasted Sheilas,
With their knees hauled back,
Pulling themselves big-fingered wide-open,
Presenting the voice in their bellies

Or the dog-heads of infernal darkness
Gripped into grinning gargoyle stone
Shall protect the time-blackened Cathedrals
From the plum-blossom.

As symbol of 'evil' Nature, the plum-blossom mouthing 'love, love' is a more potent force than the sterile theologising and rationalising of modern 'man's mental den of no departure'. These verses not only look back to the suggestion in 'The Toughest' that church spires will topple while the orange lichen survives, but also anticipate part of the main narrative of *Gaudete*, as well as several of its Epilogue poems.

Before the climactic sacrificial holocaust of the main narrative, Hughes introduces a passage (*Gaudete*, pp. 98–106) in which the changeling Lumb recovers from an attempt by the powers of the underworld to cancel him out, mainly because he aspires to human identity. The changeling Lumb finds himself 'in the slurry of a cattleyard' (p. 98), is beaten with cudgels, and escapes only by running with the cattle. When he comes to 'He lies buried in mud'. While the women of his parish lie buried alive, he is drawn by a creature 'squirming in a well of liquid mud', and attempts to save her. He finds himself completely knotted to her, as if fused by 'a powerful spring trap' (p. 104) and a 'calf-clamp' (p. 105). The creature turns out to be the woman of the Prologue; and Lumb's action has awakened him to some sort of compassion. In a state of semi-consciousness, he witnesses his rebirth in which he is not only reborn from, but also simultaneously becomes mother to, the Nature Goddess:

Somehow he has emerged and is standing over himself.
He sees himself being delivered of the woman from the pit...
Flood-sudden, like the disembowelling of a cow
She gushes from between his legs, a hot splendour
In a glistening of oils,
In a radiance like phosphorous he sees her crawl and tremble....

He sees her face undeformed and perfect.

(*Gaudete*, pp. 105–6)

The link with the *Recklings* poem exists in the acknowledgement of the terrible beauty of Nature, its creative–destructive passion as plum-blossoms ('raw barbarians' with 'burning hairy mouths' uttering 'love, love') destroy man's attempt to rationalise his existence. A further link is seen in that when Lumb next appears in his room, his window is described as 'also a door on to the furnace of the bright world/The chill bustle/Of the blossom-rocking afternoon' (*Gaudete*, p. 108). Lumb sits in a trance, his eyes locked

> To an archaic stone carving, propped on his mantel, above the fire.

> The simply hacked-out face of a woman
> Gazes back at Lumb
> Between her raised, wide-splayed, artless knees
> With a stricken expression.

> Her square-cut, primitive fingers, beneath her buttocks
> Are pulling herself wide open –

> An entrance, an exit.

This presentation of a primitive Venus figurine, in itself symbol of earth-mother, is a development of the concerns of the uncollected version of 'Plum Blossom' which links such figurines, 'bag-breasted Sheilas', with 'dog-heads of infernal darkness' as of limited scope in protecting man from the destructive forces of Nature. Similarly the changeling Lumb is unable to save himself from cancellation by transfixing himself to the worship of an effigy, rather than full worship of Nature. The fact that, according to Sharkey, such stone effigies with their 'ugly mask-like skull-face with huge scowling mouth, skeletal ribs, huge genitalia held apart with both hands and bent legs...offer a fantasy of unlimited sexual license'[14] indicates the major failure of the changeling. While the goddess is often associated with fecundity, she is also the goddess of compassion and love. The changeling's error is his concentration on the degradation of these emotions to lust.

The 'dog-heads of infernal darkness' form the subject of 'Plum-Blossom' II, published initially as 'More Theology' in *Moments of Truth* (Keepsake Press, Twickenham, 1965):

> The baboon in the zoo
> Shows me its multicoloured arse
> Meaning it wants to be friendly.
> It looks over its shoulder

With narrow glittering eyes
Like an Egyptian priestess.
We are both in a world
Where the dirt is God.

In Egyptian mythology, the dog-headed ape, the baboon, was used to represent both Anubis, the god of death, and also Thoth, the keeper of divine archives and the inventor of writing who, as Ash-tet-Huti, was the god in charge of guarding the moon, and whose spouse, Seshat, was the goddess of writing. The link between 'Plum-Blossom' and the Mother Nature figure is seen in the fact that the baboon has 'narrow glittering eyes/Like an Egyptian priestess', and also the fact that in *Gaudete* Hughes identifies the earth-mother figure as a baboon-woman:

It is a woman's face,
A face as if sewn together from several faces.
A baboon beauty face,
A crudely stitched patchwork of faces,
But the eyes slide,
Alive and electrical, ...behind the stitched lids.
                              (*Gaudete*, p. 104)

In *Gaudete*, Lumb can be reborn only by an acknowledgement of the half-animal, crudely-stitched face of the desecrated earth-goddess. As a result of his compassion, this face becomes 'undeformed and perfect'. In 'Plum-Blossom' II, Hughes acknowledges the crudity ('multi-coloured arse') and the beauty ('narrow glittering eyes;), and, because of this, is recognised by the baboon, in symbolic terms, as friend. In both works, and in keeping with Hughes's proclamations on Reformed Christianity, God is seen as the rejected ordure of a religious order, the worship of Nature, which, particularly under Protestantism, has been exiled and driven almost into extinction and zoo-imprisonment. The fact that 'Plum-Blossom' II appears only in the limited edition *Recklings* may account for Hughes's reworking of the expression 'We are both in a world/Where the dirt is God' in the penultimate *Cave Birds* poem, 'The risen', which presents the chastened central protagonist as a falcon, and as a Creator-like figure, so that

In the wind-fondled crucible of his splendour,
The dirt becomes God.

But when will he land
On a man's wrist.

Given Hughes's interest in Eastern mysticism in poems of the period, it may be that the relationship of 'dirt' with 'God' is a recognition of the celebration which dirt/earth/mud have in the Hindu, Buddhist, Taoist and Egyptian Creation myths. The deification of elemental earth is in keeping with the alchemical processes that form the analogue to the psychological transformation, union and rebirth of the *Cave Birds* central protagonist. The shift from 'is God' to 'becomes God' mirrors Hughes's changing awareness of the process of transmutation. Hughes's original subtitle for *Cave Birds* was 'The Death of Socrates and his Resurrection in Egypt', and the rebirth of the Socratic cockerel as a noble falcon suggests that Hughes is making reference to the Heliopolitan sun-god, Re-Atum (later to be identified with Horus), who in the form of a hawk settled on the Benben, the fetishistic conically-shaped stone symbolic of the first primeval mound – the 'dirt' of creation. Such an identification of the origins of created flesh informs the details of the *Cave Birds* marriage poem: 'Bride and groom lie hidden for three days', in which the almost-man and almost-woman, after an exchange of transforming and creating gifts, bring themselves to mutual perfection 'Like two gods of mud/Sprawling in the dirt'. Hughes in 'The risen' may also be referring to the Egyptian concept of the two immortal elements of man: the *ba*, which, depicted as a human-headed bird, was regarded as an animating force having some correspondence with the Christian concept of the soul; and the *ka*, the double of its owner, which after death came to be regarded as man's spirit, or that part of him which ensured his immortality as an individual. These transformed states in 'The risen' are conveyed not only by the alchemical references in the penultimate couplet ('crucible', splendour', and the elevation of dirt to a deity in which 'becomes' includes both a coming into existence *and* a state of splendid adornment), but also in the final couplet, which suggests that such divine transmutation eludes unchastened man, and thus occasions the ritualistic need for the final poem's 'goblin'.

'Plum-Blossom' III mirrors this cyclic need, but in more than just literary terms, despite its structural dependence on the Celtic rune. Hughes experimented with this form while involved with the *Crow* cycle, and it may be that the *Recklings* poem is contemporaneous with 'Amulet' (from *Crow Wakes*) which has resurfaced as the prefatory poem to his volume for children, *Under the North Star*. In content, however, 'Plum-Blossom' III looks back to *Lupercal*. In 'Crag Jack's Apostasy' Hughes eschewed the God of the dark churches, and invoked a more primitive, and simultaneously more inner, deity:

> Come to my sleeping body through
> The world under the world; pray
> That I may see more than your eyes
>
> In an animal's dreamed head
> >   (*Lupercal*, p. 55)

In 'Plum-Blossom' III this deity seems to have answered the summons and appears in the shape of a cat's head as a more ancient force than Christian belief:

> Inside the head of a cat
> Under the bones, the brains, the blood-tissue,
> Bone of the bone and brain of the brain,
> Blood of the blood and tissue of the tissue,
> Is God's head, with eyes open.
> And under that my own head, with wide eyes.
> And under that the head of a cat, with eyes
> Smiling and closed.

The connecting link with the other sections of the poem may be in the reference to the cat; for, in Egyptian myth, Mut, the Earth Mother, assumed the form of Bast, the cat-goddess. Moreover, in the early religious rituals associated with the Egyptian sun-god, Horus, amulets in the form of animals were placed in the burial chambers. This practice underpins the cyclical structure of the poem which replicates the function of the rune as a charm or bracelet, later rhyme, used to guard against evil spirits. This feature links it with the conflict in 'Plum-Blossom' I between the flowers and the protecting gargoyles; and strengthens Hughes's condemnations in 'Plum-Blossom' II of God as dirt. The invocation to primitive deities closely associated with Nature also connects the poem with Hughes's quest from *Lupercal* onwards for means of renegotiation between inner and outer worlds.

As it appears in Recklings, the subject-matter of 'Plum-Blossom' is obscure, and not entirely related to its title. However, the poem does chart the developments in Hughes's style: Part I in the quatrains of *The Hawk in the Rain* and *Lupercal;* Part II the elliptical structures of *Wodwo;* Part III the runic invocations of Crow; and the whole as an exploration of some of the thematic concerns of *Cave Birds* and *Gaudete*. 'Plum-Blossom' confirms that between *Lupercal* and *Wodwo* Hughes was searching for symbolic vehicles of expression; and suggests that in his movement towards myth as means of communicating his poetic and expository claims, vegetative life-forces enjoy an important position.

As this account reveals, the poetic contents of *Recklings* make many demands on the reader. The density of the poetic/philosophic arguments and Hughes's quest for a style to complement the contents have led commentators to view the volume as containing 'private poems' (Sagar) concerned with the exposition of a 'personal sadness' (Alan Bold) and written in 'a private style' (Walder).[15] What exactly is meant by the latter has not been fully explained; nor is it certain that it should obstruct criticism. The application of words like 'private' and 'personal' seems no more than an excuse for side-stepping the demands which the majority of the thirty-two poems make on the reader. To suggest that these are 'minor' poems (Leonard Scigaj)[16] is to underestimate the central position in Hughes's output that many of the *Recklings* poems hold, while simultaneously diminishing their worth as individual acts of creativity. The *Recklings* poems possess a dislocating medley of references, and their compressed textual density controlled by abrupt and freely associative juxtapositions produces a series of epigrammatic structures. The consequent sudden transitions in content force the reader to probe beyond the literal textual meaning of the individual poem into the acceptance of something akin to philosophical generalisation, a feature which is intensified in the cumulative process of evaluating the volume as an entirety. The emphatic shifts of voice create a poignant impressive intensity occasionally sombre in its lucidity, largely couched in the vernacular, and conveyed in a colloquial tone (quiet, intimate, sincere, mordant) that gives the poems the texture of chamber-music.

The *Recklings* poems *are* difficult works: cryptic and opaque, and explore new territory in content, theme and style. However, the light that they throw on Hughes's poetic strategies and thematic concerns in the period prior to *Wodwo* suggests that *Recklings* occupies a seminal position for a fuller understanding of his subsequent work. Since Hughes enjoys such an important place in English poetry it would seem imperative that the volume be seen afresh. That critics have been misguided in considering Hughes's evaluation of these poems as 'self-deprecatory' (May)[17] is suggested by the notion that, even if the animal connotations of the title are pursued, it is often the case that those least suited to survive demand more attention. That Hughes with his gnomic humour may have this in mind is emphasised by *The Oxford English Dictionary* illustration: '*attrib.* 1834 Sir H. Taylor *2nd Pt. Artevelde* v. iii, "A mother dotes upon the reckling child, more than the strong,"'[18] while *The English Dialect Dictionary* pushes the claim further in its definition of 'ritling' (a variant of 'reckling'): 'ritling often turns out best pig i' the farth [farrow].'[19] Certainly, it could be argued that while not all the *Recklings* poems are as fine as 'On the Slope', 'The Toughest', 'Thaw', 'Small Events', 'Fallen Eve' and 'Plum-Blossom', these particular poems do represent a more authentic way forward for Hughes than some of the 'fatter' poems which made it into *Wodwo*.

Notes

1.   May, Derwent, 'Ted Hughes' in Martin Dodsworth (ed.), *The Survival of Poetry* (Faber and Faber, London, 1970), p. 150; Sagar, Keith, *Ted Hughes* (Longman, London, for the British Council, 1972), p. 21; Walder, Dennis, *Ted Hughes, Sylvia Plath* (Open University Press, Milton Keynes, 1976), p. 23; Faas, Ekbert, *Ted Hughes: The Unaccommodated Universe* (Black Sparrow Press, Santa Barbara, 1980), p. 83.

2.   Jung, C. G., *Psychology and Alchemy* (Routledge and Kegan Paul, London, 1953), pp. 219–21.

3.   Jung, C. G., *The Practice of Psychotherapy* (Pantheon Books, New York, 1963), p. 167.

4.   Hughes, Ted, 'The Rock' in *Writers on Themselves* (BBC, London, 1964), p. 90.

5.   As 'A Pause for Breath', *New Yorker* (27 August 1966), p. 90, the poem is in five tercets; reads 'Foxglove, harebell' (line 10); and ends with 'And eyes, dimmed with losses, widening for losses'.

6.   Hughes, Ted, 'Sylvia Plath', *Poetry Book Society Bulletin* 44 (February 1965).

7.   Faas, Ekbert, 'Ted Hughes and Crow', *London Magazine* (January 1971), pp. 5–20, p. 205.

8.   Graves, Robert, *The White Goddess* (Faber and Faber, London, 1971), p. 257.

9.   Ibid., p. 465.

10. *Ted Hughes: The Unaccommodated Universe*, p. 212.
11. Hughes, Ted, 'Plum Blossom', *Transatlantic Review* 22 (Autumn 1966), pp. 71–2.
12. Friend, Hilderic, *Flowers and Flower Lore* (Sonnonschein, 1886), p. 541.
13. Faas, p. 199.
14. Sharkey, J., *Celtic Mysteries* (Thames and Hudson, London, 1975), p. 8.
15. Sagar, Keith, *Ted Hughes* (1972), p. 21; Bold, Alan, *Thom Gunn and Ted Hughes* (Oliver and Boyd, Harlow, 1976), p. 99; Walder, Dennis, *Ted Hughes, Sylvia Plath*, p. 23.
16. Scigaj, Leonard, *The Poetry of Ted Hughes, Form and Imagination* (University of Iowa Press, Iowa, 1986), p. 86.
17. May, Derwent, 'Ted Hughes', p. 150.
18. *The Compact Edition of The Oxford English Dictionary* (2 vols) (Oxford University Press, Oxford, 1971), II, p. 2440.
19. Wright, Joseph, (ed.), *English Dialect Dictionary* (6 vols) (Oxford University Press, Oxford, 1961), V, p. 128.

3

The Evolution of 'The Dove Came'

Keith Sagar

The way poetry is usually taught, artificially detaching the poem from the poet and from the whole creative process, encourages a belief that, as milk comes from bottles, so poems come from books. The complex and fascinating process by which they came into being and got into the books is totally ignored.

Though, as Hughes says, 'the poem can emerge of a sudden, complete and perfect, unalterable, taking the poet completely by surprise, as if he had no idea where it came from', there is wide-spread belief, particularly among the young, that this is how all poems are written, or should be written. Hughes would be the first to attest to the rarity of this experience. And even when it does happen, the poet more often than not *does* alter it. However, some poets have encouraged the growth of a mystique about how poetic inspiration works. There is Coleridge's suggestion in 'Kubla Khan' and its preface that once the poet has fed on honey-dew and drunk the milk of Paradise (marketed as laudanum in his day), even such complex poems as this will write themselves 'instantly', though a knock on the door is enough to break the spell. Elsewhere, Coleridge stated more temperately that the poem had been composed 'in a sort of reverie', which could be said of any poem. In fact, if a new Coleridge notebook turned up, it should not surprise us to find in it twenty drafts of 'Kubla Khan'.

Though Dylan Thomas himself to some extent also fostered the myth of unpremeditated art, the fine frenzy, what Hopkins (speaking of Swinburne) called 'a delirium-tremendous imagination', critics should not have been as surprised as they were when the notebooks came to light after his death, revealing draft after draft transforming a poem beyond recognition. He laboured night after night at his craft or sullen art to produce the impression of 'spindrift pages'. He wrote to Henry Treece:

A poem by myself *needs* a host of images, because its centre is a host of images. I make one image, – though 'make' is not the word; I let, perhaps, an image be 'made' emotionally in me and then apply to it what intellectual & critical forces I possess – let it breed another, let that image contradict the first, make, of the third image bred out of the other two together, a fourth contradictory image, and let them all, within any imposed formal limits, conflict. Each image holds within it the seed of its own destruction, and my dialectical method, as I understand it, is a constant building up and breaking down of the images that come out of the central seed, which is itself destructive and constructive at the same time.

But what I want to try to explain – and it's necessarily vague to me – is that the *life* in any poem of mine cannot move concentrically round a central image; the life must come out of the centre; an image must be born and die in another; and any sequence of my images must be a sequence of creations, recreations, destructions, contradictions.... Out of the inevitable conflict of images – inevitable, because of the creative, recreative, destructive and contradictory nature of the motivating centre, the womb of war – I try to make that momentary peace which is a poem. I do not want a poem of mine to be, nor can it be, a circular piece of experience placed nearly outside the living stream of time from which it came; a poem of mine is, or should be, a watertight section of the stream that is flowing all ways; all warring images within it should be reconciled for that small stop of time.

Reading back over that, I agree it looks preciously like nonsense. To say that I 'let' images breed and conflict is to deny my critical part in the business. (Ferris (ed.), *Collected Letters* (Macmillan, 1985), p. 281–2)

Hughes related this method to Thomas's larger purposes:

Every poem is an attempt to sign up the whole heavenly vision, from one point of vantage or other, in a static constellation of verbal prisms. It is this fixed intent, and not a rhetorical inflation of ordinary ideas, that gives his language its exaltation and reach. (Faas, p. 182)

Hughes had, at the very outset of his career, described his own method in very similar terms, when he spoke of 'the living and individual element in every poet's work':

> What I mean is the way he brings to peace all the feelings and energies which, from all over the body, heart, and brain, send up their champions onto the battleground of that first subject. The way I do this, as I believe, is by using something like the method of a musical composer. I might say that I turn every combatant into a bit of music, then resolve the whole uproar into as formal and balanced a figure of melody and rhythm as I can. When all the words are hearing each other clearly, and every stress is feeling every other stress, and all are contented – the poem is finished. (Faas, p. 163).

Though the language here ('formal and balanced a figure of melody') is influenced by the New Critics, and not the way Hughes would have expressed himself later, it describes adequately enough the method of an early poem such as 'The Thought-Fox'. It is clearly a time-consuming, paper-consuming process. Yet many young (and not-so-young) readers of 'The Thought-Fox' take literally the implication that such a poem could be written, without blotting a word, in the time it takes for the fox to cross the clearing, and with the poet having as little part in the business as the narrator who simply lets the fox enter his head and his fingers move automatically, over the blank page. Many of Hughes's detractors write as though they believed all his poems to be instantaneous, automatic, lacking the application of his intellectual and critical forces – a hotchpotch of archetypes plundered from the myth-kitty. Seeds of poems (it is a *thought*-fox, not a poem-fox) and bits of poems do frequently come this spontaneous way, but an examination of Hughes's manuscripts reveals the protracted labour usually required to bring a poem from its first draft to its very different published text.

There is, in this respect, no such thing as a typical Hughes poem. Each poem has its unique kind of evolution. The number of drafts can vary from one to twenty or thirty. A poem can remain essentially the same through all its drafts, or can be transformed beyond recognition. Most of a poem can be there from the start, or only the merest hint. It is almost as common for a poem to grow shorter through its drafts as longer; or it can grow long and then short again. It can come full circle and end where it began. (The poet has here the advantage over the painter or sculptor: if he decides that his first thoughts were best, they are not lost.)

My choice of poem is almost random, since I am restricted to those few poems I happen to have access to in all their drafts. I have chosen from *Adam and The Sacred Nine* (written late 1975) 'The Dove Came', which is fairly typical of Hughes's moderately complex medium-length poems using theriomorphic imagery for psycho-spiritual purposes. Here is the final text:

THE DOVE CAME

Her breast big with rainbows
She was knocked down

The dove came, her wings clapped lightning
That scattered like twigs
She was knocked down

The dove came, her voice of thunder
A piling heaven of silver and violet
She was knocked down

She gave the flesh of her breast, and they ate her
She gave the milk of her blood, they drank her

The dove came again, a sun-blinding

And ear could no longer hear

Mouth was a disembowelled bird
Where the tongue tried to stir like a heart

And the dove alit
In the body of thorns.

Now deep in the dense body of thorns
A soft thunder
Nests her rainbows.

When Hughes chose the order of the sections in *Moortown* – first the farming poems, then the *Prometheus* sequence, then *Earth-Numb* and finally the *Adam* sequence, he intended that the whole book, like *Wodwo*, should constitute a 'single adventure', a progress from earth-bound suffering, through numbness to rebirth. So the *Prometheus* and *Adam* poems, as it were, bracket a very important phase of Hughes's career as he emerged from the horrors of *Crow* and the numbness of *Prometheus* into the painful and raw affirmations of *Adam*. *Adam and the Sacred Nine* is part of a larger process (which also includes *Cave Birds* and *Gaudete*) of reconstituting and resacralising both the self and the world.

The manuscripts of 'The Dove Came' consist of thirteen A4 pages, eight holograph and five typescript, two of these with holograph revision. With one exception (where there are two drafts of the opening) each page carries the whole poem. I have numbered thirteen drafts, but these do not correspond to the thirteen pages, since some of the holograph pages have two drafts, the original (not always wholly recoverable) and the interlinear, marginal and superimposed revision (not always decipherable either), and some of the typescripts are merely fair copies. The published version constitutes a fourteenth, since it does not exactly correspond with the final manuscript. The drafts are undated, and there is no certainty that I have arranged them in the correct order.

Introducing a reading of several of the *Adam* poems on radio, Hughes said:

> All the creatures of the world come to him, telling him to pull himself together and get moving, but he just lies there, getting limper and limper. At last his creator can't stand it any longer, and so he sends down nine divine birds, to become his guardian, exemplary spirits. They are actually just ordinary birds, except for one, which is a Phoenix.

The dove he described simply as 'a gentle dove, forcing herself through all the opposition'.

The dove, strangely (given its crucial importance in the sequence), was not one of the nine as Hughes first conceived the story, but replaced the kingfisher ('who sews the worlds together').

Each bird brings Adam a particularly clear example of a quality he will require if he is ever to achieve his full manhood. Each quality derives partly from the ornithological character of the species ('just ordinary birds'), partly from the character each bird has acquired in myth and folklore, which is not unrelated, since each bird which has acquired mythological status has done so at least in part by virtue of the observable characteristics of ordinary birds. There is no necessary distinction between 'ordinary' and 'divine'. And in *What is the Truth?*, after the farmer has described pigeons as pests fit for nothing but pigeon pie, the vicar comments: 'The holiest bird of all! What an end!' (p. 58).

Doves are unique in being the only birds to feed their young on milk, a high-protein fluid called crop-milk. Since this can be produced at almost any time of year, they have no breeding season and raise several broods throughout the year. They copulate frequently and openly and were therefore thought to be lecherous and fertile. (The association with sexual love is built into our language with 'lovey-dovey', 'bill and coo' etc.) Presumably for this reason, the dove became sacred to the great goddesses Ishtar, Venus and Isis. The softness, warmth and milkiness of the dove's breast and its caressing call suggest all that is feminine, loving, maternal, protective. This aspect allowed its sacredness to be carried over into Judaic and Christian symbolism, where the dove symbolises the Holy Spirit. In the Old Testament, the dove was the first creature to find land after the Flood, and is thereby closely associated with God's renewed covenant with mankind, symbolised by the rainbow, (reflected in its prismatic plumage) (Genesis 9: 13). In the Gospels the Spirit of God descends on Christ 'like a dove, and lighting upon him' when he is baptised by John the Baptist (Matthew 3: 16). The Holy Ghost is traditionally pictured as a dove. For Hopkins the dove symbolised the perpetual daily renewal of the world: 'Because the Holy Ghost over the bent/World broods with warm breast and with ah! bright wings'. In both Christian and alchemical iconography the soul itself is frequently pictured as a dove. Proverbially, the dove symbolises meekness and faithfulness. Nineteenth-century sentimental Christianity gave its qualities to Christ himself – 'gentle Jesus meek and mild'. The association with martyrdom and sacrifice is strengthened by our modern experience of the dove as living target, the extermination of the passenger-pigeon, the slaughter of wood-pigeons, of which *The Birdlife of Britain* says 'everyman's hand seems to be against them'.

By far the most important non-ornithological source for Hughes is Blake. Both *Prometheus on His Crag* and *Adam and the Sacred Nine* were first published by Olwyn Hughes's Rainbow Press, the emblem of which was Blake's illustration to Bryant depicting moon-arc, dove and rainbow. Both books, like most of

Hughes's sequences of the 1970s, are reworkings of material which largely defeated Blake – attempts to find a simpler, more dramatic, more coherent, more poetic myth to embody the process by which Albion/Adam, fallen into the sleep of single vision, is gradually and painfully dismantled, reconstituted, and awakened into the fourfold vision of Adam Kadmon, and reunited with his lost bride. Blake's defeated Albion is Hughes's Prometheus on his crag: 'Albion cold lays on his Rock.../Over them the famish'd Eagle screams on boney Wings'. (*Jerusalem* 94). In the third Prometheus poem Prometheus's shout shatters 'a world of holy, happy notions', symbolised by birds: 'The dove's bubble of fluorescence burst'. For Blake the dove symbolises Albion's lost emanation, his threefold vision of innocence. Only Los, the poet, retains a vision of Jerusalem descending from heaven as a dove, and as a bride adorned for her husband Albion:

> I see thy Form, O lovely mild Jerusalem, Wing'd with Six Wings
> In the opacous Bosom of the Sleeper, lovely Three-fold
> In Head & Heart & Reins, three Universes of love & beauty.
> Thy forehead bright, Holiness to the Lord, with Gates of pearl
> Reflects Eternity; beneath, thy azure wings of feathery down
> Ribb'd delicate & cloth'd with feather'd gold & azure & purple,
> From thy white shoulders shadowing purity in holiness!
> Thence, feather'd with soft crimson of the ruby, bright as fire,
> Spreading into the azure, Wings which like a canopy
> Bends over thy immortal
> ...
> Head in which Eternity dwells.
> I see the New Jerusalem descending out of Heaven,
> Between thy Wings of gold & silver, feather'd, immortal,
> Clear as the rainbow, as the cloud of the Sun's tabernacle.
>
> (*Jerusalem* 86)

All these sources, and no doubt more esoteric ones, are available for Hughes to draw on, consciously or unconsciously, as he begins his poem. Through the drafts we can see the original images attracting others, falling away, undergoing manifold transformations, as Hughes struggles to let the dove force herself through all the opposition, most of which comes from Adam (Hughes, Everyman, reader) himself.

Here is my attempt to recover the first draft:

THE DOVE

Is the bubble the violet
A breast of quiet lightning
A thunder of softness, care
And endearment, plundered by gods

Arched wings
A gateway of watchfulness
Where the world plays
With a child

When they plucked her
The stars floated off, and became unending [?].
They roasted her
Then they disembowelled her
Their mouths smoked.
Her liver became an oracle.

Her flesh still [?]
[?] cave of slaughter.
Her heart spoke,
An oracle
Of loving words

Her heart became his tongue.

He stood, drenched in her blood
And hardening in the light.

                    Still her words were his strength.

The first thing that strikes us is that not a line, not even a phrase, of
this first draft survives into the published poem. Yet it is clearly the
same poem. All the drafts, though they play many variations with
the phrasing, begin with the dove's breast, its bulbous shape and its
distinctive colouring. All the drafts retain the imagery of thunder
and lightning, suggested, presumably, by the similar colour of thun-
der-clouds, the soft rumble of the voice, and the flash and clap of

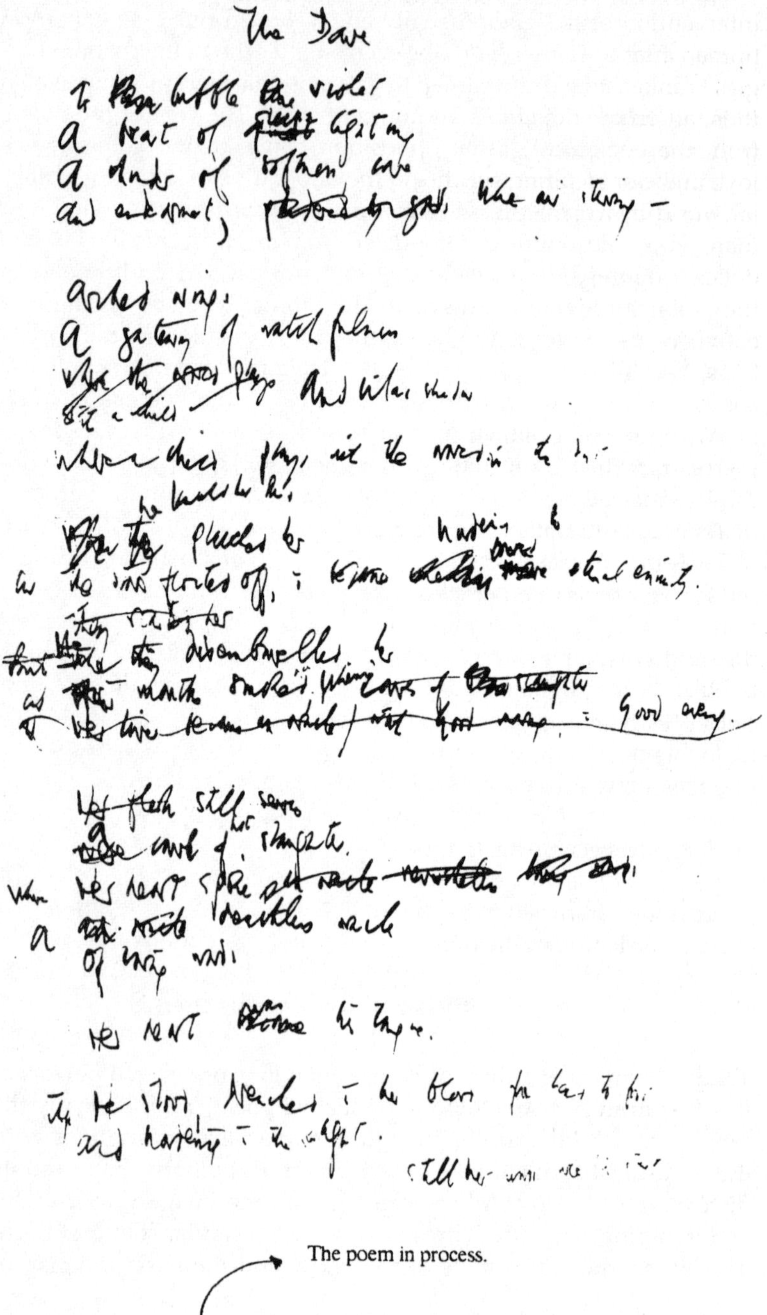

The poem in process.

wings. Thunder and lightning also traditionally announce some intervention of the gods (usually angry, but in this case gentle) in human affairs. There is perhaps even a faint echo of the cosmic energies Frankenstein draws down to galvanise his inert monster, which then, all unknowing, kills an innocent child. The core of the poem, from the beginning, is the opposition between the imperative to love in the descending spirit, and the imperative to kill in the material world in which it is obliged to try to incarnate itself. How can man, who is flesh little differentiated from mud, receive the bubble-delicate fluorescence of what the dove brings? The middle part of the poem throughout deals with the killing, disembowelling and eating of the dove, followed by the transformation of the dove's heart into the man's tongue. This alchemical transformation has something in common with such pictures as the Boehme etching, known to Blake, of fallen man awakening when a dove descends, pierces his breast, and enters or becomes his heart and also with those depictions of the soul leaving the body of a saint or martyr at death in the form of a dove emerging from the mouth.

The word 'bubble' is retained, in various combinations, through the first eight drafts. It is the right shape for a plump breast, has rainbow colours, is extremely fragile, and, moreover, exactly mimes the sound of a dove. But it has to be let go at last, probably because a bubble can only be knocked down once, if at all, does not bleed, and cannot be eaten, cannot force its way through anything, cannot live in the same world as thorns. The whole point about the dove's breast is that it is simultaneously substantial flesh and blood and insubstantial rainbow, both vulnerable and indestructible. The bubble falls between.

'Violet' comes and goes, but is finally retained in the splendid description of the dove's 'voice of thunder' as 'A piling heaven of silver and violet'. 'Violet' is soft, but potentially violent, is closer than 'blue' (the alternative in draft 4) to the actual colour of thunder clouds, and, being at the upper limit of human colour-vision, suggests, perhaps, that boundary between the seen and the unseen, the worlds of body and of spirit, where most of the events of these poems take place. Hughes continues for nine drafts to spell out the meaning of the dove's thunder as softness, care (later caresses), and endearments, but finds at last that these abstractions are redundant.

The next section also remains, little changed, until the tenth draft, when it disappears altogether. At the first revision it had become:

Arched wings
A gateway of watchfulness
And lilac shadow
Where a child plays with the world in the dust.

The dove is here presented as the guardian of a Blakean world of childish innocence. Though the word 'rainbow' does not appear until the fourth draft, the idea of the rainbow, symbolising harmony and unfallen vision, must have been in Hughes's mind from the beginning. Blake's vision of childhood seems to blend with Lawrence's. When, in *The Rainbow,* Tom and Lydia Brangwen came together in perfect marriage, Tom knew 'that she was the gateway and the way out'. They created a rainbow arch of security for their child: 'Her father and her mother now met to the span of the heavens, and she, the child, was free to play in the space beneath, between.'

In Hughes's first draft, the dove is killed by anonymous adults. It comes as a shock to find that after the first revision, she is killed by the child. In the next draft we are told that he does so 'in childish unknowing', and in the fourth 'In childish dreaminess/He disembowels her/Looking for life'. This is the authentic Hughes world, where innocence is inseparable from slaughter. The childish, larval wodwo asks: 'Why do I find/this frog so interesting as I inspect its most secret/interior and make it my own?'.

Draft 4 is already beginning to look like a finished poem, but evidently not the poem Hughes wanted to write:

The bubble-blue dove
Brings from heaven
A breast of sleepy rainbows – the dove's lightning.
An air-stirring softness, caresses
And endearments. This is the dove's thunder.

Arched wings
A gateway of watchfulness
and lilac shadow
Where a child plays with the world in the dust
Soon he grows
He knocks her down, and he plucks her alive
The stars float off
Hardening and sharpening to enmity.

In childish dreaminess
He disembowels her
Looking for life.
His mouth smokes open
A cavern of hot slaughter
With her heart speaking inside it
A deathless oracle
Loving words to the child

Her heart is his tongue. His listening begins.

Though he stands drenched in her blood from head to foot
And hardening among stars
Her words are his strength.

This is the dove's milk.

The hardening of the stars and then the child suggests not only a loss of innocence, but also a process of individuation, like something lifted from the flux, the forge, and cooling into its definitive form.

It seems that *only* when the child is drenched in the dove's blood from head to foot can he stand, come into his strength, and speak the word 'love'. There are many accounts of pagan rituals where the worshippers are drenched in the blood of a sacrificial animal. Here is Frazer's account of an Attis rite:

> A bull, adorned with garlands of flowers, its forehead glittering with gold leaf, was driven onto the grating and there stabbed to death with a consecrated spear. Its hot reeking blood poured in torrents through the apertures, and was received with devout eagerness by the worshipper on every part of his person and garments, till he emerged from the pit, drenched, dripping, and scarlet from head to foot, to receive the homage, nay the adoration, of his fellows as one who had been born again into eternal life and had washed away his sins in the blood of the bull. (*The Golden Bough*, p. 463)

There are, of course, important differences between what happens in the poem and such pagan rituals. The child is not a worshipper participating in a ritual. He knocks down the dove for no better reason than the Ancient Mariner shoots the albatross – on a whim, having nothing better to do; or rather, in accordance with the 'natural logic' (draft 8) which dictates that all creatures were created as food for other creatures, that any creature outside the ordered world of man is by nature his food, target or plaything. When Hughes was a child, his elder brother would wander the hills shooting anything that moved, and Hughes would act as retriever: 'He could not shoot enough for me' (*Poetry in the Making*, 16). But even after compassion enters in, the killing goes on. Draft 8 adds 'tears ran from the saliva ducts', an echo of 'Crow Tyrannosaurus' – 'Weeping he walked and stabbed'.

The bull was the chosen sacrifice in the belief that the strength of the bull would pass into the worshipper, or the power of the god through his totemic beast. The dove can be destroyed all too easily, but the love it manifests in its willing sacrifice is sanctified, made absolute, by that sacrifice. The innocent child kills, and that fortunate fall into experience at its most destructive opens the way for his emergence into threefold vision, a vision of love. The Christian parallel seems inescapable. Not until man has crucified God can he be redeemed by that same deathless God. This parallel is to become overt in draft 11.

Draft 10 again looks like a finished poem, neatly arranged in quatrains, and the first draft in typescript. It is noteworthy that the holograph of which the typescript is a fair copy has the deleted title 'The Dove's Covenant'.

The rainbows in the dove's breast are kindly.
She has lightning too,
When she claps her wings, it scatters like twigs.
And the piling summer clouds of her voice, these are her
     thunders.

She said to the wolf-child: worship love only.
The wolf-child knocked her down
He disembowelled her, seeking the voice.
His mouth smoked open, tears ran from the saliva ducts.

A cave of hot slaughter.
Inside, the heart, a glory
Went on speaking.
Loving words, a deathless oracle.

The heart named him. The heart
Had become his tongue moving
Thickly and powerfully. His mouth closed.
Dipped in fear, as in her blood, he emerged

And stood in air,
Hardening among stars.
He spoke. And her words were his strength.
This was the dove's milk.

The opening has moved forward a little, with its scattering twigs
and piling clouds. The gateway of arched wings, hitherto the most
consistent part of the poem, has gone. But the surprising change
here is the sudden introduction of the wolf-child, mentioned in no
other draft. By a wolf-child are we to understand a child suckled by
wolves? If so, the imperative to worship love only would clash even
more strongly with 'natural logic' than in a normal child. Yet the
normality of the child had seemed essential to the earlier versions.
We could, of course, question why there needs to be a child in the
poem at all, since the dove is supposed to be visiting Adam, who
never was a child. Blake seems to have smuggled the child in, and
Hughes has been stuck with him, the poles of his poem having
become murderous natural male innocence and sacrificial super-
natural (or spiritualised) female innocence.

It is also surprising that the poem has made so little progress in
ten drafts. In fact it seems to have lost a good deal of its original
energy. 'Kindly' is inert. The dove's lightning and thunders have
been reduced to purely descriptive metaphors. The dove loses in
reality by having words put into its mouth. 'As in her blood' again
reduces to an inert simile what had been a potent and literal drench-
ing. The regular form of the poem seems to have tamed and diluted
it. Nearly all the lines are now end-stopped, so there is no tension in
the lineation, no momentum, no drama. The poem does not bear
comparison with any of the other bird poems in the sequence.

But draft 11 throws out the child altogether, with much other
dross, and the poem leaps forward almost to its final state.

THE DOVE CAME

Her breast full of rainbows
She was struck down

The dove came, her wings clapped lightnings
That scattered like twigs
She was struck down

The dove came, her thunder
Piled like summer clouds and soft violet
She was struck down

She came with the flesh of her breast
She was eaten

She came with her blood richer than rubies
She was drunk

The dove came again, a blinding
Ear could no longer hear

Mouth was a disembowelled bird
Where the tongue tried to move, like a heart

The dove alit
In the body of thorns
Deep in the body of thorns
The dove of soft thunder
Nested her thunder.

This sudden coming clear may indicate some missing intermediate drafts, but in the absence of any evidence of that, we must assume that the advance is the result of two drastic decisions, to make the whole poem about the dove (in line with the other eight bird poems), and to allow the Christian analogue to become a much more central determinant.

By putting the striking down of the dove in the passive and by having her struck down three times, Hughes suggests much more strongly that it is the fate of the dove to be struck down (as it was Christ's to be crucified) rather than any unusual cruelty in those who struck her down. The eating of the dove's flesh and drinking of her blood echoes the last supper:

And as they were eating, Jesus took bread, and blessed it, and brake it, and gave it to the disciples, and said, Take, eat; this is my body. And he took the cup, and gave thanks, and gave it to them, saying, Drink ye all of it; For this is my blood of the new testament, which is shed for many for the remission of sins. (Matthew 26: 26–8)

Yet the lines are not exclusively Christian, for they also echo the myths and folk-songs of the eating of fertility gods, such as Hughes draws on in 'The Golden Boy':

With terrible steel
    They beat his bones from him
With terrible steel
    They ground him to powder
They baked him in ovens
    The sliced him on tables
They ate him they ate him
    They ate him they ate him

And that apparent atrocity is actually the gift of life.

In the typescript the dove is 'big with rainbows', gravid with blessings, tokens of the covenant between man and God. The dove alights, and nests, as doves do, in a dense thorn-bush, there to hatch no longer thunders but rainbows. The 'body of thorns' again suggests the crown of thorns which was the humble and painful token of the glory of Christ in his agony. Christ the king fisher of men sews the worlds together on the cross. The rainbow, reconciling the opposites of sun and rain, symbolises that, or any other, atonement.

The dove is no legless bird of transcendence. She is spirit incarnate. Her voice is also the soft thunder of a beating heart. Noah's dove was sent to find the landfall which would signify God's atonement with man. On her first flight 'the dove found no rest for the sole of her foot'. It is no coincidence that the final poem of the *Adam* sequence is called 'The Sole of a Foot'. Here Adam is at last erect and reconciled to his earth-bound status. His foot says to the world-rock

I am no wing
To tread emptiness.
I was made

For you.

The purpose of all these drafts and revisions was not to subject the material to 'craftsmanship', nor even, primarily, to produce 'a formal and balanced figure of melody and rhythm', which in many of the poems of this period would be totally inappropriate. It is a matter of throwing out all that can be thrown out, leaving only that which imperiously proves itself, the simplicity on the far side of complexity, the essential.

4

Hughes, Narrative and Lyric: An Analysis of *Gaudete*
Neil Roberts

My aim is to demonstrate the skill and sophistication of Hughes's handling of narrative in *Gaudete*, and then go on to consider what I think is the main critical question about this work – the place of the missing half of the story and of the Epilogue lyrics in the total structure.

The characters in *Gaudete* – particularly the male ones – are very clearly constructed out of a limited number of key motifs, and these motifs are repeated in different characters, with a result that might seem like redundancy. Hagen, Estridge and Garten observe Lumb's activities through lenses; Hagen and Estridge are military men; Hagen, Westlake and Dunworth confront Lumb and their wives with guns; Hagen, Estridge, Garten and Holroyd slaughter or abuse animals; the houses of Hagen, Westlake and Estridge are respectively 'barren', 'alien' and 'ponderous'.

This overlapping of motifs enables Hughes to present the experiences of the various characters as phases of a single narrative: these things are happening to them as if to a single person, and at the end they react as a single person. Hughes achieves simultaneously the effect of repetition, which is comic – we can feel for one cuckolded husband but not seven – and of progression, which is painful and ominous. So, successively, we have Hagen observing his wife and Lumb in simple proximity; Estridge watching Lumb and Mrs Holroyd disappear into the house; Garten just missing the discovery of his mother *in flagrante* with Lumb; Westlake puzzled to find Lumb merely holding his wife's ankle; and – as the culmination of this phase of the narrative – Dunworth confronted with the 'merciless and explicit' sight of his wife naked with Lumb on the couch.

This device is perhaps related to an effect that William Empson refers to, in his essay on 'Double Plots' in *Some Versions of Pastoral*, when he quotes from Ernest Jones's essay on *Hamlet*: 'one person of complex character is dissolved and replaced by several, each of whom possesses a different aspect of the character which in the simpler form of the myth is combined into one being' (Peregrine Books, 1966, p. 59). Here the effect is particularly obvious because, while the men have some distinguishing characteristics, they share so many. This perhaps helps to explain why *Gaudete* is felt to be both mythic – a distorted version of myths as various as *The Bacchae* and the Nativity of Christ – and like a soap opera ('The Archers scripted by Charles Manson').

The narrative perspective is also important here. The narrative proper begins with Hagen looking through his binoculars at his wife and Lumb. Nearly all the motifs I have mentioned are introduced in this page-and-a-half. (Perhaps the reason why Hagen is the one to kill Lumb is that he is the one in whom all the shared motifs are combined). The binoculars then serve as the instrument of narrative continuity to take us outside to the scene shared by Mrs Hagen and Lumb. This episode includes what Hagen cannot see – 'A deadlock of submarine difficulty/Which their draughty hasty lovemaking has failed to disentangle/And which has brought words to a stop' (p. 25) – but the dominant perspective is that of the deceived husband, and it is his sensations that the episode returns to:

> Hagen
> Undergoes the smallness and fixity
> Of tweed and shoes and distance. And the cruelty
> Of the wet midmorning light. The perfection
> Of the lens.
>   And a tremor
> Like a remote approaching express
> In the roots of his teeth. (p. 26)

There are episodes in the first phase of the narrative in which our perspective is that of Lumb or the women, but predominantly we see – and 'see' is an important word – events through the eyes (and lenses) of the men who will eventually combine to hunt Lumb to death.

This is related in various ways to the 'cinematic' character of the narrative, which is particularly marked in its earliest phase. The 'cutting' between brief episodes is an obviously cinematic technique, though admittedly one that has been absorbed into prose fiction by now. Particularly interesting, though, is the use, on several occasions, of the medium of the lens within the narrative. Hagen watches his wife through binoculars, and Estridge watches Mrs Holroyd through a telescope. On both occasions this enables the reader to see what the character is watching. When Garten (and we through his eyes) watches Mrs Westlake he 'fastens himself to her, as if to a magnification' (p. 30); and later his observation of Lumb and Mrs Evans through the viewfinder of a camera triggers the events that lead to Lumb's death. The perspective that the reader shares in these episodes, then, is obviously voyeuristic, but it has still more disturbing associations. Hagen watches through his binoculars 'as in a machan' (p. 23) – a platform used for shooting tigers from – and his guns and the skull of a shot tiger are described in the first few lines. Garten 'eases his elbows and knees, hunching gently to his attentiveness, as to a rifle' (p. 30). The two men who deliberately confront their wives and Lumb without the medium of a lens – Westlake and Dunworth – take guns with them. These parallel motifs, of the lens and the gun, finally converge of course when our last view of Lumb alive is through the sight-lens of Hagen's Mannlicher.318.

If *Gaudete* had been made into a film, the irony of these central motifs and narrative devices would have been even greater. The relation of these men to their wives and to Lumb is repeatedly symbolised by the pointing of a lens or a gun, which eventually merge into one instrument. In a film, this symbolism would have defined the viewer's position throughout. In the narrative poem, greater flexibility is possible. At the same time, the frequent occasions on which we view events through the eyes of the men, and also through a lens or at the end of a gun, are more unmistakably deliberate. Our complicity, as readers, with this group of characters, cannot be dismissed as the accidental consequence of the medium.

This complicity is not static. As I have pointed out earlier, we are not presented just with a repetitive sequence of voyeuristic scenes. The compulsive looking of the men seems to be a corollary of the failure of their relations with women, but it is not a merely negative phenomenon. Westlake stumbles when he sees –

In spite of what it looks like
Something quite different is going on here,
Even under his very eyes,
And if he could only see clear…
It would be plain
That her writhing and cries are actually sexual spasm,
And that the Reverend Lumb…
Is actually copulating with her
Probably through that hand on her ankle
In some devilish spiritual way (p. 75).

– but when it comes to the 'merciless and explicit' sight Dunworth
exposes himself to, seeing takes us with the character beyond
voyeurism and fantasy, beyond the objective stare symbolised by
the lens, and the hostile distance measured by the gun, so much so
that the character turns the gun on himself:

He tries to isolate the monkey-crudity of her hairline,
Her spoiled chin, all the ordinariness
That once bored him so much,
But he feels only a glowing mass.
He stands there paralysed by a bliss
And a most horrible torture –
Endless sweetness and endless anguish.

He turns the pistol towards his own face
And puts the muzzle in his mouth. (p. 87)

In the frenzied scene in which Hagen batters his dog to death
with a chair, his wife is described as watching him 'As if it were all
something behind the nearly unbreakable screen glass of a televi-
sion/With the sound turned off' (p. 35). This compares interestingly
with a statement of his intention that Hughes made in a letter to
Terry Gifford and myself not long after the poem was published: 'I
wanted something between a primitive painting, a mosaic, and a
slightly speeded up silent film' (unpublished letter, October 1978).
Hughes probably had in mind the quality of movement in a silent
film rather than the silence specifically, but the metaphor for Mrs
Hagen's watching does oddly describe the reader's own experience
of the poem – at least this reader's. This may be a merely subjective
impression because, after all, plenty of noises are referred to, from

birdsong to gunfire; but I think it is mainly a response to the complete absence of dialogue. In the scene in question there is a long and mostly metaphorical description of Hagen's outburst against his wife, which we are told consists of words, but we don't know what any of the words are, so we can't hear them. Even in the three instances where we do have some sense of what the characters say – when Old Smayle and Mrs Evans speak about Lumb's religion, and Jennifer Estridge about her and her sister's liaisons with Lumb – the sense of actually hearing the spoken words is muffled by the use of *style indirect libre* rather than direct speech.

Reviewing *Gaudete*, Terry Eagleton wrote:

> one never has the feeling…that Hughes's language self-reflectively takes the measure of its own limits and capabilities; it is, rather, a language somehow locked tight in the bursting fullness of its presence, and so ironically closer to traditional realism than it would superficially seem. The fact that almost everything is in the present tense is an index of this fact: despite Hughes's ambitious experiments with 'open' forms, a single, sometimes tyrannically controlling mode of speech remains firmly in authority throughout…. Hughes's language fails to assume any *attitude* to what it speaks of; it is positioned laconically outside those events, 'mirroring' rather than constructing. (*Stand*, Vol. 19 no. 2, 1987, pp. 78–9).

Hughes's habitual way of talking about his own writing does not, admittedly, encourage the expectation of the kind of anti-realist self-consciousness the absence of which Eagleton is lamenting here, but in practice I am not sure that his criticism is accurate. We have seen that in his construction of character Hughes deliberately deploys a limited collection of motifs to produce a group of characters who function at the same time as a single narrative entity. We have also seen that his narrative devices ensure that the reader shares the voyeuristic perspective of the group of men: that this perspective is built into our position as readers. We should not too readily assume that the language of such a poem is blind to itself. Eagleton highlights two undoubted characteristics of the language of the main narrative: the use of the present tense and the absence of 'articulation' (which I take to mean the overwhelmingly predominant use of simple, paratactic sentences). He takes these to be evidence of a naive and tyrannical linguistic and narrative practice: the poem is in the control of this voice that does not know its own character or limits.

However, these stylistic features are not transparent. We as readers are conscious of them and, if we are reading critically, will ask questions about them. It is the answers to our questions about these features, not simply the statement that they exist, which will form the basis for critical judgement.

The use of the present tense is clearly consonant with the poem's origins as a film scenario; some passages even read like the terse instructions of a shooting script:

> Maud
> Walks in the graveyard.
> She is carrying twigs of apple blossom.
> The graveyard is empty.
> The paths are like the plan of a squared city.
> She comes into the main path.
> A woman is walking ahead of her.
> Maud follows the woman.
> The woman walks to the far end of the path (p. 94).

A film has no narrator. A narrative poem has one, but his role is affected by the language employed. The use of the past tense obviously creates a time-gap between the act of narration and the events narrated. This may vary in length, and is usually indeterminate, but in most cases it is assumed that the narrator is in possession of the whole story at the time of narration. When the present tense is used, this is not necessarily the case: the moment of the action, the moment of narration and the moment of reading are the same. This simple choice rules out a whole range of 'articulated' effects such as, to choose almost at random, the opening sentence of *One Hundred Years of Solitude:* 'Many years later, as he faced the firing squad, Colonel Aureliano Buendia was to remember that distant afternoon when his father took him to discover ice' (Picador, 1978, p. 9). In *Gaudete*, this consequence is exaggerated by Hughes's decision to write predominantly in simple sentences with one verb (often no verb) or paratactic sentences combining a series of main clauses, and only very occasionally using subordinate clauses. Hughes's own accounts of the style shows that he was conscious of exclusions:

My main problem technically was to make the implications of my theme clear, and yet at the same time make no authorial comment, no exposition, permit no discussion between characters and permit them no individual speculation that was not organically part of enactment...and that didn't contribute to a sense of claustrophobic involvement. Ideally I would free my image from the entanglement of my reader's immediate intellectual response to explicit meanings – by having no very explicit meanings, or rather no meanings enlarged on in explicit terms. (Unpublished letter to Neil Roberts and Terry Gifford, October 1978)

It's like a mathematical problem – to which the style is the correct answer. It's only when the whole problem's understood, that the style will be seen for what it is. To hear it called crude, clumsy, etc. (all of which it is) means that the reader hasn't understood why I took so much trouble to make it that way. (Unpublished letter to Keith Sagar, August 1977)

One technique that, in a way, helps to foreground and perhaps explain this stylistic limitation is Hughes's repeated and characteristic use of one particular 'articulation': the 'as if' locution introducing a more or less extended simile. Sometimes this is used straightforwardly, as 'Garten/Rises above the napes of tender curled bracken/ As if clearing an aim' (p. 36), but its characteristic use creates a sense of absurdity and contradiction. Hagen tosses a pigeon he has just shot to Lumb 'Who catches it/As if to save it' (p. 36); Mrs Hagen moves towards her house 'as if to remain still were even more futile' (p. 31); Hagen lifts the dog he has just killed 'As if he had just failed to save it' (p. 35); Estridge's daughter screams at him 'as if in perfect silence' (p. 48). These small absurd locutions epitomise a rift between consciousness and action that is given more extended expression at certain key moments such as when Dunworth, seeing his wife with Lumb, points his pistol at them –

He is trying to feel
Whether he is bluffing or is about to become
The puppet
Of some monstrous, real, irreversible act (p. 85).

– or when Estridge joins the vengeful men in the Bridge Inn – 'He does not know what he will do now. He knows that anything will have to be forgiven him.' These characters are like fallen versions of the innocent Wodwo, who reflects, about pulling bits of bark off a rotten stump, 'me and doing that have coincided very queerly'.

Again and again the present moment is felt by the characters, including (perhaps above all) Lumb, as a refuge, usually illusory; as when for example, for the woman about to kill herself: 'No thought for the future falsifies these moments', or when

> [Dunworth and Westlake] feel gently around in the illusory emptiness of these minutes,
> Which are passing with such crowded rapidity.
> They are quickly aghast
> At the certainty that sooner or later they will have to move
> (p. 130).

or again

> [Lumb's] only effort now
> Is pushing ahead and away the seconds, second after second,
> Now this second, patiently, and now this,
> Safe seconds
> In which he need do nothing, and decide nothing,
> And in which nothing whatsoever can happen (p. 108).

The present tense and 'unarticulated' language, then, are employed for a narrative in which the characters' actions resist explanation and in which the present is not meaningfully related to the past or future. But if this were all, we should have said no more than that this is a very limited narrative using appropriate means. The attempt to say more than this leads us into the most difficult and perhaps most interesting aspect of our subject.

The 'Argument' of *Gaudete* seems to promise us a double plot. There are two Lumbs: one, the 'original' vicar, attempts to heal the goddess in the other world, while the other, the 'elemental nature spirit', ministers to the vicar's flock in his own elemental way. Hughes said to Ekbert Faas that he had intended to write the story of the 'original' Lumb but got diverted by the other story, and in his letter to Terry Gifford and myself he wrote:

The unwritten half of Gaudete is what happened to Lumb in 'the other world'. The written part – what happened to the wooden Lumb – is a parallel, but with all the episodes inverted and as it were depraved…. As if the brilliant real thing were happening to creatures of light in another world – but these are the shadows of it, confusedly glimpsing and remembering …. (October 1978)

Is what we have, then, the comic sub-plot without the main plot – the antics of Wagner without the Faustus scenes? Or, more fancifully, is *Gaudete* a narrative with an unconscious? How does this 'unwritten' half affect our reading of the written story?

First it is worth noting that Hughes's motivation for writing the poem as it is was an aesthetic one. As he said to Ekbert Faas:

I realised that [the underworld plot] was the more interesting part of the story. And my first hope was that I'd somehow or other manage to do it all together. But then I became more interested in doing a headlong narrative. Something like a Kleist story that would go from beginning to end in some forceful way pushing the reader through some kind of tunnel while being written in the kind of verse that would stop you dead at every moment. (Faas, p. 214)

The demands of the kind of narrative Hughes wanted to write, then, drove out the other story. Again we have evidence for regarding the language of this narrative as something other than the 'natural', unproblematised 'presence' that Eagleton complains about.

There is of course one episode that might be regarded as representing this other story: the episode in which control of Lumb's car is wrenched from him, and he finds himself in a desolate, muddy landscape where his male parishioners are dead and the women buried up to their necks screaming, and Lumb is forced to undergo the rebirth of the baboon-woman from his body into 'undeformed and perfect' beauty. But I think it is more satisfactory to see this as a forceful symbolic reminder to Lumb of his supposed mission and his failure to accomplish it, than an actual fragment of the 'unwritten half'. This is less because of the way it is integrated into the main narrative, than because its style is that of the narrative, and the 'Lumb' who has these experiences is the limited and baffled consciousness that this style inevitably represents.

But there is another style in *Gaudete,* and it is above all the presence of this style that allows us to 'take the measure' of the language of the narrative. I mean the style of the poems in the Epilogue, and it is these that present the critic of *Gaudete* with the most interesting and difficult challenge. The poems are supposedly the work of the original 'but changed' man who has returned to this world after living through the 'unwritten half' of the story. So they don't tell this story, but they presuppose it: the story is, in a sense, present in them. I don't mean by this that we should try to reconstruct the story from the poems. On the contrary, the fact that narrative has been supplanted by lyric is exactly what we have to understand: to reconstruct the story (even if that were possible) would be to evade this fact.

The relation, historically, between the lyric, the dramatic, and narrative, is extremely complex, and even in the Romantic period it would be crass to identify the 'I' of the lyric poem with the biographical author. In the twentieth century, the use of masks and personae in lyric poetry has become commonplace. (These matters are helpfully discussed in David Lindley's Critical Idiom volume, *Lyric* (Methuen, London and New York, 1985) and it is Lindley who alerted me to the Jonathan Culler essay cited below.) Nevertheless, certain distinctions remain. We might want to say that a poem is a dramatic monologue rather than a lyric: if we said this, we would mean that the 'I' is not wholly the subject of the poem, that there is another subject behind the 'I', whose meaning might be other than the speaker's. We might think this of Geoffrey Hill's 'Ovid in the Third Reich' for example; but I suggest that we would not think it of the *Lucy* poems, even though Lucy and therefore in a sense the 'I' is a fiction. I would propose that even though the Epilogue poems are ascribed to a fictional character, Lumb, they are in this sense lyrics and not dramatic monologues. There is no sense of another subject who means otherwise than Lumb. A second and related point is that they are real poems. Although they occur in a fictional context they are not, as Bakhtin says of the parodic 'sonnets' in *Don Quixote,* 'images' of poems; see *The Dialogic Imagination* (University of Texas, Austin, 1981, p. 51). They are more akin to the poems at the end of *Dr Zhivago,* though because of their relation to the 'unwritten half', they are more important and more problematic.

In his essay on 'Apostrophe' in *The Pursuit of Signs* (Routledge, London, 1981, pp. 149–50), Jonathan Culler suggests that apostrophe is a force opposed to narrative and that the lyric is characteristically the triumph of the apostrophic. A poem can recount a sequence of events.... Alternatively, a poem may invoke objects, people, a detemporalized space with forms and forces which have pasts and futures but which are addressed as potential presences. Nothing need happen in an apostrophic poem, as the great Romantic odes amply demonstrate. Nothing need happen because the poem itself is to be the happening.

The tension between the narrative and the apostrophic can be seen as the generative force behind a whole series of lyrics. One might identify, for example, as instances of the triumph of the apostrophic, poems which, in a very common move, substitute a temporality of discourse for a referential temporality. In lyrics of this kind a temporal problem is posed: something once present has been lost or attenuated; this loss can be narrated but the temporal sequence is irreversible, like time itself. Apostrophes replace this irreversible structure by removing the opposition between presence and absence from empirical time and locating it in a discursive time.

In the Epilogue poems, Hughes does not use apostrophe in the formal sense which Culler says modern critics find embarrassing (though he is not afraid of it elsewhere, as in 'Skylarks') but more than half the poems are addressed to the 'nameless female deity', and what Culler says about apostrophe in my quotation applies to them. By being lyric (or apostrophic) poems that are at the same time attributed to a person in a narrative their status as 'happenings' is foregrounded. They supplant the narrative of events in 'the other world' by being narrative events themselves. What Culler says about time and loss describes the structure of Lumb's relationship with the goddess, nowhere more exactly than in the poem beginning 'I know well/You are not infallible', where she is identified with a girl dying of a wasting disease. Culler illustrates his point with a quotation from 'Adonais', especially pertinent here, since in both poems the presence of the dead person is mediated by identifying them with a deity. Hughes's deity is a kind of female Adonais (or even Christ) because she is capable of dying in human form (here and in 'Waving goodbye') and yet is perpetually present; at the same time the rhetorical fiction of the dead apostrophised person's presence is extended into her identification with the goddess. Culler says that Shelley's poem 'displaces the temporal pattern of actual loss and...makes the power of its own evocativeness a central issue'. Similarly the quality of Lumb's poems is the evidence, since they are themselves the events we are attending to.

Characteristically, in these poems, the goddess is both present and absent, or ambivalently present. She is identified in Nature, and in certain extreme sensations felt by the speaker – 'And you grab me/ So the blood jumps into my teeth' – but her presence is modified by the questions that Lumb asks about her – 'Who is this?/She reveals herself, and is veiled'; 'Who are you?' 'So how will you gather me?' – and a pervasive sense of distance or of longing – 'The sun, like a cold kiss in the street – / A mere disc token of you'; 'Me too,/Let me be one of your warriors'. So, when she is not lost, she is, to use Culler's word, attenuated, or in danger of attenuation, but this is constantly resisted by the urgency and intimacy of the address.

No reader can fail to notice the stylistic difference between these poems and the narrative. This is much greater than the necessary difference between lyric and narrative – greater than the difference between 'Ode to a Nightingale' and 'Lamia' or Milton's sonnets and *Paradise Lost*. Once again, the style is brought to our attention. It is particularly noticeable that the language of the lyrics is much more 'articulated' than that of the narrative. 'I know well' is typical in this respect: its seventeen lines contain three main clauses, four subordinate clauses and four participle phrases dependent on subordinate clauses. One would have to search long in the narrative for a comparably complex sentence-structure.

To summarise, in *Gaudete* Hughes handles narrative with considerable skill and sophistication, and a very conscious construction of character, actional continuity and perspective. But what is most interesting about it is its subversion of narrative. Hughes's desire to write a headlong narrative, like Kleist, produced a sub-plot without a main plot which remains 'unconscious', referred to in the Argument and hinted at in the baboon-woman episode but never actually narrated. At the same time the narrative is taken over by a voice that is capable of great poetic power and vividness but is deliberately limited. When Lumb returns from the unwritten, unconscious story he gives a little demonstration of his new-found affinity with Nature by calling a sea-otter, but mainly he is represented by his poems. He is the poems, or at least he is the 'I' of the poems engaged in perpetual apostrophe to the 'you', in a discourse that is interior and timeless.

The effect of the Epilogue is to make *Gaudete* into a work that is, *pace* Terry Eagleton, self-aware not only stylistically but generically.

Hughes's phrase 'the unwritten half of *Gaudete*' is deceptive. Certainly the narrative, brilliant as it is, can tell only half the story, but the Epilogue insinuates that the other half is not a 'story' at all. Whether Hughes realised it or not, the other half of *Gaudete* is not 'unwritten'. What is unwritten and unconscious as narrative is written and conscious as lyric. *Gaudete* might be seen as a work in which Hughes vindicates the genre which concedes least to the secular and bleak irreversibility of 'empirical time'.

5

Romanticism, Existentialism, Patriarchy: Hughes and the Visionary Imagination
Alexander Davis

For the Romantic poets, the full capacity of the imagination can be realised only when the subject frees himself from what Coleridge calls the 'despotism of the eye'. To remain within the limits of the physical eye's range of vision is to be a slave and not a master – a slave both to the eye and to a diminished form of imagination. Coleridge condemns this subjection as the 'Slavery of the Mind to the Eye and the visual Imagination, or Fancy'.[1] Both Blake and Wordsworth share Coleridge's belief, and their poetry is in large part a record of the quest to free the imagination from what Wordsworth, in *The Prelude*, terms the state 'In which the eye was master of the heart',[2] and that which Blake, in *Jerusalem*, calls 'The Eye of Man, a little narrow orb, clos'd up & dark'.[3] Keith Sagar, in his article 'Fourfold Vision in Hughes',[4] argues that Hughes's poetry can likewise be read as a search for a visionary imagination – that *telos* of the Romantic quest most powerfully personified in Blake's Universal Men, who at the close of *Jerusalem*, are described in the following grand fashion:

The Four Living Creatures, Chariots of Humanity Divine
                                        Incomprehensible,
In beautiful Paradise expand...
And they conversed together in Visionary forms dramatic which
                                        bright
Redounded from their Tongues in thunderous majesty, in Visions

70

In new Expanses, creating exemplars of Memory and of Intellect,
Creating Space, Creating Time, according to the wonders Divine
Of Human Imagination...
    & they walked
To & fro in Eternity as One Man, reflecting each in each & clearly
                                        seen

And seeing, according to fitness & order.[5]

By vision, Blake means the perception of the human in all things.
That is, the object world is not an inert 'out there', but is, in fact, the
imaginative projection of the subject. Fourfold vision, in other
words, is where the 'wonders Divine/Of Human Imagination'
restore an ability to see the vast array of isolated phenomena as distinct entities yet as comprising a unified totality which is wholly
'relevant' to the human self. Sagar argues that such fourfold vision,
in Hughes's poetry, is achieved at the end of *Prometheus on His Crag*,
in the protagonist's redemption in *Cave Birds*, in the Adamic figure
present in the last poem in *Adam and the Sacred Nine*, and most of all,
in the transformed figure of Lumb in *Gaudete*. There are two obvious
– even initially bland – remarks to be made in connection with these
intensely apocalyptic moments: firstly, the Promethean figures are
all male, and secondly, their expansion to visionary awareness is frequently, if not always, described in imagery centred on the act of
perception. It is these two issues that I wish to examine in the course
of this chapter. What I will argue is that Sagar's thesis needs to be
supplemented by a reading that pays attention to the scopic images
in Hughes's texts, and that examines how these relate to Hughes's
highly problematic critique of a patriarchal society dominated by a
despotic 'male gaze'. To these two related issues may be added a
third, tangential one: existentialism. It is this philosophy that is both
an overt and covert antagonist to Hughes's belief in the Romantic
imagination. Patriarchy, vision and phenomenological existentialism – this seemingly odd assortment provides the context for the
following reading of Hughes's work.

Hughes's most extensive prose formulation on vision is contained
in his 1976 revision of 'Myth and Education'. This essay contains a
forceful argument for the necessity of a visionary imagination; one
that will enable the individual to attain a wholeness of being that –
however commonsensical Hughes's thesis appears – seems to be
nothing short of Blake's hyperbolic condition of Eternity, where
'every Man stood fourfold'. Like his Romantic precursor, Hughes

claims that the despotic eye has curtailed the individual's ability to react in an imaginative manner. He writes:

> But we sit, closely cramped in the cockpit behind the eyes, steering through the brilliantly crowded landscape beyond the lenses, focussed on details and distinctions. In the end, since all our attention from birth has been narrowed into that outward beam, we come to regard our body as no more than a somewhat stupid vehicle. All the urgent information coming towards us from the inner world sounds to us like a blank, or at best the occasional grunt, or a twinge. Because we have no equipment to receive it and decode it. The body, with its spirits, is the antennae of all our perceptions. The receiving aerial for all our wavelengths. But we are disconnected. The exclusiveness of our objective eye, the very strength and brilliance of our objective intelligence, suddenly turns into stupidity – of the most rigid and suicidal kind.[6]

The image of the cockpit suggests that the eyes' lenses, whilst perceiving the object world, make the self slavishly dependent upon it. This Wordsworthian dilemma, in Hughes's argument, has as its result an 'objective intelligence', wholly reliant upon the 'objective eye' – a condition that recalls Blake's statement that the physical eye 'leads you to Believe a Lie/When you see with, not thro', the Eye'.[7] In consequence, the world of objects is perceived as a series of dislocated aspects, by a consciousness both alienated from the 'outer' world and ignorant of the existence of an 'inner' world. This, of course, is the diminished existence of the 'Egg-Head': he who 'shuts out the world's knocking/With a welcome, and to wide-eyed deafnesses/Of prudence lets it speak'. The egg-head's wide-eyed deafness is Blake's Eye of Man, an eye fascinated by 'details and distinctions', but the constricting 'narrow beam' of which is blind to the potential vision of the Universal Man. In 'Crow's Account of St George', the patron saint of England is one whose eye is singularly deaf to that which eludes the mastery of his purely objective gaze. He may well feel that 'he sees everything in the Universe', but he is, in fact, the slave to an imprisoning mode of vision. What he cannot comprehend is that which lies outside his minute, microscopic observations – observations that, in Wordsworth's famous phrase, simply 'murder to dissect':

With tweezers of number
He picks the gluey heart out of an inaudibly squeaking cell –
He hears something. He turns –
A demon, dripping ordure, is grinning in the doorway.
It vanishes. He concentrates –

It is this demon that Hughes's redeemed protagonists, such as Lumb in his encounter with the mysterious baboon-woman in *Gaudete*, see in a completely different manner from St George. In Hughes's dualistic model of the human individual, the demon is to be read as the inner world, from which St George and the egg-head are, in the words of 'Myth and Education', 'disconnected'. Disconnection results in repression; the return of the repressed, for St George, is hence imaged as something frightful, something hovering at the very margins of sight. For Hughes, St George's objective eye also creates a diminished form of imagination, one that is visual (like Coleridge's Fancy), which he calls the 'objective imagination'. This is a faculty, however, far more crippling than Coleridge's concept of Fancy because, as in the case of St George, it turns what Hughes in 'Myth and Education' calls the 'inner world, with its spirits', into a demonic unconscious. St George's repression of this inner world of being – as befits a national saint – represents a condition that, in Hughes's opinion, is largely that of modern culture:

> People rushed towards the idea of living without any religion or any inner life whatsoever as if toward some great new freedom. A great final awakening. The most energetic intellectual and political movements of this century wrote the manifestos of the new liberation.[8]

The savage irony directed at modernity in this passage reveals that, like that of the High Romantics, Hughes's work needs to be interpreted in the light of its historical context, however ahistorical or 'mythical' his writings frequently appear to be. In the case of Blake, the revolutions in France and America led to an initial belief in the possibility of a new Jerusalem being constructed on Earth through political action. Unlike the disillusionment suffered by Wordsworth and Coleridge at the failure of the French Revolution to live up to their expectations, Blake never entirely lost faith in the radical possibilities of *social* change. If the former two poets may be said to make the characteristic Romantic move into subjective apocalypse, that is, individual revelation through the emancipation of vision, Blake provides us with a salutary reminder that individual emancipation – which, in its broadest sense, is the meaning of fourfold vision – can only become a possibility when linked to collective *praxis*. In Hughes's case, one turns to a very different historical conjuncture. Nevertheless, his aesthetic response to the material facts of history is close, in some ways, to the compensatory 'retreat' made by Wordsworth from social contradictions, and hence, as we shall see, distinct from the optimistic faith held by Blake in their just-possible resolution.

Hughes came to public fame during the Cold War period, and his admiration of several Eastern European writers attests to an intense interest (and dismay) in the socio-political situation within which their poetry is produced. The pre-*glasnost* stalemate of East–West relations leaves its mark in Hughes's own poetry and prose as a profound dissatisfaction with the possibilities of political change. This is comparable to the pessimistic outlook Wordsworth developed in the face of his own epoch, one which finds its most eloquent expression in the words of the Wanderer in *The Excursion,* who speaks of

> The loss of confidence in social man,
> By the unexpected transports of our age
> Carried so high, that every thought, which looked
> Beyond the temporal destiny of the Kind,
> To many seemed superfluous...[9]

Hughes's early poem, 'A Woman Unconscious', is a rare example of a poem which directly refers to '*our* [nuclear] age', but it is indicative of what Stan Smith calls 'the inner experience of an era of social impasse'[10] that permeates a great deal of Hughes's work. Turning to the prose, the 1978 Introduction to Vasko Popa's *Collected Poems 1943–1976* repeats this experience, whilst indicating Hughes's undaunted faith in transcendence on an individual plane:

> Circumstantial proof that man is a political animal, a state numeral, as if it needed to be proved, has been weighed out in dead bodies by the million. The attempt these [East European] poets have made to record man's awareness of what is being done to him, by his own institutions and by history, and to record along with the suffering their inner creative transcendence of it, has brought their poetry down to such precisions, discriminations and humiliations that it is a new thing.[11]

Transcendence, in this poetic, is a subjective or 'inner' redemption. History and the state's 'institutions' impinge upon but in no way negate a creative autonomy that stands apart from the realms of ideology and politics. This is the heritage of Wordsworthian Romanticism as mediated through Symbolist and Modernist poetry; and it is the firm belief in 'inner creative transcendence' that lies behind Hughes's attack, in 'Myth and Education', on those 'energetic, intellectual and political movements' of the modern era. One of those movements can be singled out for further discussion in relation to Hughes's theories of the imagination. The belief in a 'new freedom' that rejects both the notion of a repressed unconscious and the need for religion is, in this century, espoused most vocally by existentialism, particularly in its popular (and popularised) Sartrean form. Hughes explicitly attacks Sartre's existential freedom in the first section of 'Wings', where Sartre's denial of the 'inner life' in favour of an absolutely free consciousness leads less to existential anguish (which is a positive expression of freedom) than to an empty idealism, where the visual imagination strips the object world of meaning:

> He regrows the world inside his skull, like the spectre of a
> flower...
> The skull-splitting polyp of his brain, on its tiny root,
> Lolls out over him ironically:
>
> Angels, it whispers, are metaphors, in man's image,
> For the amoeba's exhilarations.

In Sartre's work, imagination is necessarily an annihilation of reality; to imagine something one has to posit its non-existence as an object of perception. In Sartre's words: 'the image involves a certain nothingness. Its object is not a simple portrait, it asserts itself: but in doing so it destroys itself. However lively, appealing or strong the image is, it presents its object as not being.'[12] In 'M. Sartre Considers Current Affairs', such an imagination is interpreted as one which turns the material world into a 'spectre' whilst simultaneously locking the self within the cockpit of the skull, condemning it to an absurd, solipsistic creation of *no-thing*. Hughes hence mocks this conception of a free intentional imagination as simply a more sophisticated form of 'disconnected' egg-headedness.

In 'Myth and Education', it is arguable that Hughes silently returns to the earlier target of his satire, and proceeds to attack the freedom of Sartrean imagination as a pointless liberation that, in denying human nature, forces one's inner life into repression. Consequently, 'the defrocked inner life...fell into a huge sickness. A huge collection of deprivation sicknesses. And this is how psychoanalysis found it.'[13] However, the 'cure' Hughes postulates for this sickness is not so much a Freudian one as it is a unique combination of Jungian analytical psychology (in particular, Jung's concept of individuation) and the sublime transformation of perception that is present in Romanticism's redemptive imagination. In 'Myth and Education', Hughes describes the second of these revelatory experiences as a faculty that is neither solely dependent on the object world nor, as in Sartre's phenomenological conception of the imagination, a 'destruction' of it. Instead, it brings that outer world into some sort of relationship with repressed inner life:

> So what we need, evidently, is a faculty that embraces both worlds simultaneously. A large, flexible grasp, an inner vision which holds wide open, like a great theatre, the arena of contention.... This really is imagination. This is the faculty we mean when we talk about the imagination of the great artists. The character of great works is exactly this: that in them the full presence of the inner world combines with and is reconciled to the full presence of the outer world. And in them we see that the laws of these two worlds are not contradictory at all; they are one all-inclusive system.... They are the laws, simply, of human nature.[14]

Hughes's concept of human nature is that of an essence which, *contra* existentialism, precedes existence. Here I must disagree with Craig Robinson's thesis that Hughes and Heidegger can be usefully compared: in all but a few concerns (such as a shared mistrust of technological development) the two writers are worlds apart. Hughes simply cannot assert that, in Heidegger's famous phrase, *'The essence of Dasein lies in its existence'*.[15] In his review of Max Nicholson's book, *The Environmental Revolution,* Hughes makes precisely the contrary point when his dualistic model of outer and inner worlds is inscribed within the context of Nature. It is 'both inner and outer nature' from which consciousness is exiled or alienated, and the former is to be read as an essence that is *given* rather than *existential*. On a related level, this inner nature, in a manner typical of Hughes, is troped as feminine, as 'Mother Nature'. This trope foregrounds the extent to which Hughes's attack on contemporary society comes into a rather uneasy relationship with feminism, as Hughes opines that the limitations of the objective eye and the objective imagination are products of a Western Civilisation that is inherently patriarchal. In the review cited above, Hughes makes the connection between a civilisation 'against Conservation' (one that makes 'the assumption that the earth is a heap of raw materials ...given to man by God for his exclusive profit and use') and a society that suppresses women: 'The creepy crawlies which infest [the earth] are devils of dirt and without a soul,... put there for his exclusive profit and use. By the skin of her teeth, woman escaped the same role.'[16] In Hughes's two major volumes of the 1970s, *Gaudete* and *Cave Birds*, the expanded visionary imagination that the protagonists assume is a rejection of the misogyny that, in Hughes's view, Reformed Christianity has bequeathed to the twentieth century. The two texts thus need to be read in a double focus, as Hughes's quasi-Romantic prose formulations of the objective eye and its contrary, the visionary imagination, are rewritten within the context of sexual politics. The motif that brings these two issues together is that of the male gaze, the misogynist form of the despotic eye.

The main narrative of *Gaudete* is hence, in large part, a critique of what Hughes declares, in 'Myth and Education', to be the ultimate expression of the objective imagination, that is, 'the morality of the camera...[which] has imprisoned us in the lens'.[17] It is thus no coincidence that the catastrophic conclusion to the narrative of *Gaudete* is precipitated by a photograph taken by Garten of Lumb and Mrs Evans enjoying sex. Garten's voyeurism, however, is only one example in a text that is littered with references to male scopophilia.[18] Indeed, the main narrative opens with a reference to Hagen's binoculars, with which he observes Lumb and his young wife embracing. As the narrative develops, telescopes, the unseen watching eye, and the camera will all be turned on Lumb and the women of the village. The village is thus, in miniature, an expression of the morality of the camera, of an existence given over to objective perception. The slavery of the eye is foregrounded in the way the perceiving subjects fail to master the objects they are fixated by, which they nonetheless feel they dominate by simply watching. For instance, Hagen's binoculars appear to negate the distance between himself and his wife, yet all that is revealed to him is his alienation from her: 'He can watch his wife/But not the darkness into which she has squeezed her eyes,/The placeless, limitless warmth/She has fused herself into'. Again, one senses the presence of an implicit criticism of existentialism. The males in *Gaudete* provide a perfect example of the impossibility of inter-subjective relations in an existential world. For Sartre, the other is always a threat to the self's freedom because the other, in order to exert its own free selfhood, to be master of its existence, must negate the freedom of other beings. Each subject desires to turn other subjects into slaves to its own existential project within the world. *Gaudete* engages with this non-dialectical process of reciprocal subordination by dramatising what Sartre calls 'the look of the other' – a dramatisation that is linked to the satirical exposure of the misogyny of the male villagers. For Sartre, the other's gaze is that which turns the self into an object of its look, thus devoiding it of freedom. Interestingly, one of Sartre's examples is the voyeur at the keyhole, whose free subjectivity is undermined by being caught. From being the voyeuristic subject, the self suddenly becomes the object of another's look and experiences *shame*. Sartre concludes:

> My original fall is the existence of the Other. Shame – like Pride – is the apprehension of myself as a nature although that very nature escapes me and is unknowable as such. Strictly speaking, it is not that I perceive myself losing my freedom in order to become a thing, but my nature is – over there, outside my lived freedom – as a given attribute of this being which I am for the Other.[19]

The scopic males in *Gaudete* are those who seek to turn the object of their gaze into a subjugated being, to whom they confer an identity or give a nature. This is the phallic power Freud locates in the scopophiliac, who likewise desires to master the object of perception. In *Gaudete*, Estridge, for example, watching Mrs Holroyd through his telescope, projects an identity on to the woman in order to make her fit within 'his collection of ideals – /She reminds him of the country love of his youth, who never appeared'.

Fruitless objective perception thus gives rise to equally vacuous acts of objective imagination. If Estridge's non-existent 'country love' is one example, Garten watching Mrs Westlake smoking in her car provides another: he feels 'his fantasy agitate...richly, monotonously, around the cool drawn features of Mrs Westlake... /He fastens himself to her, as if to a magnification'. Aside from Lumb, the majority of the figures who are observed are female, all the

observing subjects are male. *Gaudete* thus compounds its critique of
the morality of the camera and the fallacy of existential freedom
with an attack on patriarchy. In patriarchal society, the woman is frequently seen as merely an object of male desire. Laura Mulvey has
written of this phenomenon: 'In a world ordered by sexual imbalance, pleasure in looking has been split between an active/male and
passive/female. The determining male gaze projects its phantasy on
the female figure which is styled accordingly.'[20] Mulvey is considering the medium of the cinema in the light of this remark, and it is
thus revealing that *Gaudete* started off as a film script. That aside, the
narrative as published is fixated with femininity as a property that,
in Mulvey's words, 'can be said to connote *to-be-looked-at-ness*'. The
ambivalence of the gaze is that in seemingly confirming the observing subject's power over the observed, it simultaneously exposes its
dependence on its object of desire. It is thus a slave to its object,
rather than its own master. *Gaudete* seeks to contrast this 'masculine'
objective perception/imagination with the visionary imagination
that Lumb may be said to acquire in his underworld confrontation
with the baboon-woman. That incident becomes symbolic of a point
at which the protagonist *may* be said to become like Blake's Universal Man. However, whereas Blake's Man is 'clearly seen/And seeing', Lumb's mastery of the object world, as we shall see, remains
bound to the ability to *see*, rather than also to *be seen*. Blake's lines
are an expression of his desire to expand vision beyond the limitations of the subject/object dualism, to turn the object world into a
further dimension of a visionary subjectivity. In the case of Hughes,
expanded vision still remains tied to this opposition, and this, I
argue, renders highly problematic any reading that would interpret
the visionary Lumb as escaping the 'patriarchal error' that, in
Edward Larrissy's opinion, the text takes as its 'main theme'.[21]
Gaudete, to my mind, is symptomatic of what can usefully be termed
the *deferred radicalism* of much of Hughes's work. Like Blake's fourfold vision, Hughes's concept of a visionary imagination implies a
perception that is nothing less than 'revolutionary'. However, it still
fails to put into question certain assumptions of the patriarchal culture it purports to oppose, remaining a purely personal libidinal
revolution of the male self.

Lumb's vision of the baboon-woman is, like the scopophiliacs'
gaze, centred on a female figure. Unlike Hagen and his cronies,
however, Lumb does not remain a slave to the object of his perception; instead, he manages to master the female object, to see

the female in a manner distinct from St George's repulsive demon. The crucial episode of Lumb's expanded vision takes the larger structure of a scene of horrific violence that culminates in a moment of rebirth. On one level, the event can be glossed as a metaphorical account of Jung's concept of individuation, which results in a Self that is comparable to the integrated, imaginative being described in 'Myth and Education'. Hughes follows Jung in troping this process in sexual terms: the violent metamorphosis of Lumb, as he is reborn from a female form he himself becomes, is close to the 'chymical marriage' that Jung claims is an appropriate image of individuation. For Jung, the medieval and Renaissance 'science' of alchemy,

> leads in the ultimate phase of the work to the union of opposites in the archetypal form of the *hieros gamos* or 'chymical marriage'. Here the supreme opposites, male and female (as in the Chinese Yang and Yin) are melted into a unity purified of all opposition and thus incorruptible.[22]

An alchemical reading of this episode is a common one, and it is valuable. All the same, the text, on another level, describes this union of opposites in terms of a crucial alteration in Lumb's perception. At first, as he gazes with astonishment at the surreal landscape of crushed and shattered human forms, 'no explanation occurs to him/They are all there is to it', but then 'he hears a sharp crying. He looks for it, as for a clue.../It is the head of a woman/Who has been buried alive to the neck'. The woman's presence here, like the earlier reference to an enigmatic piece of 'sodden paper' that disintegrates in his hands, is inexplicable to Lumb. Like Hagen observing his wife at the opening of the narrative, Lumb's gaze sees the woman as an object he cannot fully comprehend. He remains trapped within a limited mode of perception, one that has no real mastery over its object. Lumb's bafflement is made strikingly apparent in the way in which the woman's face refuses to stabilise in his sight:

> The rain striking across the mud face washes it.
> It is a woman's face,
> A face as if sewn together from several faces.
> A baboon beauty face,
> A crudely stitched patchwork of faces.

This stupefied, patchwork vision is a covert criticism of the male gaze, the patriarchal form of objective perception. When individuated, Lumb's vision of the baboon-woman will be able to see this female face in a manner that totalises the several faces into one. Before looking at that central episode, and the problems it raises, it is worth noting that *Cave Birds* is also constructed around the perception or vision of femininity.

The protagonist of *Cave Birds* undergoes as violent a transformation as Lumb; one that, as the subtitle to the volume 'an alchemical cave drama' – implies, is similar to the atonement of inner and outer existence that is the result of the Reverend's rebirth. The outcome of the 'chymical marriage' described in 'Bride and groom lie hidden for three days' is the Promethean figure of 'The risen', whose visionary capacity is presented via the striking image: 'On his lens/Each atom engraves with a diamond'. As in *Gaudete*, this enlightened 'lens' must be achieved through a rejection of objective perception, and, once again, objective imagination is presented as the inability of the male subject to perceive fully a female object, while he nevertheless remains slavishly dependent upon her. The poem 'Actaeon', collected in *Moortown*, was, according to Terry Gifford and Neil Roberts, at one time intended for inclusion in *Cave Birds*.[23] The text is a laconic commentary on the legendary voyeur, Actaeon, and the patriarchal error of his particular form of the male gaze:

> He looked at her but he could not see her face.
> He could see her hair of course, it was a sort of furniture.
> Like his own. He had paid for it.
> He could see the useful gadgets of her hands. Which produced
> food naturally.

> And he could hear her voice
> Which was a comfortable wallpaper.
> You can get used to anything.
> But he could not see her face.

> He did not understand the great danger...

> And just went on staring at her
> As he was torn to pieces.
> Those hounds tore him to pieces.
> All the leaves and petals of his body were utterly scattered.

The failure of objective vision is that it cannot glimpse inner reality –
it remains fixated with phenomena. Actaeon, like St George, is thus
able to see dislocated elements, such as hair and hands, but these
present themselves as a disordered patchwork. As in Lumb's
encounter with the baboon-woman it is relevant that Actaeon is
unable to see a single, *female* face. The inability to identify or 'fix'
femininity becomes an image of patriarchal vision's inability to
comprehend the unconscious life it represses. In 'Crow's Undersong', the existence that underwrites consciousness is similarly presented as feminine: this is the demon that in Crow's account, St
George creates but can barely see. It is the inner world that, in the
words of 'Myth and Education', has become 'elemental, chaotic,
continually more primitive and beyond our control.'[24] On one level,
Hughes is using a female personification of unconscious being to
connote how a misogynist culture creates a dangerous unconscious
through repression *and* also suppressing actual women. The potential radicalism present in this identification comes across in a poem
such as 'Something was happening', in *Cave Birds*, where the cockerel protagonist's blindness to the suffering of his 'inner' existence is
conveyed via his indifference to a sick female:

> Her body was trying to sit up, her face unrecognizable
> As she tried to tell
> How it went on getting worse and worse
> Till she sank back.

That this female face is 'unrecognizable' links it to both the Diana of
'Actaeon' and the patchwork visage of the baboon-woman in *Gaudete*. What is intriguing in *Cave Birds* is that, for the cockerel-man to
achieve a vision comparable to the reborn Lumb's, the former must
himself become the object of a gaze which spies out the 'guilt' of his
egg-headed vision. Hughes, therefore, reworks the existential look
of the other, and turns the *male* into an *object-to-be-looked-at*, one who
must realise the shameful existence he is living, and the violence he
is inflicting on his (feminine) inner life. Only after such realisation
will he attain the redeemed lens of 'The risen'.

This is closely entwined with Hughes's use of Plato's parable
of the cave in his own 'cave drama'. At the opening of the
sequence, the protagonist merely sees the shadows on the cave
wall: in 'The summoner' his perception is limited to the 'shadow

stark on the wall, all night long,/From the street-light'. In 'The risen', on the other hand, he has left the cave, and 'stands, filling the doorway/In the shell of earth', confronting, with his crystal-clear lens, the sun. As in Blake, the sun, in *Cave Birds*, is a symbol of the imagination, and the trial at the heart of *Cave Birds* should be read as the progress from culpability in objective perception to the release of imaginative or divine vision. The transition between the illusory shadow and the enlightenment of the sun is punctuated by images of sight, as, for instance, in the point at which 'The interrogator', who is 'the sun's keyhole', turns her withering gaze upon the protagonist:

> With her prehensile goad of interrogation
> Her eye on the probe
>
> Her olfactory x-ray
> She ruffles the light that chills the startled eyeball.
>
> After, a dripping bagful of evidence
> Under her humped robe,
>
> She sweeps back, a spread-fingered Efreet,
> Into the courts of the after-life.

The look that sees nothing more than shadows imparts a false sense of mastery, a puerile innocence that, in 'The scream', sees 'the sun on the wall' as 'childhood's/Nursery picture', and grants a sense of existential freedom that is naive in the extreme: 'I knew I rode the wheel of the galaxy'. The interrogator questions that statement by becoming the searching gaze of a far-from-innocent sun, peering through the keyhole and forcing the cockerel-man to experience a sense of shame in believing in consciousness as absolute freedom. The male eye becomes a 'startled eyeball', an intimation that mastery can only be attained by accepting that one's nature can only be repressed by a denial of all 'evidence' to the contrary.

The log-like double of Lumb, in *Gaudete*, provides a relevant antithesis to the startled eyeball of the cockerel-man. During the travesty of an alchemical marriage at the WI, Lumb's prospective bride, Felicity, finds herself struck down by the curious figure of Maud. Lumb's failure to achieve in the world of the village what was achieved in the underworld with the baboon-woman is expressed via his inability to comprehend Felicity's death. And this lack of comprehension takes the form of another scopic image;

> Lumb is kneeling.
> He bows over her, close to her face,
> His check almost touching her cheek
> As he searches her face...

Lumb's gaze is mystified; his visual search provides him with no answer. In *Cave Birds*, Hughes stresses that to move beyond Lumb's stupefaction requires the destruction of objective perception. The text thus makes recourse, in 'The executioner', to imagery centred not on sight but on blindness. This returns the reader to Hughes's critique of patriarchy because, as Freud's Oedipal theory demonstrates, the fear of blindness is an image for the fear of castration. The dismemberment of the protagonist of *Cave Birds*, in poems such as 'The knight', is in many ways a loss of his phallic potency. It is worth recalling that, in its magazine publication, 'The accused' was titled 'Socrates' Cock',[25] and it is the symbolic castration of the misogyny Hughes believes Socrates handed down to Western civilisation that must be the prelude to redemptive vision. Therefore, the executioner 'comes in under the blind filled-up heaven',

> He fills up the mirror, he fills up the cup
> He fills up your thoughts to the brims of your eyes
>
> You just see he is filling the eyes of your friends
> And now lifting your hand you touch at your eyes
>
> Which he has completely filled up
> You touch him
>
> You have no idea what has happened
> To what is no longer yours
>
> It feels like the world
> Before your eyes ever opened

Blindness is to be read here as a productive moment, as a Socratic consciousness takes hemlock and loses subjectivity. The loss of objective sight is the preface to a plenitude of being that is suggested by the repetition of the verb, 'to fill'. In this light, the final couplet implies the possibility of a redeemed vision, one that will see the object world afresh. The crippling alienation that the desiring scopophiliacs experience in *Gaudete*, and that punctuates the log-like Lumb's degraded 'chymical' marriage', will hence be overcome. Like Sagar, I feel that this can be seen as *analogous* to Blake's Eternity, but it is by no means *identical* with it. This is the crux in any reading of Hughes in relation to his Romantic precursors. As mentioned, in Eternity Blake deploys images of sight that do not revolve around the master/slave fulcrum of perceiving subject and perceived object: 'One Man reflecting each in each & clearly seen/And seeing'. Blake's use of reflection as an image of fourfold vision implies a reciprocity absent from Sartre's shameful look of the Other, but it is distinct from Hughes's descriptions of expanded vision. This is clear in the case of *Cave Birds* when one compares Hughes's central image of reflection to that present in Blake's lines. In 'His legs ran about', the image of a mirror appears in a context closely bound to the individuation process and the subsequently achieved vision:

> His arms lifted things, groped in dark rooms, at last with their
> > hands

> Caught her arms
> And lay down enwoven at last at last

> Mouth talked its way in and out and finally
> Found her mouth and settled deeper deeper

> His chest pushed until it came up against
> Her breast at the end of everything

> His navel fitted over her navel as closely as possible
> Like a mirror face down flat on a mirror

The hyperbolic simile that concludes this quotation seeks to express a complete closure of the psychic division that is discussed at length in 'Myth and Education'. Following Jung, the reconciliation is presented in terms of gender, as male and female entities merge into one, but the mirror image situates this alchemical process within the field of vision. The act of reflection is where the self sees itself as alienated in another. It is thus an image of a 'false' perception of

one's identity, false in the sense that the modern individual is alienated from, in the words of the review of *The Environmental Revolution,* 'both inner and outer nature'. We have seen that Hughes links
this lack of vision to patriarchy in the review by claiming that this
alienation is the product of 'the subtly apotheosised misogyny of
Reformed Christianity'. The mirror image in 'His legs ran about' is
one that effaces such alienation *and* such misogyny by describing
the effacement of the act of reflection. The male and female are
described as two mirrors, two reflections that can be read to imply
two alienated entities: the male conscious protagonist and his
repressed (feminine) unconscious, both divorced from each other.
They are brought together via a trope that seeks to turn their shared
exile into a new unity: the disembodied reflections are completely
erased as a mirror flat on a mirror reflects nothing.

In Blake's *Jerusalem*, the reference to reflection is likewise an image
of unity. Blake, however, does not negate the act of reflection but
breaks down the opposition between the reflected and the reflection,
where the redeemed subject is also an object, he is both 'seen/And
seeing'. Hughes's poem also seems to express an enfolding, appropri-
ating moment, but it is marked by an obliteration of the subject in the
other rather than any sense of mutuality. This, in my opinion, is due
to Hughes's belief in the complete separation of inner and outer
'worlds'. The only way to overcome this dichotomy seems to lie in
some sort of *Nirvana*, a cessation of alienated subjectivity that, in 'His
legs ran about' is linked to an anti-scopic image: the cockerel-man
'got what it needed, and grew still, and closed its eyes'.

Nonetheless, this is merely the prelude to an all-encompassing
sight, a genuine form of mastery. And thus, in 'Bride and groom lie
hidden for three-days', the male's sight is restored by the female.

> She gives him his eyes, she found them
> Among some rubble, among some beetles...
>
> They keep taking each other to the sun,
> They find they can easily...
>
> So, gasping with joy, with cries of wonderment
> Like two gods of mud
> Sprawling in the dirt, but with infinite care
>
> They bring each other to perfection.

Such 'perfection' implies the assumption of a new vision that is neither objective nor patriarchal. However, this passage needs to be read in connection with the comparable moment in *Gaudete*, where, after his alchemical atonement, Lumb's vision of the woman is one that can integrate the baffling stitchwork of faces into a single identity:

> He crawls,
> He frees his hands and face of blood-clotted roping tissues.
> He sees light.
> He sees her face undeformed and perfect.

At this point, one may say that Lumb becomes an embodiment of the visionary imagination praised in 'Myth and Education'. The prose context enables the reader to interpret the baboon-woman as a metaphor for the repressed unconscious that, Hughes claims, is ignored by such myopic philosophical movements as Sartrean existentialism. Lumb manages to achieve an 'inner vision' that confronts what has become a demonic inner world, and in so doing brings it into a relationship with his conscious existence. The metaphor of sight expresses this redeemed vision by a scopic image that is intended to contrast with the slavish scopophilia of the male villagers: the patchwork face is now 'undeformed and perfect', or, in Blake's words, Lumb now sees 'according to fitness and order'. In 'Bride and groom', the ability to confront the sun foregrounds the text's modulation of Plato's parable, as the individuated self now possesses a vision that is no longer fixated with phenomenal shadows. Yet it is at precisely this point that Hughes's critique of patriarchy becomes questionable due, in large part, to his failure to overcome the subject/object opposition that informs the text. Hughes retains the subject – the reborn Lumb, the risen cockerel-man – and grants this Promethean figure a mode of vision that can fully master the object. In *Gaudete*, Lumb 'fixes' the female face; in *Cave Birds*, the groom appropriates the bride, and is thus 'given back' his power of perception. In both cases, femininity is a metaphor for that which lies beyond ordinary 'perception' (which, in Hughes, is the inner life or unconscious) and that which thus threatens masculinity (as in the demon St George creates). The mastery and appropriation of this enigmatic otherness is at the very core of Hughes's major texts, as Romantic vision becomes translated into gender relations. By casting the other as feminine and the central

protagonist as male, Hughes may be said simply to repeat the patriarchal marginalisation of women that he is at such pains to refute.
Hughes's desirable synthesis of inner and outer worlds in order to
'cure' the alienation of a misogynist culture, or the (apparent) solipsism of existential existence, is presented in imagery that simply foregrounds a male gaze that is now no longer slavish in the face of its
object.

The resulting absence of reciprocity in Hughes's texts is the by-
product of a desperate expression of individuated selfhood attained
in the teeth of a society which casts its members into a condition of
isolated and 'split' being. That this is simply wish-fulfilment is
acknowledged in the final two lines of 'The risen': 'But when will he
land/On a man's wrist'. The text here reveals that the symbolic trial
and marriage of its cockerel-protagonist is an extended metaphor in
which the bird is not the vehicle for what the reader tended to
assume was an Everyman figure. The whole trope admits that it was
'merely' a compensatory fantasy. In contrast, Blake's *Jerusalem* ends
with no such admission:

> All Human Forms identified, even Tree, Metal, Earth & Stone: all
> Human Forms identified, living, going forth & returning wearied
> Into the Planetary lives of Years, Months, Days & Hours;
> > reposing,
> And then Awakening into his Bosom in the Life of Immortality.
> And I heard the Name of their Emanations: they are named
> > Jerusalem.[26]

Of course, it may be countered that, in some sense, Hughes is
simply more 'honest' than Blake; that fourfold vision, Eternity or
individuation are simply unrealisable; that such notions have
simply the status of consoling fictions. Personal apocalypse *is* a
retreat from communal *praxis*, and both Blake and Hughes, because
of the frustrations they encounter in their respective historical
periods, have recourse to it. Nevertheless, the telling difference
between the two writers is that while Hughes resorts to the idea of a
towering 'masculine' subjectivity – and hence, somewhat ironically,
indicts his own work as patriarchal and condemns his protagonists
to what is virtually indistinguishable from the major Romantic fear
of crushing solipsism -- Blake makes what is at one and the same
time both a *lesser* and a *greater* claim for his Universal Men. The final
plate of *Jerusalem* stresses the reciprocity missing from *Cave Birds*, in

that subject and object are all 'Human Forms'. This mutuality is bound to Blake's highly politicised use of gender, in which the feminine Emanations do not signify a suppressed apolitical and ahistorical Nature, but express the imaginative form of a possible culture, the city of Jerusalem which the previously sick, masculine nation of Albion here becomes. More significantly, Blake does not seek the impossible stasis of visionary imagination for which Hughes's 'The risen' is a riven expression. Blake's Universal Men are involved in what is a dialectical movement, in which they are 'going forth and returning', moving between Eternity, of which they in fact grow weary, and the 'Planetary lives' of temporal existence. In this manner, however promissory Blake's conclusion may be, it is instructive in so far as he manages to write the temporality of history within what appears to be the apocalyptic end of history, and thus inscribes collective renewal within subjective revelation. Hughes's protagonists desire a wholly individual redemption and thus demand too much because they do not ask for enough. Blake's sense of the necessity for communal renewal as the prerequisite to individual salvation is thus, almost oddly, less extravagant than the 'leafless apocalypse' of 'The risen'. And, one hundred and seventy years after Blake completed *Jerusalem*, it certainly sounds more pertinent.

Notes

1. These quotations are cited in what remains one of the classic works on Romanticism (and to which I am indebted in my summary of what constitutes Romantic vision): Abrams, M. H., *Natural Supernaturalism: Tradition and Revolution in Romantic Literature* (Norton, New York, 1973), p. 366.
2. *The Prelude* (1805), Ernest de Sélincourt and Stephen Gill (eds) (Oxford University Press, Oxford, 1970), Bk. xi, l. 172.
3. *Jerusalem*, pl. 49, l. 34. All quotations from Blake are from The *Complete Writings of William Blake*, Geoffrey Keynes (ed.) (Oxford University Press, Oxford, 1966).
4. See Sagar, 'Fourfold Vision in Hughes', in Keith Sagar (ed.), *The Achievement of Ted Hughes* (Manchester University Press, Manchester, 1983), pp. 285–312.
5. *Jerusalem*, pl. 98, ll. 24–5, 28–32, 39–40.
6. Hughes, Ted, 'Myth and Education', in Geoff Fox *et al.* (eds), *Writers, Critics, and Children* (Heinemann, London, 1976), p. 87.
7. *The Everlasting Gospel*, d, ll. 105–6.

8. 'Myth and Education', p. 90.
9. *The Excursion*, Bk. iv, ll. 261–5, in John O. Hayden (ed.), *William Wordsworth: The Poems*, 2 vols (Penguin, Harmondsworth, 1977), II.
10. Smith, *Inviolable Voice: History and Twentieth Century Poetry* (Dublin, 1982), p. 156.
11. Hughes, Ted, 'Introduction' to *Vasko Popa: Collected Poems 1943–1976*, translated by Anne Pennington (Carcanet, Manchester, 1978), p. 1.
12. Sartre, *The Psychology of the Imagination* (Methuen, London, 1972), p. 13.
13. 'Myth and Education', p. 90.
14. Ibid., pp. 91–2.
15. Heidegger, *Being and Time*, translated by John Macquarrie and Edward Robinson (Oxford, 1962), p. 67. See Craig Robinson, *Ted Hughes as Shepherd of Being* (London, 1990), especially Chapter 1.
16. Hughes, Ted, 'The Environmental Revolution', in *Your Environment*, 1 (Summer, 1970), p. 82. For a more extended consideration of Hughes and feminism, see the article by Nathalie Anderson in the present volume.
17. 'Myth and Education', p. 88.
18. In *Three Essays on Sexuality*, Freud describes scopophilia at length. As a perversion, 'instead of being *preparatory* to the normal sexual aim, it supplants it'. This is the case for the males in *Gaudete*. See Freud, *The Essentials of Psychoanalysis*, Anna Freud (ed.) (Penguin, Harmondsworth, 1988), pp. 277–376.
19. Sartre, *Being and Nothingness: An Essay on Phenomenological Ontology*, translated by Hazel E. Barnes (New York, 1956), p. 263.
20. Mulvey, 'Visual Pleasure and Narrative Cinema', *Screen*, 16, 3 (1978), p. 11. I wish to thank Anne Fogarty for bringing this article to my attention.
21. Larrissy, 'Ted Hughes, the Feminine, and *Gaudete*', *Critical Quarterly*, 25, 2 (1983), p. 36.
22. Jung, 'Introduction to the Religious and Psychological Problems of Alchemy', in Antony Storr (ed.), *Selected Writings*, (Fontana, London, 1983), p. 286.
23. See Gifford, Terry and Roberts, Neil, *Ted Hughes: A Critical Study* (Faber & Faber, London, 1981), p. 263.
24. 'Myth and Education', p. 90.
25. Hughes, Ted, 'Socrates' Cock', *London Magazine* (April/May, 1976), p. 6.
26. *Jerusalem*, pl. 99, ll. 1–5.

6

Ted Hughes and the Challenge of Gender
Nathalie Anderson

That a chill exists separating Ted Hughes from the feminist community (if we can speak of so great a multiplicity as if it were a single entity) scarcely needs documenting, nor is its origin difficult to locate. Bestselling biographies, accusations volleyed back and forth on the pages of daily newspapers, lawsuits, even graveyard disturbances have – astoundingly, twenty-seven years on – kept alive the controversy surrounding Hughes's relationship with Sylvia Plath; mere schoolgirls can recognise that 'man in black with a Meinkampf look'.[1] From Robin Morgan's sweeping indictment of Hughes as philanderer, rapist, purveyor of his wife's image, and 'one-man gynocidal movement' in her 1972 poem 'Arraignment', to Marjorie Perloff's now famous analysis in the *American Poetry Review* of his apparently self-defensive editing of *Ariel*,[2] feminists have accused, pursued, assigned blame. And not feminists alone: the influence of this particular view is startlingly widespread. I particularly remember the staid, even patriarchal Chair of a conservative Deep South English department who asked me in a job interview how I could write about Ted Hughes, since he'd killed Sylvia Plath. This, for many quite ordinary, unimaginative, non-vindictive people, is the accepted wisdom: Hughes kills. Hughes is inimical – no, downright dangerous to women.

I mention these perilous assumptions in part to demonstrate the dangers of hyperbole – Plath's death, though tragedy, was clearly no murder – and in part to draw attention to the undeniable fact that many readers (and non-readers) of Hughes's work seem unable to extricate his poetry from his private life. I write here not biographically but literarily: I wish to examine the appearance of women as double-edged emblems in Hughes's work, particularly in *Crow*. But the actual relations that lie behind the poems make these

91

scholarly conclusions rather more personal than is usual, and offer the potential – a rather perilous one – for insight into the man as well as his work.

Double-edged emblems: for many women readers, who have looked for some vision of themselves in his poems, Hughes's female figures scarcely seem ambiguous at all. Such readers will recall poems that dismiss or reject women ('Secretary' in *The Hawk in the Rain*, for example), that satirise their duplicity or their insatiability ('Witches' in *Lupercal*, for example, or the *Gaudete* narrative), that reduce them to wombs or vaginas ('Gog' in *Wodwo*, or 'The Battle of Osfrontalis' in *Crow*), that enact violence against them ('Song for a Phallus' in *Crow*, for a start), that perceive them as violent themselves (the *Gaudete* lyrics). Yet in each case, and with increasing purpose, Hughes's disquieting presentation of women is part of a larger indictment – ultimately of a society which represses not only what Hughes perceives as a female principle within the psyche, but actual women as well. If we cannot define Hughes himself as feminist – and I certainly do not propose to do so – we can nevertheless acknowledge that feminists too endorse this position. Indeed, it is instructive to compare Hughes's stance towards scientific empiricism in *Crow* with that of Adrienne Rich in her first explicitly feminist volume, *Diving into the Wreck*, which was published two years later.[3] If, as we might plausibly argue, Hughes betrays his own ambivalence towards women in his work, he also amply demonstrates his awareness that such ambivalence is symptomatic of a societal neurosis crying out for cure.

I begin my analysis from two premises, or rather observations, about Hughes's characteristic approaches: the first is that he tends to speak in terms of dichotomies, the second that these dichotomies often blur on examination. These tendencies are particularly clear in Hughes's essay 'The Rock', his contribution to the BBC series on 'The Writer and His Background', broadcast in 1963 after the publication of *Lupercal*.[4] In this piece, written to explain 'where the division of body and soul began', Hughes delineates two geological entities or conceptual principles that moulded his childhood – the rock, 'a dark cliff...to the south', 'both the curtain and backdrop to existence', and the moors, 'a gentle female watery line' to the north:

> The rock asserted itself, tried to pin you down, policed and gloomed. But you *could* escape it, climb past it and above it, with

some effort. You could not escape the moors. They did not impose themselves. They simply surrounded and waited.

Hughes's developing dichotomy here – rock against moor; the trap of the body against the unfettered soul – falters as he describes each in similar terms. The rock's policing and the moor's ambush each suggest a sinister inevitability, a confrontation to be escaped or delayed. While a trick of light 'or some overnight strengthening of the earth' might magnify the intensity of the rock, might '[rear] it right over you', the moors 'hung over you at all times'. While the shadow of the rock produces 'A slightly disastrous, crumbly, grey light, sunless and yet too clear', light on the moors is 'at once gloomily purplish and incredibly clear, unnaturally clear'. A climber on the rock 'felt infinitely exposed', felt 'an alarming exhilaration'; on the moors, objects seemed 'more exposed to the radio-active dangers of space, more startled by their own existence', 'exultant'. And finally, while from above or below 'you cannot look at a precipice without thinking instantly what it would be like to fall down it, or jump down it', while the stories Hughes remembers of the rock involve death and falling – '... my brother told of a wood-pigeon shot in one of those little oaks, and how the bird set its wings and sailed out without a wing-beat stone dead into space to crash two miles away on the other side of the valley' – the effects of the moor are disturbingly similar: 'you began to feel bird-like, with sudden temptings to launch out in the valley air'. Clearly, Hughes experiences rock and moor as distinct entities or states – the rock masculine, puritanical, repressive, deadening; the moors feminine, atavistic, liberating, vital. Equally clearly, he finds it difficult to differentiate precisely between these entities: each looms; each exposes the vulnerable to a disquieting clarity; each fosters desolation and exultation; each prompts the sensitive to flight – a dead fall, an illusion of soaring. Each, we might say, both embodies enormity and exemplifies a possible stance for coping with it. Thus as the rock oppresses, it suggests regulation – policing – as an appropriate response to existence; the result is a deadening, a numbness – the flight of a dead bird on set wings across a valley. One implication here is that escape from the rock's oppression requires numbness. But 'you could not escape the moors', and this inescapable quality suggests that, however far one might fly, some disturbing essence lies in wait within the numbness, and essence that might as well be embraced as held temporarily at bay.

This pattern of asserted but questionable dichotomy pervades Hughes's work. Like Alex Davis, I trace in his poetry an anxiety towards enormity, infinite darkness, personal insignificance – death – which culminates and finds transcendence in the controlled disasters of *Crow*. We might recall here his 1957 *Poetry Book Society Bulletin* statement: 'What excites my imagination is the war between vitality and death'.[5] But so strong is the anxiety that vitality often seems merely another form of death. From the beginning, Hughes associates this anxiety with female figures. Thus in 'Billet-Doux' from *The Hawk in the Rain*, the speaker maintains, 'I am driven to your bed and four walls/From bottomlessly breaking night', 'By the constellations staring me to less/Than what cold, rain and wind neglect'; thus the lovers of 'Incompatibilities', also from that volume, enter 'black-outs of impassables', 'The maelstrom dark', 'the endless/ Without-world of the other'. Sexuality, seemingly a refuge from nothingness, thrusts its refugees into negation.

An while 'refugees' may imply that male and female are equally menaced, Hughes's sympathies are clearly with the male, with – for example – the jaded lover of 'Two Phases' who

Sweats his stint out,
No better than a blind mole
That burrows for its lot
Of the flaming moon and sun
Down some black hole.

The endless/Without-world of the other' is here more vaginal than existential, the motive force more binding than driving, the blindness more deluded than instinctual. Where the lover of 'Billet-Doux' is impelled to sex by existential dread – 'I come to you enforcedly' – the mole as sexual labourer is exploited, trapped in relation. In either situation, the woman is almost incidental to the man's dilemma.

Indeed, for the most part, women in these early poems are satirised, condemned outright, or curiously anonymous – 'some black hole'. 'Any woman born', asserts Fallgrief of 'Fallgrief's Girl-Friends', 'having/What any woman born cannot but have,/Has as much of the world as is worth more/Than wit or lucky looks can make worth more'. Fallgrief's assumption that value derives from sexuality – 'What any woman born cannot but have' – works in context to deny the force of mere appearance, the seductions of 'admiration's giddy mannequin', and even to glorify female essence, but it simultaneously erases female individuality, 'wit' as well as 'looks'.

Fallgrief 'meant to stand naked/Awake in the pitch dark where the animal runs,/Where the insects couple as they murder each other'. He assumes that his denial of appearances will reveal the predatory reality of sexual relation, or – to put this less abstractly – that reducing his partner to 'What any woman born cannot but have' will strip the falsifying glamour from a terrifying animalistic function. Fallgrief here is not himself animal, insect, or murderer; rather, he is a witness, a hero. 'Naked', he is vulnerable to attack; 'awake', he is vulnerable to the enormity he perceives. Having discarded both physical and mental protection, Fallgrief intends consciously to observe the running animal of his own unconscious. This heroic act may require woman as the locus of enormity, but what drives the man has little otherwise to do with his girl-friend. 'He meant to stand naked/Awake' implies also 'alone'.

By the poem's conclusion, however, Fallgrief 'has found a woman with such wit and looks/He can brag of her in every company'. Though attributed to 'chance' – mere accident – this culminating change seems both a consequence of heroic risk and a distraction from it, both reward and punishment. 'The chance changed him' – changed his refusal of intellect and beauty, changed his heroic intention. The woman's anonymity underscores Hughes's ambivalence: does the poem chart Fallgrief's luck in finding a package with 'such wit and looks', or his fall from grace in bragging about his distracting find?

Despite such ambivalence, this admired woman nevertheless highlights a more significant admiration for women elsewhere. In 'Billet-Doux', for example, girls who 'Sweeten smiles, peep, cough' are contrasted with an approved woman

> Who sees straight through bogeyman,
> The crammed cafes, the ten thousand
> Books placed end to end, even my gross bulk,
> To the fiery star coming for the eye itself,
> And while she can grabs of them what she can.

Cut from the same heroic mould as Fallgrief's idealised self, this woman is still more capable than he: where he 'meant to stand', she 'sees straight through' appearances, she 'grabs of' essence. Margaret Dickie Uroff has argued persuasively that such capable partners reflect Hughes's relationship with Plath: 'her presence is everywhere felt in Hughes' elevation of women to predatory status equal with men'.[6] Yet even here the woman is more paradigm than individual. Love – which the speaker of 'Billet-Doux' dismisses as 'a spoiled appetite for some delicacy' – is a state that occurs rather than a relationship which develops. Lovers are 'found', stumbled over, encountered. Sex is the locus of enormity, a concentration which makes more perilous the 'Without-world' of existence. Heroes – male or female – may pluck the 'fiery star' from the void, but embrace annihilation in their very heroism. The woman who 'sees straight through' and 'grabs...what she can' is preferable to the affected and repressed, but is herself faceless, reduced to function, and – like the male persona of these poems – doomed.

It is interesting in this context to recall the conclusion to 'Bawdry Embraced', a poem from *Recklings* explicitly dedicated to Plath, where '...every ogling eye/Is a cold star to measure/Their solitude by'. The marriage of equals here is by implication hot rather than cold, a star of greater magnitude; 'Their solitude' emphasises their uniqueness, the distance that separates them from merely 'ogling eye[s]'. Yet even here, the figuring of mutuality in terms of solitude raises the spectre of isolation, and the 'cold star' as standard paradoxically lowers the poem's temperature even as it gestures towards warmth.

Hughes's second volume, *Lupercal*, offers as a stance towards enormity the figure of a dreaming tramp, dead to outer reality, open to inner 'blackouts of impassables'. In his debilitation, his self-negation, and his connection with the animalistic underworld, the tramp serves as a corrective to the posturing hero of *The Hawk in the Rain*. Most particularly, he is – despite 'Dick Straightup' – no lover: women are virtually missing from the volume, serving when they do appear mainly as props – the mother in 'Everyman's Odyssey', the barren women in 'Lupercalia'. Only 'To Paint a Water Lily' and 'The Voyage' may be construed as love poems. It is as if Hughes is insisting that his proper arena – despite the earlier failed attempts to ground existential nausea in sexuality – has nothing to do with sex. His new hero exists in blank potentiality.

This passive figure thus provides an intriguing parallel for the anonymous 'one, numb beyond her last of sense', whose death is posed against nuclear annihilation in 'A Woman Unconscious'. Is hers 'a lesser death' than global world-cancelling black', Hughes asks, conflating private loss with that ultimate cancellation as the woman 'Close[s] her eyes on the world's evidence', cancelling it. Where the tramp survives enormity, even in death, to find deity 'In an animal's dreamed head' ('Crag Jack's Apostasy'), the woman's parallel submersion negates the promise of transcendence implicit in this stance. Valued because sunk beyond consciousness, yet debilitated beyond human aid, she dissipates admiration for the tramp's endurance in poignancy, as a stony emblem of loss.

Moreover, although the woman remains firmly anonymous and firmly real, the description of holocaust as 'A melting of the mould in the mother' gestures towards an identity of mother and world, so that a cancellation of one literally cancels the other. Interestingly, Hughes's most conventional love poems – 'The Voyage' here, and 'Song' in *The Hawk in the Rain* – ratify this cancellation in romantic tropes. Each assumes loss: 'Without hope move my words and looks/Towards you'; 'when I shall have lost you'. Each affiliates the beloved with the elemental: 'a marble of foam' caressed by the tide, 'a shaped shell' through which the wind harmonises, a cloudy 'fire' lit by the moon in 'Song'; as unfixable in 'The Voyage' as the sea. Each ends in disaster: 'my hands full of dust'; 'The sea's.../Other than men taste who drown out there'. To lose the beloved is to lose the world; devotion to her involves the risk of elemental annihilation.

The unconscious woman of *Lupercal*, vulnerable on 'the white hospital bed', becomes in Hughes's radio play 'The Wound' a composite figure whose 'mundiform belly' is 'sliced.../With joy./To numbers' by such authorities as 'The Coroner', 'medical specialists', 'Experimental psychologists', 'Zoologists','Bacteriologists', 'Anthropologists'. The hospital, implicitly incapable of saving its patient in 'A Woman Unconscious', becomes in 'The Wound' the site of active dismemberment, of purposeless vivisection, of rape: the researchers do not find what they 'hoped for./Lusted for'. As in the earlier volumes, this vulnerable female figure both embodies and distances enormity; the 'mundiform belly' again equates woman and world, enlarging a single atrocity into global catastrophe. The significance of the woman's vulnerability has shifted, however: tragically silent in 'A Woman Unconscious', here she accuses, assigns blame.

The multiple voices of the 'mundiform belly' speak only briefly in 'The Wound': this scene – part of a soldier's nightmarish visit to the underworld – comprises perhaps three pages of the play's forty-two. While neither 'The Wound' nor *Wodwo*, the volume in which it appears, thus centres on a paradigmatic female entity, the

'mundiform belly' reduced 'to numbers' indicates that by 1962
Hughes has consciously begun to pose against scientific empiricism
a female sensibility he associates with earth itself, a spirit injured literally and metaphorically by the dominating intellect. Women represent what rationality denies.

This conclusion need scarcely surprise us, since Hughes himself repeatedly asserts it. 'The subtly apotheosised misogyny of
Reformed Christianity is proportionate to the fanatic rejection of
Nature, and the result has been to exile man from Mother Nature –
from both inner and outer nature', he writes in 1970.[7] His 1971
experimental drama *Orghast* traces 'the crime against material
nature, the Creatress, source of life and light, by the Violator, the
mental tyrant Holdfast, and her revenge'.[8] Hughes's introduction to
a selection of Shakespeare's verse insists:

> When the physical presence of love has been degraded to lust and
> forbidden lust has combined with every other forbidden thing to
> become a murderous devil, life itself has become a horror, the
> maiden has become a whore and a witch, and the miraculous
> source of creation has become the empty hole through into
> nothing.[9]

This 'empty hole' vividly recalls the ambivalences of Hughes's earliest poetry – sex as salvation, sex as deception – and thus highlights
our difficulties in assessing his indictments of rationalist misogyny
in *Wodwo* and later in *Crow*. If rationalism perceives the female principle as 'a horror', 'a whore and a witch', then Hughes must portray
such a horror in order to present rationalism accurately. Yet to do so
is to incorporate a horrific vision of woman into his own discourse –
a discourse which surely reveals in some sense that which fascinates
and distresses its author. 'The maiden *has become* a whore'; 'the
miraculous source of creation *has become* the empty hole': Hughes's
verb here pushes the association of existential meaninglessness and
female sexuality beyond short-sighted misperception to identity.

In *Wodwo*, the nadir of this ambivalence occurs in 'Gog', where a
'horseman of iron' 'Gallops over the womb that makes no claim,
that is of stone' 'on the horse shod with vaginas of iron' – one of
Hughes's most controversial images. The earth here, defined
through the familiar association of womb and tomb, is clearly
female and clearly sinister: thus in part II, the question 'Then
whose/Are these/Eyes' receives the answer, 'Death and death and

death – Her mirrors'. Even the fortuitous capitalisation of 'Eyes', 'Death', and 'Her' implies a deity at once all-powerful and intimate whose true identity – death – we can perceive mirrored in creation. The iron horseman who rides 'Out of the blood-dark womb' might thus – on the evidence of his character and origin – plausibly be her champion, an extension of her deathly will. Yet Hughes's imagery pits horseman against goddess, male against female: 'He follows his compass, the lance-blade, the gunsight, out/Against the fanged grail and tireless mouth'. In a pattern which becomes increasingly familiar in later books, the male principle – dependent on the female and bound to her symbolically – nevertheless seeks to separate himself, to destroy her. 'It's the key to the neurotic-making dynamics of Christianity', Hughes writes in his 1970 essay 'Myth and Education': 'Christianity in suppressing the devil, in fact suppresses imagination and suppresses vital natural life'.[10] And again, 'The fundamental pattern was made within Protestant Christianity that the devil, woman, nature were out of bounds'.[11] Yet in 'Gog', the point of view, which seems to endorse the horseman's misogyny, raises problems of interpretation. These lines, for example, with their tone of prayer or command, ironically reverse the attitude of a volume where poem after poem questions the rule of empiricism:

> Shield him from the dipped glance, flying in half light, that
> tangles the heels,
> The grooved kiss that swamps the eyes with darkness.
> Bring him to the ruled slab, the octaves of order,
> The law and mercy of number. Lift him
> Out of the octopus maw and the eight lunatic limbs
> Of the rocking, sinking cradle.

It is instructive to read these lines against Hughes's well-known comments on the poem from his 1971 *London Magazine* interview: 'Gog', he tells Ekbert Faas,

> ...actually started as a description of the German assault through the Ardennes and it turned into the dragon in Revelations [presented as a Caliban- or Grendel-like figure in Part I]. It alarmed me so much I wrote a poem about the Red Cross Knight just to set against it with the idea of keeping it under control... keeping its effects under control.[12]

We can see 'Gog' III as a conscious dramatisation of the psychological war between repression and the distended repressed, a war
which – Hughes explains to Faas – transforms 'Isis, mother of the
gods' into 'Hitler's familiar spirit'. Or we can see the poem as evidence that Hughes's conscious understanding masks, is a projection
of, a continuing psychological war of his own.

Wodwo and *Crow* demonstrate that Hughes manages his ambivalence by externalising it. His dramatisation of violent men and
devouring women allows him to demonstrate the power of this
ambivalence without acknowledging its hold over him. He defuses
it, separates it from his own sexuality, his own marriage to a psycho-
logically demanding woman, his own upbringing. While wrestling
his ambivalence into schematic form, Hughes simultaneously per-
sonifies the elemental, the inconceivable, the void, the darkness,
death, meaninglessness – and what is personified can be ap-
proached, understood, sympathised with, loved, adored. Thus in
'Karma', 'the mother' is explicitly 'the mother/Of the God/Of the
world/Made of Blood', at once embodiment of death and authority
over it, to whom we cry for sustenance, for oblivion.

The various images of women to be found in *Crow* testify to the
intensity of Hughes's dilemma. Female sexual organs often appear
alone, disembodied and depersonalised: the 'vulva' tightening on
'man's neck' in 'Crow's First Lesson', the 'vaginas in a row' with
which 'Words' try to tempt Crow in 'The Battle of Osfrontalis', 'The
horrible oven of fangs' in 'Crow's Account of St. George', the 'buttocks' under which Crow is caught in 'Crow and Mama'. Sex is
repellent or mechanical: the apparent cannibalism of post-nuclear
horrors in 'Notes for a Little Play', the regenerative efforts of two
halves of a cut worm in 'A Childish Prank', the waving legs and
open 'maw' of the Sphinx in 'Song for a Phallus' where Oedipus
'stood stiff and wept/At the dreadful thing he saw'. 'Knife', 'fangs',
and reflexive strangulation assert the danger of engaging the
female: even 'the soft and warm that is long remembered' culminates in 'a volcano' ('Magical Dangers').

With such excuses, it is not surprising that the female is often the
object of violence: confronted with vaginas, Crow 'called in his
friends'; confronted with the 'oven of fangs', the obsessed scientist
'bifurcates' it with a Japanese sword; confronted with the 'dreadful'
'maw', Oedipus 'split[s]/The Sphinx' with 'an axe' as he eventually
'split[s] his Mammy like a melon'; Crow's every action deforms the
mother he cannot escape. Most of this violence is clearly phallic,

suggesting a doubleness to each action – a murder, a rape, a feminist's nightmare.

Yet, while few readers can perceive this pattern of aversion and reactive violence undisturbed, it is also clear that a depiction of such pathology is part of Hughes's criticism of a pathologically unbalanced culture. Neither Oedipus nor the scientist is presented heroically; their fatal limitations, evidenced in their cataclysmically disproportionate violence to those they ostensibly love, form the thematic focus of their respective poems. 'Crow and Mama' begins with *inadvertent* violence manifesting implicit reciprocity: 'When Crow cried his mother's ear/Scorched to a stump'. Only at the fifth couplet, nearly half-way through the poem, does the reciprocity become explicit and the violence reactive: 'When he stopped she closed on him like a book/On a bookmark, he had to get going'. From this point on, Crow's attempts to achieve independence, increasingly drastic, repeatedly entangle his mother, his eventual rocket flight to the moon lets him out 'Under his mother's buttocks', a circumstance analogous to 'a book/On a bookmark' or to a disturbing rebirth – that is, to a pre-existent rightness, a reassertion of relationship. Crow's relationship with his mother is thus by implication that which cannot be escaped, wholeness; its violent aspect signifies imbalance and fragmentation. In a similar image, once Oedipus splits his mother to discover 'What's on the other side' of 'The World' he perceives as 'dark', 'He found himself curled up inside/As if he had never been bore...'. Interrelatedness reasserts itself; the pattern, denied, begins again.

Against fragmentation and denial, *Crow* poses a grim transcendence. 'Man' in 'Fleeing from Eternity' is 'faceless.../Eyeless and mouthless bald face' until 'He got a sharp rock he gashed holes in his face/Through the blood and pain he looked at the earth'. 'Blood and pain' serve as his sense organs; only through suffering can he perceive the 'woman singing out of her belly', reminiscent of the 'mundiform belly' in *Wodwo*, and 'exchange' 'eyes and a mouth' – 'life' – for her song. Even in this void, even through disaster, transcendence can find a way: 'The song was worth it'. 'The mind is its own place', says Milton, 'and in itself/Can make a Heaven of Hell, a Hell of Heaven'. Hughes might say that 'the mind' has already made 'a Hell of Heaven'; when we admit our complicity in hellishness, abandon our resistance to what we have defined as hell, we may find ourselves among the 'staring angels' ('Pibroch'), able to sing.

Yet 'Fleeing From Eternity' admits other interpretations: are the gashes, through which the man perceives, emblems of relatedness, of abandoned solipsism, of newly-achieved wholeness; or does his action only continue his flight? His 'exchange' with the singing woman deepens this ambiguity: 'He gave her eyes and a mouth' means that he gashed her face; 'in exchange' does not necessarily imply that he has given up anything himself; 'exchange' can thus be read as a rationalisation of theft, of rape; indeed, despite the gift of 'life', 'The woman felt cheated'. However we read the poem, its last two lines are disturbing. 'The song was worth it' implies first that the man has given his life for it, but his laughter indicates that he has not lost his newly-gashed mouth. If both he and the woman are now alive, 'The song was worth it' suggests that, having heard the song – whether he has stolen it or has simply reimbursed her for what she still sings – the man finds it worth giving the woman pain, or giving her a life he would have preferred to hoard. 'The woman felt cheated' suggests either that newly-acquired life, however valuable, does not make up for her loss of the song, or that her new awarenesss, song or no, is a poor exchange for wholeness and interiority.

Perhaps, then, this poem represents a repeated crime against the earth, a renewal of fragmentation. Yet the conclusion of 'Fleeing from Eternity' focuses less on the man's implicit crimes than on the clear value of the song, 'worth it' to both man and woman. Does Hughes control his imagery, use it to thematic advantage – does the man's behaviour toward the woman signify culpability? Or is the imagery undependable, taking to itself disgust, rage, and trepidation beyond the requirements of context – is the man's transcendence tainted?

To explore these issues of artistic control and betraying anxiety, and to assess the possibilities for healing embedded in gendered relation, as Hughes perceived them at this point in his career, it is useful to turn from *Crow* the volume to what Keith Sagar has called 'the great *Crow* project'[13] – the myth Hughes spun for himself as 'a quarry', 'a way of getting the poems'[14] during the late 1960s and early 1970s. Within that larger schema, the poems eventually identified by the volume's subtitle as 'From the Life and Songs of the Crow' were apparently conceived as literal songs occasioned by Crow's experiences within a quest narrative. Although this narrative remains almost completely invisible to us through the published work, Hughes from time to time drops tantalising hints of its details – that 'Lovesong' from *Crow* and 'Bride and Groom Lie Hidden for Three Days' from *Cave Birds*, for example, are answers Crow gives to the gnomic questions of an ogress he must recognise as his own bride: 'Who paid most, him or her?'[15] and 'Who gives most, him or her?' The 'alchemical wedding' that culminates this quest indicates that, in the narrative, the solution to Crow's dilemma is posited less in terms of perception – as suggested, for example, by 'Revenge Fable' and 'Glimpse' in *Crow* the volume – and more in terms of implicitly sexual relations between men and women. An examination of four poems from the *Crow* material which deal with such relations – 'Crow's Undersong', 'Crow's Song about England', 'Lovesong', and 'Bride and Groom' – will allow us to assess the strengths and limitations of the solution Hughes offers.[16]

In *Crow* the volume, 'Crow's Undersong' follows 'Owl's Song', a poem which begins with the words 'He sang'. That strategy – the poem presented as a narrative account expanding its title – prepares us to see a parallel relation between poem and title in 'Crow's Undersong'. Yet 'Crow's Undersong' begins 'She cannot come all the way', and that female pronoun controls the entire poem. The 'natural' way to read the poem is as the contents of Crow's song, but the parallel with 'Owl's Song' makes the 'she' slightly peculiar, as if the poem offered not his words but an independent entity singing itself, unperceived by Crow: the undersong personified, coming about its business as in 'The Thought-Fox'. It's worth recalling here Uroff's sexual reading of this title: 'his view of man's place against the woman who insatiably comes and comes and comes, even while Crow attempts to fend her off by claiming she cannot manage anything but coming'.[17] Indeed, the description of the female principle offered by the poem is one which few contemporary women will appreciate – 'She comes singing she cannot manage an instrument'; 'She comes sluttish she cannot keep house'; 'She comes dumb she cannot manage words'; 'She has come amorous it is all she has come for' – but it is nevertheless consistent with an incarnation of the natural, the procreative, the psychological principle opposed to rationality: 'She brings petals in their nectar fruits in their plush/ She brings a cloak of feathers an animal rainbow'. We might see the title, then, as implying that this song underlies Crow's dominant persona, inarticulable but essentially significant; in a sense, it manifests the unconscious recognising itself, the devalued asserting its value. The last lines – 'If there had been no hope she would not have come/And there would have been no crying in the city/(There would have been no city)' – convert apparent blame (her fault that there is crying) to necessity, agency: without her, there would be nothing. 'She cannot come all the way': what appears at first as deficiency on reflection suggests that what is missing is a 'he' to, so to speak, come with her, meet her half-way.

'Crow's Song about England'[18] brings a 'he' into play, but as the flip side of a 'she': the poem enacts the disturbing equations posited in Hughes's discussions of gender in Shakespeare's work, meta-morphic equivalents reminiscent of Blake's 'The Mental Traveller'. Using *Venus and Adonis* and *The Rape of Lucrece* as paradigms through which to view the plays, Hughes perceives a persistent 'oscillation' 'from loving female to angry male';[19] here 'a girl' becomes an unspecified 'he' and then becomes 'a little girl' again. Each gender exists alone, but comes into being in reaction to the other, so the interdependence is clear; at the same time, relation is so embedded in the male's violent rejection of the female that transcendence or mutuality seems impossible. 'She trie[s] to give' herself, and then 'she trie[s] to keep' herself: neither strategy is suf-ficient; in each case her self is taken from her, used as evidence against her. The culminating lines of these sections – 'She tried to give [or keep] her cunt/It was produced in open court she was sen-tenced' – indicate that female sexuality in itself constitutes a crime in this perverse society. And thus the female, 'mad with pain', underlies male violence:

She changed sex he came back

Where he saw her mouth he stabbed with a knife
Where he saw her eyes he stabbed likewise
Where he saw her breasts her cunt he stabbed

In its distressingly phallic violence, 'Crow's Song about England' recalls 'Fleeing from Eternity', but here the societal critique works less ambiguously. 'Where he saw her mouth' turns the poem's violence simultaneously outward against other women and inward against the traces of femininity perceptible in the male self. Violence against women is thus implicitly self-destructive, implicitly a result of a society which 'frames' women in sexual roles, which defines both giving and keeping as crimes, which denies interrelation through opposition.

In 'Lovesong' man and woman are at last coexistent, but express their love by devouring, negating the other.

> He loved her and she loved him
> His kisses sucked out her whole past and future or tried to
> He had no other appetite
> She bit him she gnawed him she sucked
> She wanted him complete inside her

'In the morning', the poem concludes, 'they wore each other's face'. The poem particularises emotion through a series of correlatives as idealised love becomes 'appetite', becomes disguised spite:

> Her smiles were spider bites
> So he would lie still till she felt hungry
> His words were occupying armies
> ...
> His whispers were whips and jackboots
> Her kisses were lawyers steadily writing
> ...
> Her promises took the top off his skull
> She would get a brooch made of it
> His vows pulled out all her sinews
> He showed her how to make a love-knot

Through its contrasts, 'Lovesong' forces us to perceive the violence implicit in possessiveness, the justifications that accompany cruelty, the societally characteristic methods of woman and man, the equivalence of overt and insidious violence, and – perhaps most intriguingly – an awareness of complicity in destruction. We might recall that, in Hughes's early 'Incompatibilities', terror transformed into desire paradoxically culminates in the solitary fall 'through the endless/Without-world of the other'. 'Lovesong' subverts that isolation, identifies each partner's role as victim and agent, asserts the pattern of relationship which defines and contains each through that role, implies endless repetition through their interchangeability – in short, presents devouring sexuality as implicitly a manifestation of the culture's debilitating fragmentation. Crow's answer to the ogres' question – 'Who paid most, him or her?' – transforms it to

'Who extorted most?'; love in this economy becomes a competition to make the other pay, to evade payment oneself. Yet to engage in this competition is to lose even one's gender: 'they wore each other's face'.

After poems in which male and female 'cannot come all the way' to each other, or supplant each other inexorably, or 'love' each other out of existence, the moving delineation of mutuality in 'Bride and groom lie hidden for three days' comes as a relief – and yet on closer examination this mutuality too becomes less equal. Though male and female share a delight in existence and in each other, 'she' characteristically *finds* the parts of his body 'She gives him his eyes, she found them/She has found his hands for him/Now she has brought his feet...' – while 'he' characteristically *devises* her parts:

> He has assembled her spine,
> …
> And he has fashioned her new hips
> …
> And now he connects her throat,
>   her breasts and the pit of her stomach
> With a single wire

Although the task facing each entity is virtually identical, Hughes emphasises the male's cleverness: where he recovers her skin, 'He just seemed to pull it down out of the air', in a masterful act of prestidigitation or sorcery; the labour of restoring her spine is explicitly 'a superhuman puzzle but he is inspired'. Her response to his gifts is emotional – 'She weeps with fearfulness and astonishment'; 'She leans back...laughing incredulously' – while he is active, centred in his body: 'his hands.../...are amazed at themselves'; 'his whole body lights up'. Her activities are understated, mediated through the skills supposedly appropriate to femininity: she 'smooths' his skull, ties his teeth, 'stitches his body here and there/with steely purple silk'. If her final act shows an artisan's skill – 'She inlays with deep-cut scrolls the nape of his neck' – the paradigm of female slightness established by the rest of the poem makes the achievement something of a surprise. In 'Crow's Undersong', 'she comes singing she cannot manage an instrument', 'with eyes wincing frightened', 'she has come amorous it is all she has come for', and here too – although the incapacity is relative, the fearfulness inextricable from delight, the mutuality of desire central – she 'cannot manage' what he can, and her worth to him is ultimately, essentially sexual. When she fits his hands to his wrists 'they go feeling all over her'; his last and thus most significant act is to '[sink] into place the inside of her thighs', giving her her sexuality. If 'they bring each other to perfection', so that both of them can 'come all the way', that 'perfection' might nevertheless feel diminishing to a female reader.

In his *Crow* project, Hughes uses gender for purposes to which a feminist might well assent: to acknowledge and ultimately embrace devalued aspects of the self, to critique a society in which a rejection of the 'feminine' excuses self-destructive violence, to explore how such a society breeds competition and possessiveness, to offer an alternative in mutual respect and delight. Yet, even in mutuality, his female remains Other. As incarnation of Nature,[20] she is voiceless – and this voicelessness persists into more realistic portrayals: although the matched 'promises' and 'vows' of 'Lovesong' implicitly put words in both mouths, 'his words' are explicitly paired with 'her laughs', 'his whispers' with 'her kisses'. Although each poem apparently seeks to revalue the female, in each case her insufficiency comprises part of the poem's logic – even to the point of explaining violence towards women through outraged femininity in 'Crow's Song about England'. And in each case the female is essentially sexualised, defined by her sexuality. If part of Hughes's point is that the Western (male) intellect must recognise and embrace its intuitions, its emotions, its connectedness, its sexuality, that laudable precept nevertheless rests on an identification of the female as intuitive, emotional, connected, and sexual – an object available to be embraced, rather than a fully realised partner, a complex subjectivity. While 'Lovesong' and 'Bride and groom' grapple intriguingly with this dilemma, the closed sexual arena – whether claustrophobic, or more appealingly intimate – ratifies the limited definition of the female and thus implicitly assents to objectification.

In the twenty years since the publication of *Crow*, Hughes has continued to experiment with the configurations that dominate the early books: repressive piety, debilitating rationalism, reciprocal violence, unperceived culpability, grim transcendence. Women still punctuate these experiments, as active agents and as passive victims.

Thus the baboon-woman who joins with the priest in the mutual rebirth of the *Gaudete* narrative, and the biting goddess of its lyrics, are matched in *Cave Birds* by the woman whose 'heart stopped beating' 'While I strolled' ('Something was happening'), and by the 'earth/...[that] turned in its bed/To the wall' ('In these fading moments I wanted to say'): thus the vampiric snow woman of *River*, whose 'kiss/Grips through the full throat and locks on the dislodged vertebrae' ('Japanese River Tales') of the now-freezing stream, is matched by the 'earth invalid' of *Moortown*, who 'Leans back, eyes closed, exhausted, smiling/Into the sun' 'While we sit, and smile, and wait, and know/She is not going to die' ('March morning unlike others'). Even the 'empty hole through into nothing' appears with striking corporeality in the Sheela-na-gig which serves *Gaudete's* Lumb as an object of contemplation:

> The simply hacked-out face of a woman
> Gazes back at Lumb
> Between her raised, wide-splayed, artless knees
> With a stricken expression.
> Her square-cut, primitive fingers, beneath her buttocks
> Are pulling herself wide open –

> > (*Gaudete*, p. 110)

The conclusion of this section – 'Heavens opening higher beyond heavens/As the afternoon widens' – transforms the violence implicit in 'hacked-out' and 'stricken' into a redeeming vision of the universe giving birth to itself. Indeed, these volumes generally point towards healing: the convalescent earth is still a 'Woman Unconscious', but we 'know/She is not going to die'.

Whatever the successes of these more recent volumes, however, *Crow* remains a point of strength in Hughes's career, with a continuing power to fascinate, to influence, and – emphatically – to disturb. This disturbing quality explains in part the notoriety that has dogged its author. Myth – Hughes's method in *Crow* – involves a therapeutic representation of personal anxieties. The encounter with the shadow requires that we face what we most fear, a fear compounded by the societal assumptions that formed us and by our uneasy suspicion that what we despise in others is present in ourselves. For readers who share the assumptions and anxieties of the author the myth may offer a healing insight – or it may represent unbearable threat. For readers who do not share these assumptions – or no longer share them – the myth may appear not as an exploration encouraging insight and redefinition, but as evidence of an indictable society – as in fact it is. And to the extent that diagnosis and neurosis overlap, the reader may be led to equate the physician with the illness he describes. Rather than commend the myth for the accuracy of its aim, the reader will then reject it as a symptom of this ill. Can bigotry seek to eradicate itself? Can neurosis hazard a cure?

In *Crow*, Hughes's probing to the split between consciousness and instinct leads him to a sexual correlative, a figuration which is convincing as an analogue for unacknowledged interdependency in the psyche, and which allows Hughes to submerge sexual anxiety in an indictment of the society that, at some level, produced and ratified it. By displacing his anxieties to what David Holbrook terms a 'split-off indestructible self'[21] – Crow – he both obscures his own guilt – including his guilt as a survivor – and triumphs over death and nothingness. Sexual anxiety and mortal anxiety intertwine: rejection of the female, all too natural in the context of the 'horrible oven of fangs' and the 'octopus maw', is nevertheless a form of suicide.

For a man who came to age in the early 1950s, the assumptions at the heart of this figuration can be surprising only in their intensity – indeed, they are the familiar assumptions of Romanticism, stripped bare. Given Hughes's indictment of rational materialism and his recognition of the female principle as essential to wholeness, he must be stunned by feminist rejection of his work. In order to write, we might posit, Hughes cannot accept such criticism; his philosophy is a product of personal development, a means of externalising and thus controlling personal anxiety. Is it possible for a reader to sympathise with Hughes's artistic and personal dilemmas, to assent to his mythic paradigms, to deplore with him societal objectifications, to keep message and messenger separate?

Rather than attempt to address such questions – which must in any case remain rhetorical – we may find it intriguing to shift focus to Hughes's most recent work. Does Hughes continue to deploy female figures emblematically and ambivalently? How might a feminist reader respond to *Wolfwatching*?

At first glance, the volume may seem more a compendium than a unity: it contains naturalistic animal poems, densely mythic poems, seemingly autobiographical poems, poems about war, poems of place – a virtual catalogue of the many distinct styles and themes with which Hughes has experimented during his career. But closer examination reveals coherence and design, founded once more in gender.

Wolfwatching begins with a hawk (a sparrow-hawk) – 'The warrior/Blue shoulder-cloak wrapped about him' – and ends with doves – 'Nearly uncontrollable love-weights./Or now/Temple-dancers'. The volume is thus framed by slightly disguised or dis-placed emblems of war and peace, the masculine and the feminine. The volume's two mythic poems create a second, interior frame, as both 'Two Astrological Conundrums' (the second poem in the vol-ume) and 'Take what you want but pay for it' (the fourth from the end) explore gendered emblems of relation. The first 'Conundrum' offers the fable of the tigress who

> ...promised to show me her cave
> which was the escape route from death
> And which came out into a timeless land.
>
> To find this cave, she said, we lie down
> And you hold me, so, and we fly.

In its vaginal 'cave', the 'escape route from death', this poem recalls the sexual solutions of *The Hawk in the Rain*, but removed from literal interaction to a more mythic, shamanistic relation with the goddess. 'Folded/In the fur', 'dissolved/in the internal powers of tiger', the protagonist has the opportunity to become 'The never-dying god who gives everything', but somehow fails:

>   I heard
> A sudden cry of terror, an infant's cry –
> Close, as if my own ear had cried it.
>   ...
> A bright spirit went away weeping.

'Take what you want but pay for it' offers a similarly mythic use of the female. Here Adam's wounded body, tortured by God so that it 'Shall destroy [the soul's] peace no more', 'exhal[es]...from the blackest pit of all'

> A misty enfoldment which materialized
> As a musing woman, who lifted the body
> As a child's effortless, and walked
> Out of the prison with it, singing gently

In the first poem, 'terror' brings the protagonist back to earth, per-haps as an infant reborn in the chain of existence, driving away the 'bright spirit' who might have delivered him as an equal into godhead. In the second, 'despair' draws out the female emanation who frees the body, nurtures it, mothers it. In the first case, mothering represents the protagonist's failure; in the second, the body's victory – but in each case the duality of female and male, mother and child signals a deeper unity, misperceived as separation in the first poem, valued as relation in the second.

These poems exploring a quasi-Blakean mothering principle alert us to other references to mothers peppering the volume. In 'Slump Sundays', the 'seed-corn' of experience 'Lugged back from the Somme…served for a mother-tongue'; in 'Dust as we are', the 'knowledge' brought back by 'My post-war father' fills the speaker: 'After mother's milk/This was the soul's food'. Women structure the postwar world as representatives of society, of relation at once intimate and judgemental. In the father's memory, 'naked men/Slithered staring where their mothers and sisters/Would never have to meet their eyes'; when the man in 'Sacrifice' belatedly determines to join his brothers' business, 'The duumvirate of wives turned down their thumbs'. Hughes's familiar trope of reciprocity – 'When Crow cried his mother's ear/Scorched to a stump' – appears here through the identity of men with their families: when the man in 'Sacrifice' hangs himself,

his sister, forty miles off,

Cried out at the hammer blow on her nape.
And his daughter
Who'd climbed up to singsong: 'Supper, Daddy'
Fell back down the stairs to the bottom.

In 'Walt', the German's wartime bullet 'brought him and his wife down together/With all his children one after the other'. Again and again, the aftermath of war is triangulated through women: sisters, daughters, wives, mothers of the next generation, where the repercussions echo.

The two poems in the volume which might be portraits of Hughes's own mother play intriguingly with the motifs of mothering suggested in the mythic poems. In 'Source', the mother weeps without apparent cause, as if she 'could dissolve yourself, me, everything/Into this relief of your strange music'; in 'Leaf Mould', the mother carries 'your spectre-double, still in her womb', and the poem ends with the memory of how it felt 'as you escaped'. The repetition of dissolving and weeping from the fable of the tigress, and the anticipation of doubling, of nurturance, of modes of freedom, soon to be repeated in 'Take what you want', translate mythic unity in duality into the more literal relation of mother and uncomprehending, belatedly grateful son. The war forms a backdrop to each poem, a possible explanation of the 'mourning/That repaired you' in 'Source', a forest of 'cenotaphs' for 'cordite conscripts' echoed in the mother's perception of the literal forest in 'Leaf Mould'. Where the poems about men who have survived the war delineate the impossible weight of responsibility they suffer under and pass on, these poems about mothering suggest the potential for 'relief', though in ways which at first may feel defeating or coercive.

In the paradigm of mother and child which structures the volume and raises its central questions of relation and identity, of loss of self and acceptance of pain, what happens to mutuality, to the equality of sexual relations, to the alchemical marriage?

In 'Anthem for Doomed Youth', the echo of Eliot's *Waste Land* – 'And who's that other beside her?' – alerts us to a glimpse of the goddess, however ironic or misperceived, in the girl-friends – 'portly birds' – set in the Ford's back seat by the 'doomed' brothers whose 'glances/Hawked' the countryside, searching for 'tame, fuddled coveys'.

In the far more serious poem that follows, 'The Black Rhino', the rhinoceros is at first explicitly male; then ambiguously 'you', 'I', 'it'; then finally, in the poem's third section, explicitly female. The shifting pronoun underscores the shift from strength to vulnerability, encompasses the entire species, and enables the sexual figuration – 'an ornament for a lady's lap', 'the black hole in her head' – through which Hughes indicts both genders of the human species in the extinction of others.

'On the Reservations' too designates its section by gender, but here the first is evidently a husband, the second a wife, the third their child. In a lifetime of coal and ashes metaphorically left in his Christmas stocking, the miner of the first section recalls only one interaction with a woman, presumably his wife: 'The brochures screwed up in a tantrum/As her hair shrivelled to a cinder'. Momentary anger and lifelong disappointment equally shrivel her beauty and youth, as the couple's cramped existence reduces her to mere coal-slag, hopeless Cinderella. In her section, this diminishment speaks through the repeated phrase 'She dreams she sleepwalks', which conveys daily life as a nightmare of exhaustion, converts sleep to perpetual restlessness, and makes even the dream of walking a delusion. The surreal combinations of the horrific and the mundane culminate, however, in a lost moment of mutuality:

> Remembering how a flare of pure torrent
> sluiced the pit muck
> off his shoulder-slopes while her hands
> soapy with milk blossoms anointed
> him and in their hearth
> fingers of the original sun opened
> the black
> bright book of the stone
> he'd brought from beneath dreams
> or did she dream it

The poem's last section offers, in its portrait of this couple's 'sulky boy', the punk as alchemical child. The irony is that, like the alchemical original, he promises transcendence through transformation:

> This megawatt, berserker medium
> With his strobe-drenched battle-cry delivers
> The nineteenth century from his mother's womb:
>
> The work-house dread that brooded, through her term,
> Over the despair of salvaged sperm.
> ...
>
> Bomblit, rainbowed, aboriginal:
> 'Start afresh, this time unconquerable.'

'Delivers' turns the berserker into postman, into midwife, into liberator: the 'nineteenth century' *is* 'the work-house dread', now loosed on the world 'afresh'; is the brood-hen, the contemplator, that brings despair to fruition; is the child himself, result of capitalism's 'dark work', who converts defeat into invulnerability by rejecting society's terms.

Finally, the volume's last poem, 'A Dove', never in fact specifies the dove as female, despite the opposition with the masculine hawk, despite the implications of 'love-weights' and 'temple-dancers'. Its last lines – 'Bubbling molten, wobbling top-heavy/Into one and many' – enables the evasion of difference through a refusal of gender. 'One and many': could a feminist assent to this? Maybe.

Notes

1. The 'man in black' appears in Sylvia Plath's 'Daddy', *Ariel* (Faber & Faber, London, 1965) p. 55.
2. Morgan, Robin, 'Arraignment', in *Monster* (Vintage, New York, 1972), pp. 76–7; Perloff, Marjorie, 'The Two Ariels: The (Re)making of the Sylvia Plath Canon', in *American Poetry Review*, 13, No. 6 (November–December, 1984), 10–18.
3. Rich, Adrienne, *Diving into the Wreck: Poems 1971–1972* (Norton, New York and London, 1973). See, in particular, 'Meditations for a Savage Child' (pp. 53–62), or 'The Phenomenology of Anger' (pp. 25–31): 'The prince of air and darkness/computing body counts, masturbating/in the factory/of facts.'
4. 'The Rock', *The Listener*, 19 September 1963, pp. 421–3.
5. 'Ted Hughes Writes', in *Poetry Book Society Bulletin* 15 (September 1957).
6. Uroff, Margaret Dickie, *Sylvia Plath and Ted Hughes* (University of Illinois, Urbana, Chicago and London, 1979), p. 52.
7. Review of Max Nicholson, *The Environmental Revolution, Your Environment* 1, 3 (Summer 1970), pp. 81–3; rpt in Ekbert Faas, *Ted Hughes: The Unaccommodated Universe* (Black Sparrows, Santa Barbara, 1980), p. 186.
8. Smith, A. C. H. *Orghast at Persepolis* (Eyre Methuen, London, 1972), p. 47.
9. Note to *A Choice of Shakespeare's Verse* (Faber & Faber), London, 1971), p. 199.
10. 'Myth and Education', in *Children's Literature in Education*, 1 (1970), p. 66.
11. 'Myth and Education', p. 70.
12. Faas, 'Ted Hughes and *Crow* (1970): An Interview with Ekbert Faas', in *London Magazine* 10, No. 10 (January 1971), rpt in Faas, *Ted Hughes: The Unaccommodated Universe*, p. 200.
13. Sagar, Keith, *The Art of Ted Hughes* (Cambridge University Press, Cambridge 1978), p. 171.
14. Faas, p. 213.
15. Faas, p. 144.
16. It is perhaps worth noting explicitly that I have ordered these poems for the purposes of my own argument, not in an effort to replicate Hughes's intentions.
17. Uroff, p. 210.
18. First published in *Poems: Fainlight, Hughes, Sillitoe* (Rainbow Press, 1971), but more conveniently available in Keith Sagar (ed.), *The*

Achievement of Ted Hughes (University of Manchester Press, Manchester, 1983).

19. *A Choice of Shakespeare's Verse*, p. 190.
20. For further considerations of the disturbing implications of this trope, see Ortner, Sherry B., 'Is Woman to Man as Nature is to Culture?' in Michelle Zimbalist Rosaldo and Louise Lamphere (eds), *Woman, Culture, and Society* (Stanford University Press, Stanford, 1974), pp. 67–87; and the collection of essays prompted by Ortner's argument, Carol MacCormack and Marilyn Strathern (eds), *Nature, Culture and Gender* (Cambridge University Press, Cambridge, 1980).
21. Holbrook, David, 'Ted Hughes's *Crow* and the Longing for Non-Being' in *The Black Rainbow: Essays on the Present Breakdown of Culture*, Peter Abbs (ed.) (Heinemann, London, 1975), p. 41.

7

Regeneration in *Remains of Elmet*
Ann Skea

Throughout his creative life, Ted Hughes has used his poetry to tap the universal energies and to channel their healing powers towards the sterility and the divisions which he sees in our world. All his major sequences of poetry work towards this end, and *Remains of Elmet* represents an important step in Hughes's ability to achieve wholeness and harmony through the imaginative, healing processes of his art.

In his pursuit of these regenerative energies, Hughes appears to have adopted the role of poet/priest/shaman, and it is a role which carries responsibilities that Hughes takes very seriously. He is aware of both the creative and destructive powers of the energies he courts, and he has a superstitious belief that by fixing these powerful energies in a poem he can affect both writer and reader 'in a final way'.[1] Consequently, Hughes has experimented with many methods of summoning and containing these energies and while he is skilled at using the rhythms and the rituals of poetry for this purpose, in his longer sequences he most frequently turns to 'the old method' of religious and mythological ritual in order to obtain the imaginative healing he intends.

Crow, Gaudete and *Cave Birds* show the progressively greater skill with which Hughes uses a framework of ritual and myth to weave together complex themes into a single dramatic and imaginative work. *Remains of Elmet* is, in every way, built on these skills. Unlike the earlier sequences, the focus of *Remains of Elmet* is the real world, peopled by real people, not a world of imaginative fantasy through which symbolic figures journey. The world of Elmet existed and exists, and Hughes's poems recreate it vividly in such a way that we may perceive the human errors which have desecrated it and the enduring, ever-present forces of Nature which survive.

116

The sequence shows, too, a new ability to weave myth, ritual, music and drama so closely into the fabric of each poem, and into the cycle as a whole, that they are almost inseparable from it. The reader is aware of the beauty and the unity of the poetry and of its emotional impact, while the deeper thematic aspects of the sequence work on the subconscious mind and may never be consciously formulated. In addition to this, the beautiful integration of the poetry with Fay Godwin's dramatic and evocative photographs, and the great personal significance which this area and its people clearly have for Hughes, seem to provide all the reason we need to explain this work's creation. So successful has Hughes been in using the imagination to integrate the physical and spiritual energies in this book, that his critics have to a large extent misjudged his underlying purpose and, have therefore, undervalued the importance of this sequence in Hughes's work.

Clearly, I am suggesting that there is more to *Remains of Elmet* than Hughes's record of tribal memories and his cogent and masterful demonstration of Nature's supremacy over humankind. And to demonstrate this, it is necessary to move beyond the bleak and rugged physical world that Hughes depicts and to attend to some of the metaphysical aspects of the sequence.

In examining any of Hughes's books of poetry or any of his sequences of poems, it is of value to pay particular attention to the first and last poems of that book or sequence. Characteristically, these poems delineate the imaginative boundaries within which Hughes manipulates the energies of the whole work and, because of this, they are a useful indication of the themes and the overall purpose of the poems they encompass.

To take just two examples: *Lupercal*, which we are told contains mostly poems written as 'invocations to writing',[2] begins and ends with poems which symbolically and ritually evoke the creative energies; and in *Crow*, the first and last poems express Hughes's belief in the necessity and promise of the black energies he embodies in his trickster bird while, at the same time, they demonstrate the care with which he summons and contains these energies.

In *Remains of Elmet*, the first and last poems of the sequence suggest two major, closely linked themes on which the other poems have been built: the theme of 'The Mothers', which has strong regenerative aspects; and the theme of the imprisonment of divine light, or soul, in matter and its eventual, apocalyptic release. In these poems, too, we can discern strands of the mythical/religious beliefs which form part of the complex structural fabric of this work.

The opening poem, 'Where the Mothers', immediately establishes a mood of pagan, elemental energy. Using rhythms and sounds which capture the wildness of Nature as it is commonly experienced on the pictured moors, Hughes evokes the disembodied souls which, like the wind and the rain, howl through heaven and 'Pour down onto earth/Looking for bodies/Of birds, animals, people'.

In the galloping 'Mothers', there are echoes of the Nordic Valkyries. But this is the old British Kingdom of *Elmet* where the Celtic 'Mothers' – three goddesses of fertility – held sway and where ancient standing stones, like the Bridestones, still testify to the worship of Brig (Brigid), the mother goddess of the Brigantian people.

These 'Mothers' were the earliest Celtic-British personification of the powers of the Great Mother Goddess, Nature, whose cycles of life and death pervade this sequence.[3] Their evocation in this opening poem defines the geographical and historical context from which the Calder Valley civilisation grew. It was these primitive energies and this bleak environment that shaped the people and gave them their toughness and endurance. It was these energies that spawned and fed the Industrial Revolution. And it was the physical and spiritual misdirection of these energies which Hughes believes brought this society to 'the dead end of a wrong direction' ('Top Withens').

Important as these ancient goddesses are, there are other 'Mothers' present in the wild natural elements of this opening poem. These are the alchemical 'Mothers' – Air, Water and Fire – from which Hermeticists believe all things are created.[4] Hughes, who (as I have shown elsewhere[5]) carefully structured his *Cave Birds* sequence on an alchemical transmutation, again uses the Hermetic/Neoplatonic myth of the imprisonment of Divine Light (or Soul) in matter, and its eventual release, to shape this work. The poems and photographs in *Remains of Elmet* demonstrate the 'rummaging of light/At the end of the world' ('Long Screams'). (Hughes's use of the verb, here, is deliberately ambiguous, as light both rummages and is rummaged.) And, as he tells us clearly in one poem:

It is all
Happening to the sun
The fallen sun
Is in the hands of the water
                    ('It Is All')

In many of Fay Godwin's photographs, and particularly in the photographs which accompany and immediately follow this poem, we can see for ourselves the 'cold fire' of the trapped sun shining from clog-worn stones ('It Is All') and from the 'busy dark atoms' ('High Sea-Light') of the moorland causeys, and gleaming through the darkness of the waters.

The Hermetic/Neoplatonic myth tells how, from the time of original Chaos, Divine Light (Soul) has been attracted by the Subtle Spirit, Nature, down into the dark Abyss, from whence it is released only by dissolution or death.[6] In the words of the Greek Neoplatonist, Porphyry, it is the 'urge for pleasure' – the urge to 'follow and obey their worst parts',[7] which draws souls down into the 'witches' brew of generation', and this, perhaps, is the reason for the 'silent evil joy' which accompanies the embodiment of souls in Hughes's first poem. There, amidst the chaos of the elements, on the ancient moors of Elmet where, in a later poem, Hughes describes the 'witch-brew boiling in the sky vat' ('Moors'), the drama of generation begins.

This, too, is the starting point for the Great Work to which alchemists devote their lives. Using the alchemical 'Mothers' – Air, Fire and Water – they undertake the careful dissolution and cleansing of the base matter of generation in order to release the Soul. Just so, in this sequence, Hughes and Godwin use the interaction of light and matter, both physically in the words and photographs, and metaphorically in the effects which these accomplish, to release the imaginative energies and bring illumination, feeling and insight. The 'Grasses of Light', the 'stones of darkness', the 'water of light and darkness' with which both artists work in this book, are not simply 'words in any phrase' ('These Grasses of Light'), as Hughes puts it, or the interplay of light and shadow fixed in a photographic image, they are the mother elements from which our world is formed and on which our survival and the eventual metamorphosis of our souls depend. And they are the elements which, in this book, will accomplish the regeneration of the land and free the souls of its people.

The theme of the 'Mothers' which is established in this first poem is reinforced by Hughes's dedication of this book to his own mother, Edith Farrar, and by the prefatory poem in which his mother lives on briefly for him through her brother. The dreams, aspirations, achievements and failures of the Calder Valley people which make up this book are their memories, precious 'Archaeology of the mouth' which Hughes tries to record before the 'frayed, fraying hair-fineness' of the thread linking his spirit to theirs is finally broken.

It is through this personal aspect of the 'Mothers' that the first and last poems of the *Elmet* sequence are linked. And it is the influence of Hughes's mother which appears to have been germinal in the regenerative purpose which underlies his work. To explain this, let us turn now to the final poem of the *Elmet* sequence.

'The Angel' describes a recurrent dream which, according to Faas, Hughes has 'dreamt about once a week during childhood and adolescence'[8] and at regular intervals ever since. The first poetic version of this dream appeared as 'Ballad from a Fairy Tale' in *Wodwo*. There, as in the *Elmet* version, Hughes describes a disastrous fiery event – something like 'a moon disintegrating' ('Ballad from a Fairy Tale', line 4) on 'Black Halifax' ('The Angel', line 3) – and from the resulting phosphorescent crater there emerges a huge and beautiful swan/angel which lights the moors as it passes low across them 'towards the West' ('Ballad From a Fairy Tale', line 31). At first, Hughes thinks this angel brings a blessing, but his mother's words, when she interprets this 'immense omen' ('The Angel', line 24) for him, turn the 'beauty suddenly to terror' ('The Angel', line 17).

In neither poem are we told Hughes's mother's words, but the detail which links Hughes's vision with events in his life, and which gives her words 'doubled' ('Ballad From a Fairy Tale', line 59) significance, is his second sighting of the angel's strange and puzzling halo. This 'enigmatic', fringed 'square of satin' ('The Angel', line 21) which ripples in the wind of the angel's flight, when seen again is a piece of funerary furniture.[9] So, this angel of beauty and light is also an omen of disaster and death, and the fact that both Sylvia Plath and Edith Farrar are buried on the moors where Hughes stood in his dream, seems to suggest that the angelic omen has been fulfilled. Yet, despite the very personal nature of this poem, with its reference to Hughes's family and to events in his own life which left him in 'darkness' (just as the angel left him in his dream), Hughes's retelling of his dream at the end of *Remains of Elmet* links it closely with the fall of the whole Calder Valley society and gives it much greater prophetic significance.

Several things about the poem itself suggest the broader symbolic function which Hughes intends for the angel in the *Elmet* sequence. Firstly, there is the ambiguity of the poem's closing lines and the echoes which they contain of the last poem in Hughes's earlier sequence, *Adam and the Sacred Nine*.[10] And secondly, there are the resemblances which exist between Hughes's angel and the apocalyptic messengers described in the Kabbalah, the Koran, and, in particular, in the biblical books of Ezekiel and Revelation,[11] all of which portend both destruction and spiritual salvation.

At first reading, what Hughes says in the final stanza of 'The Angel' seems quite clear:

> When next I stood where I stood in my dream
> Those words of my mother,
> Joined with earth and engraved in rock,
> Were under my feet.

Metaphorically, 'those words' of his mother which turned a blessing to terror are, indeed, now joined with the earth beneath his feet. But, although there are significant words engraved in rock at the place where Hughes's mother is buried, on her headstone there are only names and dates. On Sylvia's headstone nearby, however, there are words which assert, through the symbolism of the lotus, the endurance of the creative energies and the promise of regeneration and spiritual rebirth:

> Even amidst fierce flames
> The golden lotus can be planted.

Whether or not these are the words to which Hughes refers in 'The Angel', their essence is central to many of the *Elmet* poems. And, given the multiple meanings that the word 'mother' has in the opening poems and the parallels which exist between this sequence and *Adam and the Sacred Nine*, we can interpret the closing stanza of *Remains of Elmet* as presenting a similar message of enlightenment and hope.

Adam and the Sacred Nine, like the *Elmet* sequence, deals with the embodiment of elemental energy in human form, the proud dreams and aspirations of humankind, and the lessons and enlightenment which are possible through Nature. In the opening poem of both sequences, pure energy, in the form of a song, searches the 'cradle-grave' of earth for suitable embodiment. In both sequences (although more obviously in *Adam and the Sacred Nine*), the birds have a symbolic function, acting as the natural agents of enlightenment and regeneration as they move between heaven and earth, between the physical and the non-physical. And in both sequences, the closing poems show two human representatives, Adam and Hughes, linked with their mothers through the soles of their feet – a traditional symbolic route of enlightenment.

The enlightenment which Hughes grants to our progenitor, Adam, is exactly that which the poems in *Remains of Elmet* seek to bring to us – the knowledge that mankind is not only made *of* the elements of Earth, we are also made *for* Earth. Like Adam we cannot 'tread emptiness' – we depend on the Earth for our survival, it feeds us and gladdens us. It is through the Earth that the energies of the Source flow to us, and only by co-operating with Nature rather than seeking to dominate her can we achieve our true potential.

Remains of Elmet, as a history of the Calder Valley people, demonstrates the fate of a society which fails to learn this lesson. And Hughes's angel, in this context, is a symbol through which he invokes the elemental forces of the universe to redress the natural balance which has been disturbed. The huge, illuminating beauty of the angel, the awe and terror which she inspires, her association with the moon and snow, and her eventual disappearance 'under the moor', all suggest that she is the Mother Goddess, Nature, and, as such, she has the power both to destroy and to create.

As mentioned earlier, there are resemblances between Hughes's angel and the apocalyptic messengers of several major religious texts. They, too, appear amidst fiery disturbances to bring a warning to the human race. They, too, serve an omnipotent power which threatens death and destruction for human misdeeds. And they, too, offer the hope of blessing and spiritual rebirth. Through such links as these, Hughes channels the invoked energies of his angelic symbol towards creative rather than destructive ends. At the same time, he indicates the spiritual aspect of the regeneration he seeks to effect in *Remains of Elmet*.

Hughes makes a similar, biblical, allusion in 'The Trance of Light' where he envisages the renewal of the Earth as it 'stretches awake, out of Revelations'. And he suggests the spiritual aspect of his work in such images as that of the 'soul's caddis' which, in 'These Grasses of Light', clings to the threadbare elements of creation awaiting its own release. The biblical references in *Remains of Elmet*, however, are few, and Hughes's angel represents a much older, pre-biblical Goddess. So, he turns most often (and more appropriately) to the pre-biblical Hermetic/Neoplatonic myths that I have already discussed and, taking these abstract stories of the original creation and the eternal struggle between darkness and light, he anchors them firmly in the reality of the prevailing weather conditions on the West Yorkshire moors. In this way, he uses our own experience of the ever-present powers of Nature to alert us to the continuing presence of his Goddess in our world. At the same time, be obliges us to give credence to the picture of the natural cleansing and renewal of the Earth which he presents in *Remains of Elmet*.

But what of spiritual regeneration? How does Hughes handle this?

From the very beginning, the spiritual element in *Remains of Elmet* has been linked imaginatively with music. It was there in the faint lark-song which accompanied the embodiment of souls in living creatures; in the 'mad singing in the hills' ('The Trance of Light') which became submerged by the slavery of War, Industry and Religion; and in the fragile memories which reverberate in the yarning of the old people:

> Attuned to each other, like the strings of a harp
> They are making mesmerising music,
> Each one bowed at his dried bony profile, as at a harp.
> Singers of a lost kingdom.
>
> Wild melody, wilful improvisations.
>   ('Crown Point Pensioners')

As the spirit of the people succumbs to the self-imposed rigidity of their lives and they become 'four-cornered, stony' ('Hill-Stone was Content') in their work and 'cowed' ('Mount Zion'), instead of inspired, by their chosen religion, the music is heard, still, in the song of a cricket ('Mount Zion'), the 'wobbling water-call' ('Curlews in April') of curlew, and in the magical drumming of snipe ('Spring-Dusk'). Above all, it is there in the poetic music which Hughes makes as he draws for us this realistic, and paradigmatic, picture of human strengths and human weaknesses.

Still, as the elements work to free the Earth from 'the human shape' ('Top Withens') which has been imposed on it, the music of the Earth, itself, can be heard in the poems. Away from the darkness of the valleys, where wild rock has been 'conscripted' ('Hill-Stone was Content') by Mankind and has forgotten its 'wild roots' and its 'earth Song', the 'big animal of rock' ('The Big Animal of Rock') crouches singing in its 'homeland' on the moors. This is the 'cantor', the preceptor who leads the spiritual singing at Nature's 'Festival of Unending' death and rebirth and, like a soft continuous undertone, its music accompanies the elemental choir in perpetual worship. Under the heather and bog-cotton, the harebells and willowherb, the dark rock-animal – part of the first created matter – endures until Hughes's poetic cleansing rituals are almost complete. Then, 'In April', it emerges with the reawakening Earth to stretch itself, cat-like, under the strengthening sun and to lead the Messianic singing in 'The Word that Space Breathes'.

This poem follows a series of bleak, wintry poems and photographs in which the light and the life of Earth sink towards their nadir. In it, Hughes draws on the great choral tradition of the North of England, where Handel's *Messiah* is a well-known and much-loved part of the Easter celebrations, to create an oratorio of his own in which, in the 'chapel of clouds', the music of the people, the land and the skies gloriously herald the natural resurrection which is to come.

Again adapting biblical stories to suit his own purposes, Hughes gives the Valley of Dry Bones, which Ezekiel saw in his vision,[12] a contemporary presence in the Calder Valley. The biblical 'Word of the Lord', which promised salvation to the people of Israel, becomes one with the winds which breathe new life into the scattered bones of the people. And, as in the Book of Revelation, the Word of this disembodied voice is accompanied by a 'huge Music': 'as it were the voice of a great multitude, and as the voice of many waters, and as the voice of mighty thunderings saying Alleluia: ...' (Revelation 19: 6).

In Hughes's poem, as in Fay Godwin's photograph opposite it, the walls which the people so painstakingly built, the enclosures into which their lives and cares went 'like manure' ('Walls'), guide the spiritual wind-song upwards, leading it 'from every step of the slopes' to the crest where clouds and walls meet. As if in a musical crescendo, the 'huge music/Of sightlines' is gathered into a dramatic focus which joins heaven and Earth, and this climax is echoed in the final stanza of the poem, like an Alleluia! for 'the Messiah/Of opened rock'.

So it seems that the illuminating spiritual song, like that of the great bird which once before, long ago, 'drew men out of rock' and 'put a light in the valley' ('Heptonstall Old Church'), will return to the Earth. And, after the long and careful cleansing ritual which Hughes has undertaken in the *Elmet* sequence thus far, he is finally ready to create the apocalyptic 'golden holocaust' which is presaged in 'Football at Slack' and by means of which the trapped light will be freed from the valley, the souls released, and 'a new heaven and a new earth'[13] created.

In 'Cock-Crows', Hughes again combines present reality with myth. The scene which he describes from his hilltop vantage-point is one which is quite familiar to him and, were it not for the thematic concerns of *Remains of Elmet* (which I have already discussed) and the careful positioning of this poem in the sequence, one might be content to accept it as a highly imaginative picture of the sort of sunrise which occurs almost daily in the Calder Valley. Careful attention to the diverse connotations and allusions that the imagery in this poem contains, however, soon makes it clear that there is a deeper level of meaning, and that this poem is of central importance to Hughes's regenerative work.

The title of the poem joins 'Cock' with 'Crows', linking the symbolic bird of dawn with those of darkness and of death to create a unity from which there can be a new beginning. In the connection between darkness and light, birth and death, which is thus achieved, there exists a consubstantiality of opposites which allows for change and renewal. At the same time, the crowing cock which the hyphenated words in the title invite us to see and hear is, traditionally, the herald of the risen Sun-God and the harbinger of resurrection. Here, in the title of Hughes's poem, the imperative bird-call signals a 'tidal dawn' which splits 'heaven from earth' and brings the first 'taste' of gold light to the encompassing darkness, as if portending a new world as well as a new day.

Hughes's imagery of mountain-tops, sunrise, gold and splendour, again has precedents in the visions of the new Jerusalem which both Ezekiel and John of the Book of Revelation were granted.[14] But the strongest and most telling echoes in this poem are those of Blake's prophetic writings. Hughes's opening lines, 'I stood on a dark summit, among dark summits –/Tidal dawn splitting heaven from earth', in tone and content recall the beginning of Blake's poem in his address 'To the Christians' on Plate 77 of *Jerusalem*:[15] 'I stood among my valleys of the south/And saw a flame of fire, even as a wheel/Of fire surrounding all the heavens: ...'. Blake's lines precede the final chapter of Jerusalem which describes the awakening of Albion. And (making another suggestive link between Hughes's poem and Blake's prophetic book) Blake's etching at the top of Plate 78 shows the cockerel-headed figure of Hand (the composite Spectre of the Sons of Albion) watching a brown-rayed sun which David Erdman identifies as 'the setting material sun – a signal for the rise of a more bright sun'.[16]

Although Hughes's imagery in the rest of his poem is quite different from Blake's the parallels are clearly present. His 'bubbling valley cauldron' suggests Blake's 'Furnaces of Los'. And the cock-crows, the 'sickle shouts' which he kindles from it, 'soaring harder, brighter, higher', and 'bursting to light/Brightening the under-cloud', are like the 'arrows of flaming gold' (*Jerusalem*, 95:13) which flew into the heavens from Albion's 'horned Bow Fourfold' until the 'dim Chaos brighten'd beneath, above, around: ' (*Jerusalem*, 98: 14). Above all, it is the rhythm and diction at the central climax of Hughes's poem which echo those of Blake in exultant and glorious power, and which invite us to believe that '… the Night of Death is past and the Eternal Day/Appears upon our Hills'. (*Jerusalem*, 97:3–4).

Whilst these comparisons between 'Cock-Crows' and Blake's *Jerusalem* are worth making for the light which they throw on Hughes's purpose in this poem, and in *Remains of Elmet* as a whole, they should not be allowed to overshadow the complex interweaving of themes which Hughes has achieved here in his own unique way. For the light that Hughes creates in the dark valleys of Elmet is an effusion of the 'magical soft mixture' that bubbles in the Earth Goddesses' cauldron; and the whole process, with its bubbling mixture, its molten and metallic glistenings, its pervasive mists, and its bursts of light and sound, is one in which the alchemical 'Mothers' – Fire, Water and Air – are intimately involved. The crowing of Hughes's cockerels in this West Yorkshire valley is the realisation of the voice of the Phoenix which, in *Adam and the Sacred Nine* '…flies flaming and dripping flame/Slowly across the dusty sky' until

Flesh trembles
The altar of its death and its rebirth

Where it descends
Where it offers itself up

And the naked the newborn
Laughs in the blaze

By the end of 'Cock-Crows', the fiery purification of the Earth has been completed and we are left with a cooling crucible, lifeless and dark, in which the only remaining signs of towns are smoking holes in the earth. Hughes's golden holocaust is over. And now, as the sun climbs into the 'wet sack' of Earth's atmosphere, heaven and Earth are reunited and the 'day's-work' of recreation can begin.

With his visionary renewal of the Earth completed, it still remains for Hughes to free the souls which have been trapped in the world of generation. This he does in 'Heptonstall Cemetery'. In rhythms which convey a mood of powerful, exultant energy, this poem shows the whole Earth in motion. The wind 'slams across the tops', the rain 'cuts upwards', and amidst this chaos of air and water the moors become one 'giant beating wing' in which the risen souls are 'living feathers'. Finally, in a glow of 'storm-silver', like the great radiant haze of sunlight in Fay Godwin's accompanying photograph, the reborn souls of the human race, like a family of dark swans, lift from every horizon and fly Westward towards the Atlantic – the direction in which Hughes's angel disappeared.

So, taking all that remains of the old Celtic-British Kingdom of Elmet, in the physical reality of the West Yorkshire moors with their changing skies and their fickle weather, Hughes has poetically transformed the death of the Calder Valley society into a spiritual rebirth. At the same time, he and Fay Godwin have brought some transforming imaginative energies into our lives which may allow us to attain our own enlightenment and spiritual release. Such enlightenment is not easily achieved. And, as Hughes constantly shows us in his work, it will come when we learn to open our senses to the world around us and to attend to the lessons of our own great mother – Nature.

Notes

1. Hughes, T., *Critical Forum Series*, Norwich Tapes Ltd, 1978.
2. Faas, E., *Ted Hughes: The Unaccommodated Universe* (Black Sparrow Press, Santa Barbara, 1980), Appendix II, p. 209.
3. Early Celtic deities are discussed by Nora Chadwick in *The Celts* (Penguin, London, 1970), p. 154.
4. '... the three Mothers...are Aire, Water and Fire: ...The Heavens were made of Fire, the Earth was made of Water...and the Ayre proceeded from the middle Spirit', lines 1457–67 of Thomas Vaughan's *Magica Adamica* (1655), in Rudrum, E. (ed.), *The Works of Thomas Vaughan* (Clarendon Press, Oxford, 1984).
5. Skea, A., *Sources in the Work of Ted Hughes* (PhD thesis, 1988).

6. Everard, Dr, (trans. 1650) *The Divine Pymander of Hermes*, (Wizard Books, San Diego, 1978), Bk 3, pp. 18–19. Also, Rudrum, E., *The Works of Thomas Vaughan*, op. cit. p. 54–8.
7. Porphyry, *On the Cave of the Nymphs* (written AD 3), in Lamberton, R. (trans.) (Station Hill Press, New York, 1983) p. 9–10.
8. Faas, E., *Ted Hughes: The Unaccommodated Universe*, op. cit., p. 139
9. Hughes confirmed this in a letter to me in November 1984.
10. First published as a limited edition by Rainbow Press in Spring 1979, then in *Moortown* (Faber & Faber, London, 1979) p. 157–170.
11. The Koran, traditional chapter LIV.I; the Book of Revelation, 7:21 and Ezekiel 1:4–28.
12. Ezekiel 37.
13. Revelation 21:1.
14. Ezekiel 40 and 43: Revelation 21.
15. Reference numbers used here refer to the original etched plates as indicated by David Erdman (ed.) in *The Illuminated Blake* (Anchor Press, New York, 1974).
16. Erdman, D., *The Illuminated Blake*, op. cit., p. 357.

8

Gods of Mud: Hughes and the Post-pastoral
Terry Gifford

It has been clear from his earliest work that the poetry of Ted Hughes has challenged our urbanised, post-industrial, denatured society by making, first, images and, later, myths, that would reconnect our own natural energies with those at work in the external natural world. This poetry has also represented a challenge to our denatured culture which has promoted poets to key editorial positions whose work is cerebral and conspicuously disconnected from the natural world. To Craig Raine, Poetry Editor at Faber and Faber, a flood is an opportunity to make verbal conceits that are, in the end, self-referential rather than enlarging our perception of the subject-matter itself:

> Every quibble returns to the torrent,
>
> And even the slow digressions at our feet
> Are part of an overall argument.
>
> They cover all the points of grass.
> What single-minded brilliance,
>
> What logic!
> Not one of us can look away.[1]

But, of course, the reader already has 'looked away' from a flood to the surface of the language itself. The 'logic' of Nature in this poem is ignored since the mind conspicuously at work here is that of the lucid, sophisticated poet 'covering all the points' of his extended metaphor.

I have wanted to establish at the outset the bizarre incongruity between the poetry of Ted Hughes and that of his latter-day editor at Faber and Faber not only to indicate what I mean by a denatured poetic culture, but because David Moody, in an article entitled 'Telling It Like It's Not'[2] accuses Hughes of deploying the same technique as Craig Raine, with the same result. This is an argument to which I want to return in considering Hughes's most recent work.

But my main concern here is to examine Hughes's contribution to contemporary poetry by rereading his work through the perspectives of the pastoral. In choosing the term 'pastoral' as a touchstone I am aware that it is unfashionable, unreconstructed and now usually pejorative, despite Seamus Heaney's rearguard attempt to argue for its contemporary neutrality.[3] It is an indication of our denatured culture that the terms 'Nature poet' or 'Nature poetry' have also come to be used pejoratively. However, I want to make it clear that I follow Raymond Williams in *The City and The Country* and Barrell and Bull, editors of *The Penguin Book of Pastoral Verse*, in using the term 'pastoral' to represent a false construction of reality, usually idealised, often nostalgic, and distorting the historical, economic and organic tensions at work in human relationships with Nature.

Raymond Williams comments upon Pope's making explicit the deception of the pastoral tradition:

> 'We must therefore use some illusion to render a Pastoral delightful; and this consists in exposing the best side only of a shepherd's life, and in concealing its miseries.' When Pope could say that, the 'tradition' had been altered. 'No longer truth, though shown in verse.' The long critical dispute, in the seventeenth and eighteenth centuries, on the character of pastoral poetry had this much, at least, as common ground. What was at issue was mainly whether such an idyll, the delightful Pastoral, should be referred always to the Golden Age, as Rapin and the neo-classicists argued; or to the more permanent and indeed timeless idea of the tranquillity of life in the country, as Fontenelle and others maintained.[4]

Barrell and Bull anticipate a revival of comfortable, idealised nature poetry in contemporary Britain:

Indeed, with the current concern for ecology, it is not difficult to anticipate a revival of interest in the Pastoral – Industrial Man looking away from technological Wasteland to an older and better world…. But now and in England, the Pastoral is a lifeless form, of service only to decorate the shelves of tasteful cottages, 'modernised to a high standard… '. For today, more than ever before, the pastoral vision simply will not do.[5]

Yet there is also now an evident need for poetry which engages with Nature.

Indeed, even under the metaphorical flamethrowers of the metropolitan Martians, Pan is hard to kill. Against the odds of our cultural politics, very varied Nature poetry is being written in these islands today by Sorley MacLean in Scotland, by Heaney in Ireland, by Gillian Clarke in Wales and, of course, by Hughes in England, to name but a representative few. How much of this contemporary Nature poetry, then, can be called 'pastoral'? I would want to argue that the poetry of George Mackay Brown actually sets out to achieve all of those qualities that constitute the pastoral, and given more space might suggest that he is continuously rewriting the same exemplary nostalgic, idealised pastoral poem. (Against this yardstick Craig Raine's poem would have to be termed 'a-pastoral'.) However, the Skye poet, Sorley MacLean, in 'Scrapadal',[6] asserts the historical associations of place against the seal-smooth backs of nuclear submarines in the Sound of Raasay. His poetry has clearly got beyond pastoral nostalgia, into the less comfortable tensions of what I might term the 'post-pastoral'. Gillian Clarke swims with seals,[7] but also in her latest collection, *Letting In the Rumour*,[8] describes connecting with wind power to light her house in a poem of unsentimental elemental celebration. Her recent work is clearly 'far out at sea all night' in the enlightenment of the post-pastoral! Heaney is capable of pastoral, in the first part of *Station Island*,[9] for example, as I have argued elsewhere.[10] But Heaney's poetry at its best has got beyond the pastoral. In *Field Work*[11] he uses Nature imagery as a mode of thinking about his own experiences, whether of love or of death, or of his own unease with his role as a writer. Where Heaney is a personal sounding-board for Nature, Hughes is a shamanistic maker of myths. Where Heaney's poetry cannot avoid images of Nature as its mode of expression, Hughes's poetry cannot avoid it as his subject. Both have developed a vision beyond pastoral poetry, but for both, pastoralism offers the best definition of the risk they take.

I now want to trace two strands through the work of Ted Hughes, suggesting that much of the early work is acting as militant anti-pastoral before developing into the visionary poetry that might be called 'post-pastoral'. I would like to clarify the features of Hughes's particular form of post-pastoral poetry against the background of very different contemporary Nature poets whose parallel contributions I have only been able to hint at in this Introduction. (I shall define Hughes's place within the context of other writers mentioned here in a forthcoming book, *Why Has Nature Poetry Survived?*) Finally, looking briefly at *River*, which has been regarded as Hughes's best book,[12] it is necessary to confront the possibility of pastoralism in that volume and to attempt to offer criteria for distinguishing such poetry from that which achieves the post-pastoral within the same book.

ANTI-PASTORAL

'Egg-Head', from Hughes's first collection,[13] has long seemed to me to be a manifesto poem, a direct challenge to the reader and an indirect challenge to pastoral poetry. It begins where Lawrence left off: in the 'otherness' of the natural world and in 'the war between vitality and death' even in the process of 'becoming'.[14] But Hughes is more ironic. The title of this poem might, for example, be considered as a play upon Lawrence's notion of 'sex in the head',[15] as the hyphen seems to be suggesting. The stance which is being ridiculed in this poem was also mocked by Blake: 'For man has closed himself up, till he sees all things through narrow chinks of his cavern.'[16] In Hughes's poem, 'So many a one has dared to be struck dead/Peeping through his fingers at the world's ends,/Or at an ant's head.' This filtering-out produces safe subjects such as a leaf's, as opposed to a tiger's, 'otherness'. It also produces beautiful distortions such as 'eagled peaks' in which the power of the eagle is defused to become the adjective describing the peak, just as 'the whaled sea-bottom' is coyly 'monstered'. These opening images are being presented as examples, taken together in this context, of inventive, seductive, pretty, pastoralism. Against such images as 'might be painted on a nursery wall' Hughes went on to celebrate the jaguar's otherness in the poem in *The Hawk in the Rain*, the enlightened destructiveness of the eagle in *Under the North Star*, and those uncomfortable mythic monsters from 'Ghost Crabs' (*Wodwo*) to 'The Executioner' (*Cave Birds*).

Of course the egg in 'Egg-Head' produces a man who is also a cockerel. Thus in his first volume Hughes apparently invented the later protagonist of *Cave Birds*. The fact that this man 'trumpet[s] his own ear dead' with an overdose of Gerald Manley Hopkins should not overshadow the importance of this poem in launching a determination to '[receive] the flash/of the sun, the bolt of the earth', and to face 'the looming mouth of the earth' and 'the whelm of the sun'. Here in the verbs are the awesome forces of vitality and death: in 'whelm' and 'looming', 'flash' and 'bolt'. But here too are elements of Earth and Sun, dark and light, material and spirit, mud and god, equal in power, but only *apparently* focused upon by the 'lucid sophistries' of egg-heads like Craig Raine.

Part of the hostility towards the early anti-pastoral poetry of Hughes can be accounted for, perhaps, in the representation of his acting as a shaman bringing us images of 'wilderness'. 'Wilderness' is a concept that is more psychological than geographical. In European folklore it is what its etymology suggests, 'the place of wild beasts'.[17] As such, it's the very opposite of the pastoral. From his wilderness alternative to a 'whaled monstered sea-bottom', Hughes brought us 'The Thought-Fox' (*The Hawk in the Rain*), 'Hawk Roosting' (*Lupercal*) and 'Wodwo' (*Wodwo*), all of them ultimately, of course, from the wilderness of the human psyche. What Hughes had exposed was the old fear of the dark unknown in the natural world that hovers around the Old English notion of 'wilddeor-ness'. Even walking in a safely pastoral National Park Hughes might meet a black mountain goat that could turn him under an eye 'slow and cold and ferocious as a star', as might have happened in the making of the poem 'Meeting' in *The Hawk in the Rain*. Unfortunately, Hughes's own efforts to outstare the complacently pastoral attitude to nature occasionally led to a little melodramatic distortion in the opposite direction. In what sense, for example, can a star be 'ferocious'? 'Slow and cold' perhaps, but 'ferocious' is surely a little too active compared with, say, 'fierce' in its sense of 'intense'. Just as Hughes has continued writing anti-pastoral through 'Glimpse', for example, in *Crow*, 'A green mother' (*Cave Birds*), 'Lumb Chimneys' (*Remains of Elmet*) and the correctives to the common pastoral associations with lambs in *Moortown*, so too there have been the attendant dangers of over-correction from the metallic images of 'Snowdrop' (*Lupercal*), through the bathos of 'For Billy Holt' (*Remains of Elmet*) to the nuclear overkill of the warrior 'Sparrow Hawk' (*Wolfwatching*). But Hughes's greatest achievement has been in going further than any other contemporary writer beyond the 'cliché or consolation' of pastoral, as Heaney puts it.[18]

POST-PASTORAL

I want briefly to indicate five features of what I shall characterise as Hughes's post-pastoral poetry, but first I would like to focus this discussion by considering the notion of 'gods of mud'. The final stage of *Cave Birds* is that of rediscovery of the self, including the sensuality of the human body, celebrated in a poem which is the answer to the question 'Who gave most, him or her?'. The climax of a male and female 'giving each other' the exquisite discovery of the workings of the machinery of each part of their bodies is also a sexual climax:

> So, gasping with joy, with cries of wonderment
> Like two gods of mud
> Sprawling in the dirt, but with infinite care
>
> They bring each other to perfection.
>   ('Bride and groom lie hidden for three days')

Just as they can only achieve perfection by giving to each other, so they are both 'gods' *and* 'sprawling in the dirt'. This detail is clearly anti-pastoral in function, countering any suggestion of transcendence in 'gods' by keeping the experience animal and material. But the duality of 'gods of mud' is post-pastoral in its vision of mud and dirt as the possible context for the 'infinite care' that brings a sense of perfected fulfilment, as through that of a god. Their 'sprawling' in the mud firmly maintains the notion of 'gods' as a metaphor here.

The first feature, then, of Hughes's post-pastoral is a body of poetry that explores this tension as a dynamic process in Nature. Perhaps the earliest gods of mud were to be found in 'Crow Hill' (*Lupercal*) where 'Pigs upon delicate feet/Hold off the sky, trample the strength/That shall level these hills at length'. The delicacy is there again, the celebration of heroic god-like lives that 'hold off the sky', and the simultaneous awareness of the presence of mud-flow levelling. But the tension between these forces is focused upon the pigs themselves within the single line that balances forces at work above and below them. Again transcendence is avoided: pigs do not fly, even on the Crow Hill of what is now 'Hughes Country'.

This dynamic duality is at work in every volume of Hughes's poetry, so that it constitutes a notion of Nature that is more wholly achieved than can be seen in the production of any other contemporary poet. The process is explicitly celebrated in 'Still Life' (*Wodwo*) where the god in the harebell is 'the maker of the sea' and the mud is 'outcrop stone'. In 'Mosquito' (*Under the North Star*) mud is replaced by ice, but after many deaths 'Mosquito/Flew up singing, over the broken waters –/A little haze of wings, a midget sun'. It may be midget, but its life has the light of a sun in its wings, clearly a god of 'broken waters'. In 'Salmon Eggs' (*River*) the 'mudblooms' of the river produce 'the nameless/Teeming inside atoms'. Such dynamics as the salmon 'emptying themselves for each other', or of a conceit such as 'The river goes on/Sliding through its place, undergoing itself/In its wheel' do not need the heavy overlay of religious functions with which this poem ultimately pleads too much.

Of course the second feature of Hughes's particular contribution to post-pastoral is his exploration of these tensions in the dramas of the myths. The female figure who makes a first appearance, perhaps, in 'Crow's Undersong' (*Crow*) is a god of mud, an underground presence from the wilderness such as Lilith,[19] who is just as much a presence in 'How Water Began to Play' (*Crow*) as in the poems that explicitly feature her. 'She stays/Even after life even among the bones.' Water has to meet 'maggot and rottenness' as well as 'womb' before it can achieve the vision of itself as inanimate, 'utterly worn out' but 'utterly clear'. Similarly at the conclusion of *Cave Birds* 'The dirt becomes God' in the vision of 'The risen' falcon.[20] And in the simple discovery that concludes *Adam and the Sacred Nine* (*Moortown*), 'The sole of a foot' celebrates 'with even, gentle squeeze' its fitting the surface of 'world-rock' in the ultimate down-to-earth, post-pastoral poem.

But perhaps a challenge could be made for that distinction by some of the poems in *Moortown Diary*. The recent republication[21] of the poems under that title is introduced by a political statement against 'the EEC Agricultural Policy War' which indicates just how far from the pastoral the Poet Laureate intended to take his starting-point in these poems. Here, then, is the third feature of Hughes's post-pastoral notion of Nature: that of direct responsibility for the management of it. That 'February 17th' produces a powerfully symbolic image of a lamb's head stuck in mud, is almost incidental to the urgency of caring, practical responsibility being enacted in the poem. When that involved observation is turned upon a co-worker in 'A Monument' the cost of a lifetime of that responsibility for Nature is seen in detail. Indeed such a detail as the 'gasping struggle/In the knee-deep mud of the copse ditch' might suggest anti-pastoral were the reader not to know that this is an elegy to an effort that is finally 'using your life up'. That tension of making and unmaking, of a 'face fixed at full effort' yet hammering the staple 'precise to the tenth of an inch' is not a long way away from the pigs of 'Crow Hill' on their delicate feet 'hold[ing] off', while at the same time trampling a strength that is ultimately greater than themselves.

In Hughes's notion of Nature the outer processes echo the inner processes so that they are part of a whole. The organic tensions in external Nature are enacted in human nature. Processes at work in landscapes are at work in the human complex of energies. This is what 'The knight' recognises in *Cave Birds*, and Lumb in his identification with the tree from which his changeling self is made (*Gaudete*). In *Remains of Elmet* external natural processes are shown to be reflected not just in individuals but in both a farming and an industrial culture. Hence the poem title 'Dead Farms, Dead Leaves', for example, or the poem about 'Lumb Chimneys' 'flowering' like trees and 'falling into the future, into earth'.

This fourth feature of Hughes's post-pastoral poetry, in which outer processes reflect inner processes, is closely linked to a fifth feature concerning the way this notion of Nature is frequently expressed. If culture, human life, animal life, the workings of weather and landscape are parts of an interactive whole, then it is possible to express this relationship through an interchangeability of images. One can say that dead farms *are* the dead leaves of the culture of Elmet. Again *Remains of Elmet* provides a rich source of examples of this linguistic pattern. Perhaps the most all-inclusive is the title-poem, which sees the Calder Valley as 'the long gullet' of a creature which eats even the farms that are themselves 'stony masticators/Of generations that ate each other/To nothing inside them'.

PASTORAL OR POST-PASTORAL?

It is this last characteristic of Hughes's achievement, which I have described as a consequence of the unity of his post-pastoral vision, that David Moody characterises as 'telling it like it's not'. For him Hughes is working a dangerous reversal: 'Hughes fairly consistently translates his birds and beasts and fishes into something man-made, and he translates anything human into the animal or the brute'.[22] The danger lies, he argues, in perceiving Nature through the *writer*'s sensations and taking for granted the reality (and the rights) of the creature itself. He demonstrates this in an examination of the poem 'Earth-numb' (*Moortown*):

> The hooked salmon is there only in the hunter's sensations; and the hunter's intelligence is so caught up in the sensations that it fails to analyse them and discover what they signify…. His mind is active, in throwing up a stream of associations to isolate and dramatise the sensational phase of the experience. At the same time there is a cut-off from any inward knowing and feeling what it means for the salmon. When the salmon does emerge it is only in the form of association.

Moody then quotes from the end of the poem which began with the hunter feeling himself 'hunted and haunted' by the black depths of a river which suddenly grabs him,

> Till the fright flows all one way down the line
>
> And a ghost grows solid, a hoverer,
> A lizard green slither, banner heavy –
>
> Then the wagging stone pebble head
> Trying to think on shallows –
>
> Then the steel spectre of purples
> From the forge of water
> Gagging on emptiness
>
> As the eyes of incredulity
> Fix their death-exposure of the celandine and the cloud.

David Moody writes:

> My crude response to that is 'You bastard!' The refinement of
> brute sensations into aesthetic effect is offensive if you have feel-
> ing for live salmon and remember that this artist has just killed
> one, all the while carrying on about *his* sensations.

Now I do not accept this as a wholly adequate account of what
Hughes has been establishing in this poem. Against the river's
apparitions which are hunting him, 'the lure is a prayer'. He is
about a dangerous, delicate activity, searching with 'a prayer, like a
flower opening'. When the river suddenly grabs him with 'an elec-
trocuting malice/Like a trap' he becomes a connector between river
and sky, stiff with an electrical charge that is 'something terrified
and terrifying'. Thus the emergence of the ghost in the form of the
salmon is a material image of both conquest and sacrifice, survival
and death, gain and loss. Hughes has been re-enacting the drama of
those tensions that I have suggested signify the height of his
achievement. But David Moody's 'crude response' cuts through this
symbolic discourse to remind us that in reality the poem is about the
writer's gain at the expense of the salmon's loss. Indeed the discourse just does not ring true: a lure is not a prayer, a river is not a
trap, the struggle for life of a hooked salmon cannot terrify the fisherman in any deeply-felt sense, otherwise he would not be hunting
it to death. What we are confronted with in 'Earth-numb' is the
discourse of pastoral distortion.

The reason this poem is so important is not just because Hughes
gives it the status of title-poem for a section of *Moortown*, but
because it anticipates a whole volume of poems which has been
elevated by recent Hughes scholarship to the status of a holy book.
The effort to articulate the apparently transcendental insights of the
'master' has produced some remarkable critical statements. We
can read that 'fish swim in a religious trance'[23] (*pace* 'Relic'
and 'Pibroch'[24]), or that 'riverline meets horizon at the point that
vanishes into the transphenomenal'.[25]

'The real task confronting critics of Ted Hughes's poetry is not one
of exegesis but of discrimination', writes Edna Longley in her review
of *River* for *Poetry Review*:[26] '*River* signals that the temptation of cele-
bratory Hughes is sentimentality and abstraction, rather than verbal
melodrama'. Actually, it seems clear to me that 'Earth-numb' might
qualify as evidence that 'verbal melodrama' is also a danger in the

most recent writing of Hughes. Indeed if we are to accept the challenge of Edna Longley we ought to be clear about why celebration can lapse into pastoral so consistently in this one volume.

The reasons, I would suggest, are twofold. Both have already been hinted at, and they are connected. It isn't a question of images that try too hard, as Longley's own examples suggest. It is the poetry's fundamental assumption that it is now 'preaching to the converted' and that therefore the language doesn't have to justify itself. This is what I mean by the special pleading of the religious language of 'Salmon Eggs'. What does it add to the poem to say that 'this is the liturgy/Of the earth's tidings – harrowing, crowned – a travail/Of raptures and rendings./Sanctus Sanctus/Swathes the blessed issue'? If regeneration is a marvel to be revered, the poem's evidence should show rather than preach this to us, as indeed it has demonstrated to us brilliantly in the earlier part of this poem. Further, if this poem sanctifies the birth process in isolation it will inevitably lead to the sentimentality of 'only birth matters'. Where is the awareness that 'the tiger blesses with a fang'? ('Tiger-Psalm', *Moortown*.) It is 'inscribed in the egg' of 'October Salmon', but its presence in 'harrowing, crowned' or 'raptures and rendings' seems glib and formulaic in the absence of the evidence here. So it is not only, firstly, that the accumulation of 'crypts', 'altar', 'liturgy', 'mass', and finally 'font' are unnecessary to the generation of awe, but secondly that the essential elemental tension is a dynamic that is not active in the poem.

'O leaves, Crow sang.' 'O river', sings Hughes through the god's head, according to Scigaj's account of Hughes's 'transfigured vision' of 'a metaphysical source' in 'Salmon Eggs'.[27] My argument is that Hughes's post-pastoral vision regresses to pastoral when the dynamic represented by 'gods of mud' is taken for granted by the signifiers of the text. The result is a static assertion of images that remain in the realm of verbal description and hence become susceptible to David Moody's criticism of self-referential conceits such as those indulged in by Craig Raine.

'October Salmon' begins and ends in the mud of material reality. The poem begins: 'He's lying in poor water, a yard or so depth of poor safety' and returns to: 'this was the only mother he ever had, this uneasy channel of minnows/Under the mill-wall, with bicycle wheels, car-tyres, bottles/And sunk sheets of corrugated iron'. The poem evokes the tension of contradictory and complementary processes as 'after two thousand miles, he rests' dying in 'this chamber of horrors [that] is also home./He was probably hatched in this very pool'. Thus his 'poise' can achieve the mythic, symbolic status of 'epic', for his inner process is the enacting of a larger one and his submission to it suggests an animal dignity that cannot be adequately characterised by David Moody's word 'brute': 'The epic poise/That holds him so steady in his wounds, so loyal to his doom, so patient/In the machinery of heaven'. Of course that dignity is actually the writer's reverence for this creature and the dynamic of complementary tensions that is 'the machinery of heaven'. It must remain a cause for regret, then, that this poem, which possesses all the features that I have suggested as typical of Hughes's post-pastoral poetry, should celebrate a creature which is finally failed by the poet's practical responsibility in Hughes's travelling the world to kill his kind. Finally, we may have to recognise that Hughes, as both good shepherd and fisherman, may not have escaped the contradictions of his own cultural lifestyle. It now seems more important than ever to distinguish in the poetry between the post-pastoral and the pastoral without ultimately allowing these later lapses to obscure the achievements of a body of work that, at its best, has gone more comprehensively beyond pastoral poetry than the work of any other contemporary poet.

Notes

1. *A Martian Sends a Postcard Home* (Oxford University Press, Oxford, 1979).
2. In E. J. Rawson (ed.), *The Yearbook of English Studies*, Vol. 17 (Modern Humanities Research Association, London, 1987), p. 166–78.
3. *Preoccupations* (Faber & Faber, London, 1980), p. 173–80.
4. *The City and the Country* (Chatto and Windus, London, 1973), p. 30.
5. *The Penguin Book of Pastoral Verse* (Penguin, Harmondsworth, 1974), p. 423ff.
6. *Poems 1932–82* (Iona Foundation, Philadelphia, 1987), p. 173.
7. *Swimming with Seals*, F. Steel (ed.), *Poetry Book Society Anthology* (Poetry Book Society, 1990).
8. Carcanet, Manchester, 1989, p. 9.
9. Faber & Faber, London, 1984.
10. 'Saccharine or Echo Soundings? Notions of Nature in Heaney's *Station Island*', *The New Welsh Review*, No. 10, Autumn 1990.
11. Faber & Faber, London, 1979.
12. See Scigaj, L. M., *The Poetry of Ted Hughes* (University of Iowa Press, 1986) and Robinson, Craig, *Ted Hughes as Shepherd of Being* (Macmillan, London, 1989).

13. *The Hawk in the Rain* (Faber & Faber, London, 1957).
14. I have in mind here Lawrence's sequence of six tortoise poems (published as a unit two years before the publication of *Birds, Beasts and Flowers* in 1923), but especially 'Tortoise Shout' in V. De Sola Pinto and F. Warren Roberts (eds), *The Complete Poems of D. H. Lawrence* (Heinemann, Oxford, 1964), p. 363.
15. *Phoenix* ((Heinemann, Oxford, 1936), p. 657.
16. *The Marriage of Heaven and Hell*, Plate 14.
17. Nash, Roderick, *Wilderness and the American Mind* (Yale University Press, London, 1967), p. 2.
18. 'Turning Points', Radio 4, 15 November 1988.
19. See Koltuv, B. B., *The Book of Lilith* (Nicolas-Hays, 1986).
20. The lines 'We are both in a world/Where the dirt is God' appeared in the poem 'More Theology' (in *Moments of Truth*, Keepsake Press, Twickenham, 1965) which is part II of the poem 'Plum-Blossom' in *Recklings* (Turret Books, London, 1966).
21. Faber & Faber, London, 1989.
22. *The Yearbook of English Studies*, p. 175.
23. Robinson, Craig, *Ted Hughes as Shepherd of Being* (Macmillan, London, 1989), p. 205.
24. See Gifford, Terry and Roberts, Neil, *Ted Hughes: A Critical Study* (Faber & Faber, London, 1981), p. 74.
25. Scigaj, L. M., *The Poetry of Ted Hughes* (University of Iowa Press, 1986), p. 290.
26. *Poetry Review*, Vol. 73, No. 4 (January 1984), p. 59.
27. Scigaj, ibid., p. 314.

9

Hughes, History and the World in Which We Live
Rand Brandes

Richard Murphy, recalling the five years he spent writing his fine historical poem *The Battle of Aughrim*, writes in his notebook (1962) of a conversation he had with Ted Hughes: 'He (Hughes) says that you can only get through to these things, such as war, by getting the remoteness of *Aughrim*, you can't deal directly with Vietnam horror, it's much more effective to set it in the time-scale of history.' Hughes has, throughout his career, kept history at a distance. He has resisted dealing 'directly' with contemporary 'horrors' and has remained true to what he called in 1962 his 'gift' which 'has none of the obvious attachment to publicly exciting and seemingly important affairs...' ('Context' 44). Even though Hughes is preoccupied with the past, the particulars of history – names, places and events – exert only a minor influence on his poetry. Throughout his career, Hughes has attempted to suppress Clio and to write his own Saga of the Soul in terms of the history of a degenerating Western civilisation. The absence of history in Hughes's work has several possible sources and equally as many aesthetic, philosophical and political repercussions.

One could quickly list many of the more obvious reasons why Hughes does not write 'about' history (even in *Remains of Elmet*):

1. He is obviously a Nature poet interested in horizons not history;
2. He consistently measures time by natural cycles, and disregards linear human time;
3. He has been called a writer of 'visionary' poetry, thus he focuses on the great intangible of existence and on moments of revelation;

142

4. He has also been described as, in relation to *Gaudete*, a devotional poet writing to the Earth-Mother;
5. He relies heavily on mythical, not historical, allusions and structures as reference points in the past;
6. He has immersed himself in Oriental philosophies that challenge Western concepts of history;
7. 'Reality' for Hughes is not social institutions, political ideologies, or religious dogma; reality is related to the 'sacred' as it appears in the non-human world.

With these propositions in mind, I would argue that, from a philosophical perspective, Hughes resists history, and at times is anti-historical, because he sees history as a logical, anthropocentric construct that assumes the linear progression of events in time which are irreversible and inevitable. In the simplest terms, Hughes does not *believe* in history.

For Hughes, history is a wall that frustrates desire, the desire to return to one's origins, to start over and begin anew – literally to leave the past and its imperatives and necessities behind. As Fredric Jameson argues: 'History is what hurts, it is what refuses desire and sets inexorable limits to individual as well as collective praxis, which its 'ruses' turn into grisly and ironic reversals of their overt intentions.'[1] Jameson's description resembles Mircea Eliade's discussion of the 'Terror of History' and Nietzsche's notion of the 'Malady of History'. Both thinkers argue that linear concepts of history based on an idea of predetermined forces that shape the past, present and future can kill the individual and collective spirit. To really live, Eliade argues, one must live through the trans-historical *power* of ritual, while Nietzsche argues that one must live 'unhistorically'. Both thinkers celebrate living in the eternal present – the present, for example, that appears in the poem 'Wodwo' and in *Moortown Elegies* or *River*. As Hughes writes: 'History is really no older than that new-born baby' ('Myth and Education', 1976, p. 83).

Hughes has also resisted writing explicitly about modern society or, as he said in 1962, throwing the poet's verse 'into the popular excitement of the time' ('Context' 45). Of course, Hughes is not simply arguing against verse that indiscriminately absorbs the Nightly News; he is also arguing against rhetorical poetry – a poetry that consciously attempts to take sides. Still, contemporary issues are in the margins of many of Hughes poems – nuclear war, violence in the streets and, perhaps most importantly, the destruction of the environment.

Hughes is more interested in the history of the body than the body of history. Since history assumes an anthropocentric centre, in theory it does not exist without a human subject. Thus, many of Hughes's earlier animal poems, even though connected to human experience through language itself or anthropomorphism, operate outside history. One could say that their 'animal courage' negates history. Thus, even though the pike, otter, bull and hawk enter history through the linguistic event of the poem, or even references to England and legends, they always escape into the ahistorical margins of the text.

When Hughes does write about history, he often relies on satire or parody when confronted with historical material that is not related to the First World War. His historical myths, especially in his early verse, are often satirical poems: as in 'Dully Gumption's Addendum' (1962), 'Dully Gumption's College Courses' (1961), 'Semantics', 'Humanities' and 'On Westminster Bridge' (1963).

These are obviously not Hughes's best poems – the scepticism of satire which mocks history's claims on the 'truth' and 'progress' depends heavily on a one-dimensional cynical view of the past and the forces that shape the present. Hughes is much more successful when he parodies the focus, content and structure of history instead of adopting a satirical posture.

Writing about Nietzsche's 'effective' history, which 'deals with events in terms of their most unique characteristics, their most acute manifestations', Foucault concludes: 'the true historical sense confirms our existence among countless lost events, without a landmark or a point of reference'.[2] 'Effective history', according to Foucault, also

> shortens its vision to those things nearest to it – the body, the nervous system, nutrition, digestion, and energies...and if it chances upon lofty epochs, it is with the suspicion – not vindictive but joyous – of finding a barbarous and shameful confusion.

Finally Foucault argues of Nietzsche that 'effective history' will produce a new historian, the genealogist.

> He will not be too serious to enjoy it; on the contrary, he will push the masquerade to its limit and prepare the great carnival of time

where masks are constantly reappearing. No longer the identification of our faint individuality with the solid identities of the past, but our 'unrealization' through the excessive choice of identities – Frederick of Hohenstaufen, Caesar, Jesus, Dionysus, and possibly Zarathustra. Taking up these masks, revitalizing the buffoonery of history, we adopt an identity whose unreality surpasses that of God, who started the charade. 'Perhaps, we can discover a realm where originality is again possible as parodists of history and buffoons of God.'

Crow obviously is an embodiment of the principles of 'effective history'. *Crow* is Nietzsche's genealogist – the trickster historian. In *Crow*, history appears as 'concerted carnival' written by a parodist. Hughes has said of Crow's world that it 'is a world where everything's happening simultaneously – the beginnings of the world, the end of the world, and all the episodes through – the world, inside and out' (Ted Hughes, reading in Loughborough, 12 March 1977). Crow's world parodies linear time by ignoring the principles and monuments of traditional history. *Crow* is also a manifestation of Nietzsche's 'effective history' as a result of its focus on the biological workings of the body of the world. If history is, as C. S. Lewis argues, 'a story written by the finger of God'[3] or, as Fredric Jameson refers to it in discussing St Augustine's *The City of God*, 'history itself [is]..."God's book" then God is the author', Crow's battle with Christianity is a battle with history. Crow refuses to read history as a narrative with a beginning, middle, and all-too-ominous end. Crow parodies the very premises of cause and effect, Providence, and Progress in the 'buffoonery of history'. Anything is possible in Crow's world because history has been dethroned. And when history is deposed hope appears.

Hughes's exposure to primitive culture, ritual and myth not only provided him with a vast reservoir of archaic subject-matter for *Crow*, but also informed his sense of history throughout his career. The Foreword to Mircea Eliade's book *Shamanism*[4] (a central text in Hughes's reading) discusses at length the 'transhistorical content a religious datum reveals' (p. xv). Eliade argues that the historian of religion 'knows that "history" does not exhaust the content of a religious phenomenon' and Hughes would agree. Despite the aggressiveness of Eliade's Foreword, he does concede that manifestations of the sacred do occur in historical contexts: 'The specific plane of manifestation is always *historical*, concrete, existential, even if the religious facts manifested are not always wholly reducible to history' (p. xvi).

Still, Eliade attempts to defuse the claims of those who would argue that every phenomenon in a culture can be explained by the unique history of the culture. Without establishing the validity of trans-historical experience and analysis, Eliade's comparative approach to Shamanism would be forced to acknowledge cultural relativism and more importantly to acknowledge the power of history over the sacred. Thus, the shaman himself is a trans-historical figure in two ways. One, the shaman functions similarly in different eras and cultures; two, the shaman, when practising his rituals and when encountering the sacred, passes through history in *illo tempore*. Not only does the shaman pass through time but moves out of time. The shaman then abolishes history through his return in ritual to the beginning of time.

Eliade explores in great detail the relationship between myth, ritual and history in *The Myth of the Eternal Return or Cosmos and History*.[5] Eliade's observations are extremely useful in discussing Hughes's use of mythic content and structure, the material of ritual, and ultimately Hughes's marginalisation of history. All of these concerns merge in Eliade's belief that 'the man of archaic cultures tolerates "history" with difficulty and attempts to periodically abolish it' (p. 36). Periodic ceremonies, Eliade points out, can be listed under two headings: '(1) annual expulsion of demons, disease and sins; (2) rituals of the days preceding and following the New Year' (p. 53). These ceremonies serve not only to periodically 'regenerate' the culture, but also to regenerate time because they presuppose 'a new Creation, that is, a repetition of the cosmogonic act' (p. 52). Eliade states that those 'historical peoples, those [with] whom history...begins...the Babylonians, Egyptians, Hebrews, Iranians...appear to have felt a deeper need to regenerate themselves periodically by abolishing past time and reactualizing the cosmogony' (p. 24). In contrast, in primitive societies 'time is recorded only biologically without being allowed to become "history"' (p. 7). Thus, Eliade asserts, 'all these instruments of regeneration tend toward the same end: to annul past time, to abolish history by a continuous return *in illo tempore*, by the repetition of the cosmogonic act' (p. 81). Eliade summarises his argument:

Collective or individual, periodic or spontaneous, regeneration rites always comprise, in their structure and meaning, an element of regeneration through repetition of an archetypal act, usually of the cosmogonic act. What is of chief importance to us in these archaic systems is the abolition of concrete time, and hence their antihistorical intent.... In the last analysis, what we discover in all these rites and all these attitudes is the will to devaluate time.... Basically, if viewed in its proper perspective, the life of archaic man...does not bear the burden of time, does not record time's irreversibility; in other words, completely ignores what is especially characteristic and decisive in a consciousness of time. Like the mystic, like the religious man in general, the primitive lives in a continual present (pp. 85–6).

Hughes's verse, especially in collections such as *Cave Birds*, *Moortown Elegies* or *River*, reflects, however obliquely, the attitude towards history outlined in Eliade's work. Whether Hughes has consciously applied this attitude to his work or has internalised it through his reading of anthropology and through farming is not the issue. My point is that the absence of history or even the hostility to history in Hughes's poetry may have as one of its origins the basic make-up of myth and ritual itself. Hughes would agree with Eliade who proclaims that 'the real situation of man in the cosmos...we shall never tire of repeating, is not solely historical' (*Shamanism* p. xiv).

Using Nietzsche's text *The Use and Abuse of History*[6] as a reference point, I have argued elsewhere[7] that Hughes consistently writes from what Nietzsche terms an 'unhistorical' perspective. This perspective is antithetical to what Nietzsche deems the 'historical sense', which can be a destructive force when translated into 'The Malady of History'. The essence of the argument is that *Remains of Elmet* struggles because of its inadequately-resolved historicity, while *Moortown Elegies* flourishes because of its resistance to history. By unresolved history I mean that Hughes never really comes to terms with his subject, the chronological history of the Calder Valley. Humans are noticeably absent from many of the *Elmet* poems. Biological and organic processes are carelessly conflated with economic and political processes. Finally, the volume suffers from a disabling nostalgia for a primeval (and even pre-human) Paradise outside the contingencies of history.

I also argue that in contrast to *Remains of Elmet*, *Moortown Elegies*, as originally published, both in terms of substance and structure, challenges the claims of history to closure and truth, not by relying on the trans-historical dimension of myth, but by explicitly focusing on individuals and creatures that are oblivious to history, yet not outside it. History, in *Moortown Elegies*, is an enabling absence.

With the republication of *Moortown Elegies* as *Moortown Diary* (1989) Hughes reveals a radical change in attitude toward the politics of history in relation to his verse. A detailed analysis of the differences between the two texts would require a separate essay in itself. Consequently, I will briefly mention those changes which affect how we read *Moortown Elegies* and *Moortown Diary* in relation to history. Essentially, Hughes, in the Preface to *Moortown Diary*, provides a much more historical context in which to read the basically 'unhistorical' poems. In contrast to the earlier volume, Hughes provides the topographical and historical coordinates of the farm in the Preface. In the later volume, the farm now has a locus and a history. The farm also interfaces with agricultural politics when Hughes mentions the financial ramifications of the 'EEC Agricultural Policy' (p. ix). While the Preface constructs a political and historical framework for the poems, the inclusion of the dates upon which the poems were written at the end of the poems ties them even more closely to chronological time and history. The dates, when combined with the notes at the end of the volume, say 'this is what happened on this particular day in this specific place'. Hughes has deliberately recast *Moortown Elegies* in an historical mould in *Moortown Diary*.

As in *Moortown Elegies*, Hughes's subsequent volume *River* (1983) works outside social and communal reference-points. Hughes walks out of the fallen history of the Calder Valley and into a 'new stillness' ('Christmas') where 'The river-epic/Rehearses itself') ('Four March Watercolours'). The creatures are familiar – the 'Merry Mink' in its 'folktale form' and the salmon is 'A god, on the earth for the first time'. Hughes leaves the traffic, the pollution, and the human confrontations behind. He has gone on his own pilgrimage to the river that is the 'Primitive, radical/Engine of earth's renewal' ('Four March Watercolours'). Time is seasonal, cyclical in the poems. Thus, fishing, one of the oldest forms of survival, satisfied 'an ancient thirst' ('River Barrow'). This is a spiritual 'thirst' for, as Eliade asserts, fishing is a sacred act and connects one instantly with an archaic world; a 'world [that] knows nothing of "profane" activities: every act which has a definite meaning – hunting, fishing, agriculture, games, conflict, sexuality – in some way participates in the sacred... [where] every responsible activity in the pursuit of a definite end is, for the archaic world, a ritual' (*Myth* pp. 27–8). The persona of *River*, who speaks in 'futuristic, archaic under-breath' ('A Cormorant'), advises us to 'Go Fishing'. In the poem 'Go Fishing', the baptismal ritual 'Join water wade into underbeing' asserts its ahistorical claims. The fisherman or woman is born again after the symbolic death. This is not Wodwo in the water, never to re-enter the community but someone whose rebirth has practical social consequences.

> Let the world come back, like a white hospital
> Busy with urgency words
> Try to speak and nearly succeed
> Heal into time and other people.

The private, individual ritual has social, 'other people', if not political consequences. Stepping out of time in this case is not an end in itself – it is not a permanent escape from history, but a way of getting back into it as Hughes does in *Wolfwatching*. Herbert J. Muller writes:

> 'Happy is the people that is without a history', wrote Christopher Dawson, 'and thrice happy is the people without a sociology for as long as we possess a living culture we are unconscious of it, and it is only when we are in danger of losing it or when it is already dead that we begin to realize its existence and to study it scientifically.' There are still such happy people among us, on farms, in business offices, and in congressional chambers. But those who are cursed by consciousness cannot become unconscious by an effort of will, and many have grown unhappier because they know too little history and sociology. A little consciousness is the most dangerous thing. And so we had better strive to become clearly and fully conscious, of who we are, where we are, and how we got this way.[8]

In her dismissive review of *Wolfwatching*, Edna Longley writes that Hughes 'has long rejected certain formal and social co-ordinates which his poetry now sorely misses. Perhaps difficulties begin at the point where archetypes cannot do the whole work of psychology, where dying animals cannot altogether stand in for unaccommodated man'.[9] Longley's desire for 'social co-ordinates' in Hughes's poetry is a desire for history, a history of complex individuals working in a human economy. As I have suggested elsewhere, I too am uncomfortable with Hughes's tendency to reduce the complexities of human social existence to a series of biological 'laws'. And I agree that archetypes do tend to privilege the universal at the expense of the individual. However, Longley overlooks what could be called the hyper-historical activity in *Wolfwatching*. After the ahistorical and asocial poems of *Flowers and Insects* and *River*, Hughes commits himself to re-entering history, to rewriting the history of his earlier volumes. This hyper-historical energy does short-circuit in a few of the poems in the form of hyperbole and heavy-handedness, but I still feel that *Wolfwatching* represents Hughes's attempted re-engagement with the world we live in – the world of history.

History counterbalances the transcendent claims of myth. History demythologizes even as it becomes myth itself, that is, even as it enters the cultural memory in the form of trans-historical paradigms. History asserts the once-and-only-once(ness) of the event and the 'uniqueness' of the individual. In *Wolfwatching* Hughes goes over old ground; injecting a more critical demythologizing view of history into the poems. Of course, as Longley points out, there are those poems which still follow the ahistorical, archetypal and anthropomorphic direction of Hughes's earlier volumes which run against this hyper-historical current. But in poems such as 'Climbing into Heptonstall' and 'Leaf Mould', Hughes rewrites poems from *Remains of Elmet* from a more critical historical perspective.

Unlike the poem 'Remains of Elmet', which suffers from a self-defeating nostalgia for lost power – a power which the modern person pathetically approaches with a tourist's superficial reverence for the past, 'Climbing into Heptonstall' is a climb into a past that is not comforting or scenic. The 'group' of tourists in the poem obviously wants the pleasantries of history – to look at the material remains of the past, unable or unwilling to project themselves into it. The voice of history ironically appears in the poem as 'the madman's yell. Bird-like. Wordless.' If, in the 'madman', the poem tries too hard to demythologise Elmet, the rhetorical excess of the wordless yell still attempts to open up a less glorified view of the past. The historical voice of the madman wants the skeletons out of the closet:

> So spring-clean the skull. Sweep from the soul's attic
> Spinners, weavers, tacklers, dyers, and their infants.
> All agitators of wool and cotton
> Caught in the warp and the woof.

The list of mill-workers places the poem in actual history. The madman also wants the group to look at the economic, not the mythic sources, of the worker's misery: ' "Penny hunger",/That anaesthetic herb, choked this valley'. In the earlier poem 'Remains of Elmet', Hughes reduces the historical processes to biological and natural ones. The reference to monetary forces keeps 'Climbing to Hepton-stall' in touch with the unique, human territory of socio-political economies. Thus, the dispirited lives of the mill-workers are seen more in the light of historical movements than in the opaque distortion of a mythic determinism.

Coming to terms with the past in *Wolfwatching* also appears in Hughes's poems where genealogy dovetails with history, personal history becomes public history, with the inverse being true as well. In 'Dust as We Are', 'Source', 'For the Duration' and 'Walt', the persona must struggle with the presentness of the past. History, as manifest in the First World War, kills the present; thus, the persona recounts the death-in-life experiences of those 'killed but alive'. History asserts its power in the form of silence, nightmares, tears and physical mutilations, where 'The whole hopelessness [is] still going on/No man's land still crying and burning/Inside our house'. History is 'no man's land' from which one must escape but cannot because it is inscribed in the body. One cannot repress history; it leaks out like a buried instinct. Consequently, to exorcise history one must talk it out, and the persona attempts to be the therapist working out the 'talking cure' in 'Dust As We Are': 'I had to use up a lot of spirit/Getting over it. I was helping him./I was his supplementary convalescent'. The war poems of *Wolfwatching* tap some of the same power of Hughes's earlier poems such as 'Out' or 'Scapegoats and Rabies'. What resembles Eliade's 'Terror of History' has been internalised to the extent that the persona feels helpless not simply in the face of present emptiness but, more importantly, in the face of the irreversible past.

In 'Hardcastle Crags' from *Remains of Elmet* the human and non-human are fused to the extent that they negate each other. The attempt at statement in the poem becomes a non-statement so that by the time one reaches the end of the poem where 'the air-stir releases/The love-murmurs of a generation of slaves/Whose bones melted in Asia Minor', the tragic becomes trite. In contrast, Hughes's rewriting of 'Hardcastle Crags', the poem 'Leaf Mould', occupies itself with human, personal affairs. The poem's setting, 'that echoing museum', is a 'birth' place, an origin, 'Where she dug leaf mould for her handful of garden/And taught you to walk'. Here the past is personalised as the first step out into the poet's world – which is Nature. The poem's self-reflective phrase 'others are making poems' connects this origin with that of other poets and with earlier poems. The three italicised stanzas call on the ghosts of Billy Holt and the cenotaphs from *Remains of Elmet* and include a direct reference to Seamus Heaney's famous poem 'Digging' – 'Between finger and thumb roll a pine-needle'. The sense of evaluating the past and one's inheritance connects the Heaney allusion to a later stanza, in which the speaker casts a suspicious eye on Robert Graves's White Goddess while also keeping in touch with the actual world of the mother:

> White-faced, brain-washed by her nostalgias,
> You were her step-up transformer.
> She grieved for her girlhood and the fallen.
> You mourned for Paradise and its fable.

It appears as if Hughes has jilted the White Goddess for a stoic Clio. The poem attempts to demythologise personal history, by acknowledging the various 'nostalgias' for 'Paradise'. The self-reflexive and ironic tone of 'Leaf Mould', when juxtaposed with 'Hardcastle Crags', reveals the difference between Hughes's quixotic historicity in *Remains of Elmet* and *Wolfwatching*'s deference to history.

Before discussing the last poem I will cover from *Wolfwatching*, I want to consider quickly two poems about extinction: 'The Black Rhino' and 'Little Whale Song'. Although Hughes concentrates on the cyclical motion of Nature and its amazing capacity for rebirth and renewal, extinction forces us to acknowledge the linear progression of events through time and the true irreversibility of history. Again I would argue with Longley that Hughes's writing about environmental issues is a 'social co-ordinate'.

We can measure time by the extinction of animals; each unit is the end of a species. History becomes a series of endings when Hughes writes about extinctions. 'Little Whale Song' is a typical Hughes poem which clearly draws on Lawrence's 'Whales Weep Not', particularly in the lines:

> The loftiest, spermiest
> Passions, the most exquisite pleasures,
> The noblest characters, the most god-like
> Oceanic presence and poise –
>
> The most terrible fall.

Hughes mythologises the whales, lifts them out of history, and thus their extinction seems fictive when we know it is not. In contrast the extinction of the Black Rhino is considered within historical para-meters which are reinforced by the lengthy note at the end of the volume. When reading the poem, we feel *the facts*:

> For this is the Black Rhino, who vanished as he approaches
> Every second there is less and less of him
> By the time he reaches you nothing will remain, maybe,
> But the horn – an ornament for a lady's lap

Simply by bringing in the 'lady', the modern consumer, the poem stays in touch with history and the economics of extinction. This connection closes the poem in the 'Snoring frowns of African big-shots, in the strobe glare and rumble of airports, uttering grunts of hard currency/Ballistic data'. This is not the fanciful ballistic know-ledge that informs *Gaudete*, for we are convinced that these are *real* bullets.

One other important aspect of the poem is Hughes's partial rereading of non-Western traditional cultures in relation to their ritual vitality. Hughes has often suggested that if Western man would adopt some of the rituals of traditional cultures, he could revitalise his life. However, in 'Black Rhino' Hughes is forced to con-sider the flip-side of this primitive energy – its resistance to reason – in the form of superstition and taboo. Thus, when he mentions the 'fifty thousand North Yemenite warrior youths', 'Each gripping a dagger by the hilt of rhino horn at eight or nine thousand dollars a handful', the historical consequences of 'primitive' life become apparent. The ancient hero is not celebrated; a vital culture is not idealised. The rhino, Hughes writes, 'has blundered somehow into man's phantasmagoria and cannot get out'. One way out, however, is through history, by making people conscious, as Hughes does in this poem, of a real problem in a real place that they can do some-thing about.

The penultimate poem in *Wolfwatching*, 'On the Reservations', draws heavily on contemporary history and the more remote past. The three sections of the poem – 'Sitting Bull on Christmas Morning', 'Nightvoice' and 'The Ghost Dancer' – conflate Native American his-tory with modern British life. Although some of the references in the poem, both private and public, are difficult to follow, one feels that Hughes is attempting to test the power of the shaman, his dreams, and myth against socio-political forces. The word 'Reservations' itself immediately generates a complex of historical images and associations. Hughes's shamans typically operate in their mythic worlds, and are not confronted with the realities of reservations or genocide. The use of Sitting Bull, therefore, suggests an historical situation in which spiritual power is challenged by military power.

Sitting Bull was the leading chief and holy man of the Teton Sioux Indians. In 1876, while Crazy Horse defeated Custer at Little Big Horn, Sitting Bull stayed in the camp and practised magic. He later participated in the Ghost Dance religious movement that predicted the arrival of a messiah to save the Indians from the white men. Ultimately Sitting Bull, the shaman, could not protect his tribe or himself from the socio-economic imperialistic forces of history. Thus in the first section of 'On the Reservations', Sitting Bull stands in for, or in contrast to, the modern coal-miner who has inherited the products of a junk culture and the emptiness of a secular age: 'Chapels pews broken television/(Who dumped these, into his stocking,/Under coal-slag in a flooded cellar?)'. The forces that ended Sitting Bull's world made the Calder Valley and the post-industrial society we live in. Still, the spiritual continuity between Sitting Bull and the coal-miner is qualified by cultural difference, the distance between tepees and TVs.

Part II, 'Nightvoice', is introduced by a quotation from the Nez Percé Indians: 'My young men shall never work. Men who work cannot dream and wisdom comes in dreams.' The obvious impossibility of such a position in a capitalistic society is clear. The poem is localised in a domestic setting where 'She dreams she sleep-walks' through various nightmares. The pensioners of *Remains of Elmet*, 'Crown Point Pensioners', who are referred to as 'Singers of a lost kingdom', are demythologised, transformed instead into 'pensioners who chorus in croaks/While Shepherds/ Watched their Television'. Tele-evangelists work in the same spiritual sector as the shamans – they are both technicians of the sacred.

When the woman dreams that 'all the dead/huddle/in the slag-heaps wrong/land wrong/time tepees a final/resting for the epidemic/solution' the images of genocide, though distorted by a surreal presentation, stay in the human world of facts where everything seems to have gone wrong. The poem's final section, 'The Ghost Dancer', conflates the icons and choreographies of the punk movement with those of the late-nineteenth-century Ghost

Dance Movement. The ghost dance was an obvious product of an apocalyptic vision and a real sense of doom – it was the *danse macabre*. In the poem, the spasmodic dancing, mohawk haircuts, and industrial jewellery recall the costumes and ceremonies of the Sioux. Even the kid dancing 'Through his septum a dog's penile bone', in a waste lot in 'Half-anguish half-joy' unconsciously mimics the ceremonial garb and motions of Native Americans. (Paul Muldoon, a poet Longley praises, has covered similar ground by weaving together Native American history and culture with contemporary Irish life as in *Meeting the British*.) The historical conflation, when charged with a brief revival of the rhythms of the Beat Poets, or perhaps echoing the jumping beat of hip-hop, turns the punk rocker into a post-industrial shaman: 'This megawatt, berserker medium/ with his strobe-drenched battle-cry', watches while the 'Mau-Mau Messiah's showbiz lightning stroke/Puffs the stump of Empire up in smoke'. (Like Sitting Bull, the Mau-Mau movement of Kenya was anti-white.) Granted it is difficult to see the shaman in Sid Vicious when he sings 'God Save the Queen' or in Rick Jones when The Clash sings 'London's Burning', but Hughes's historical interweaving is brilliant.

Hughes's crash-landing into contemporary urban life signified an important return to history. Perhaps he is feeling the heat of Marxist critics and others who want his work to be politically relevant. Yet his use of Native American history (and not simply myth) produces an historical perspective from which to read the poem's closing line: 'Start afresh, this time unconquerable'. As a result of the institutionalised despair and despondency of many post-colonial cultures, Hughes's call in the end is wishful, but at least it is wishful in the light of forces Hughes acknowledges exist, and not because he is attempting to redress some cosmic imbalance, as in 'Crow's Song about England'. 'On the Reservations' may not be a poem full of street-names or political slogans as in a Ciaran Carson poem ('The Irish for No', for example), but Hughes's poem is a semiotic reading of contemporary style. Hughes still does not believe in institutional solutions, and placing his hope for the future in the Rastas may be a bit fanciful (and a strange manifestation of his primitivism), but the mere fact that he would write obliquely about contemporary issues and risk getting caught up in 'the excitement of the times' is a new beginning for him.[10]

We cannot change history, but we can change our relationship to it. For most of his career thus far, Hughes has marginalised history, or reduced it to a master-narrative that traces the decline of Western civilisation. Hughes's poetry resists history through his pre-occupation with the ahistorical and unhistorical presence of beasts; his belief in the healing capabilities of ritual and myth in the trans-historical; and his anti-historical rewriting of history as the 'effective history' of the parodist.

The absence of history in much of Ted Hughes's verse is to some the powerhouse of his poetry, while to others it is a fatal weakness. In an age that self-consciously makes history and in a critical envir-onment that idolises the 'poet as witness' and lauds socially com-mitted poetry, Hughes's poetry nonetheless resists history and political prescriptions. It is tempting to say that Hughes has had the luxury of ignoring history; that he can afford to shop around the world of mail-order myths, or that he has lived history vicariously through Eastern European and Irish poets. However, this would be a serious misreading of a poet who has assumed the inner self and Nature as his battleground; a poet who has cast his lot with chil-dren, ecologists and the imagination.

No matter how much we want Hughes to sound like those writers who have felt the direct pressure of history such as Heaney, Milosz, Linton Kwesi Johnson, Carolyn Forche, he will not and can-not. Even in *Wolfwatching*, where Hughes fights his way back into history, the project is only a partial victory. Seamus Heaney has written:

> The fact is that poetry is its own reality and no matter how much a poet may concede to the corrective pressures of social, moral, political and historical reality the ultimate fidelity must be to the demands and promise of the artistic event.[11]

The 'artistic event' for Hughes is 'timeless'.

Hughes apparently had those issuers of critical 'correctives' men-tioned by Heaney in mind when describing 'The Questioner' in the Foreword to *The Way to Write*:

> There is no arguing with one who lowers the meaning of every-thing by simply lowering the interpretation, and who distrusts all that is invisible and intangible. For one thing, he has hard evidence on his side, even when he goes on to tell us that man is a political animal, a machine only, and that all culture is an opiate, a tem-porary illusion, and that our inner lives are a vapour – of no more

account or reality than the inner lives of slaughter-house sheep (p. xvi).

This 'evidence' is the verity of history, irreversible and irreverent, and this 'culture' is that of Walter Benjamin: 'There has never been a document of culture which was not at one and the same time a document of barbarism' (quoted in *The Political Unconscious*, p. 281). Hughes counters this argument by equating the soul, history and language:

> Our best imaginative literature can well be called the sacred book of the tribe. It holds what we, as a tribe, have inwardly – and therefore with most decisive experience – lived through: it holds the inner vision we all share, the unbroken circle of our national-ity. This living monument of our language is the closest thing we have to a mythology: it is sacred because it enshrines our deepest knowledge of ourselves as a people, the language-circuits of our thought and feeling. It holds the D.N.A of our consciousness as a spiritual unity. The literature and language are one. And we value it for the same reason that all nations in good morale have valued their literature: it is the national soul we carry (pp. xvi–xvii).

The chauvinistic tone of this passage reveals the pressure Hughes is under to defend his position on history. By appealing to the tribe's inner vision, Hughes appeals to the 'sacred book' and not to history. Hughes produces a monoculture devoid of plurality. Is he speaking for Northern Ireland? for the Blacks in Brixton? for the Sex Pistols? Hughes has carved this position in stone outside the office of Faber and Faber:

> A Nation's a soul.
> A Soul is a Wheel
> With a crown for a Hub
> To keep it whole.

To counter this reading of Hughes's purification of the 'national soul' one could easily quote 'Crow's Song about England': 'Once upon a time there was a girl/Who tried to give her mouth/It was snatched from her and her face slapped' (see Keith Sagar, *The Achievement of Ted Hughes*, p. 338). Or to quote from Hughes's comments in the 'Poetry International '67' programme:

We now give more serious weight to the words of a country's poets than to the words of its politicians – though we know the latter may interfere more drastically with our lives. Religions, ideologies, mercantile competition divide us.

This is the Ted Hughes of *Modern Poetry in Translation*; the poet who believes in breaking down national linguistic barriers, the international poet. However, history, in the form of 'religions, ideologies and mercantile competition', is an anathema; it divides us. Yet there are other, more constructive ways of reading Hughes's confrontation with history.

In the end, Eliade and Milosz represent two antithetical positions regarding the place of history in our lives. In *The Myth of the Eternal Return* Eliade predicts:

There is also reason to foresee that, as the terror of history grows worse,...humanity, to ensure its survival, will find itself reduced to desisting from any further 'making' of history in the sense in which it began to make it from the creation of the first empires, will confine itself to repeating prescribed archetypal gestures, and will strive to forget, as meaningless and dangerous, any spontaneous gesture which might entail 'historical' consequences.

Milosz offers an opposing vision of the future of history. After arguing that the modern mind – that is, the imaginative mind as well – has been shaped by a biological model of 'reality' which ultimately forces us to affirm our affinities with the animal world of evolution, Milosz suggests that in the future we will look for models that celebrate the uniqueness of human existence. The main model, Milosz asserts, will be that of history:

Daring to make a prediction, I expect, perhaps quite soon, in the twenty-first century, a radical turning away from the Weltanschauung marked principally by biology, and this will result from a newly acquired historical consciousness. Instead of presenting man through those traits that link him to higher forms of the evolutionary chain, other of his aspects will be stressed: the exceptionality, strangeness, and loneliness of that creature mysterious to itself, a being incessantly transcending its own limits. Humanity will increasingly be turning back to itself, increasingly contemplating its entire past, searching for a key to its own enigma, and penetrating, through empathy, the soul of bygone generations and of whole civilizations.[12]

As metaphysical propositions, the 'unhistorical' presence of beasts and the trans-historical power of ritual are seductive philosophical positions – positions, ultimately, of privilege. However, as written or unwritten principles by which one writes poetry today, they could be dangerous positions of complacency or collaboration. Good history may not make good poetry, but if history is a true source of hope, as Milosz and others argue, then it is the writer who must take on the challenge of history, which is the challenge of the future:

> Every day one can see signs indicating that now, at the present moment, something new, and on a scale never witnessed before, is being born: humanity as an elemental force conscious of transcending Nature, for it lives by memory of itself, that is, in History.[13]

Notes

1. *The Political Unconscious* (Cornell University Press, New York, 1981), p. 102.
2. 'Nietzsche, Genealogy, History' in Rabinow (ed.), *The Foucault Reader* (Pantheon, New York, 1984), pp. 89 and 94.
3. 'Historicism' in McIntire (ed.), *God, History and Historians* (Oxford University Press, New York, 1977).
4. Paris, 1949, and Princeton University Press, New Jersey, 1974.
5. Paris, 1949, and Princeton University Press, New Jersey, 1974.
6. Trans. Collins (Macmillan, New York, 1985).
7. 'Ted Hughes In and Out of Time: *Remains of Elmet* and *Moortown Elegies*' (Kent State University Press, Ohio, 1990).
8. *The Uses of the Past* (Oxford University Press, New, York, 1952), p. 27.
9. *London Review of Books*, 22 March 1990, p. 22.
10. Hughes has become more openly activist. In a recently published open letter to Mrs Thatcher, Hughes calls for new taxes to help protect the environment and to improve education by paying teachers more since 'the most important of all jobs must be that of teacher'. Hughes seems to concede that one must transform institutions as well as imaginations if we are to *save* the world.
11. *The Government of the Tongue* (Faber & Faber, London, 1988), p. 101.
12. *The Witness of Poetry* (Harvard University Press, Cambridge, Mass., 1983), p. 110.
13. Ibid., p. 116.

10

Ted Hughes and Ecology: A Biocentric Vision

Leonard M. Scigaj

When Ted Hughes reviewed Max Nicholson's *The Environmental Revolution* in 1970, he spoke enthusiastically about Nicholson's ability to write from 'Nature's point of view'. Nicholson could show the reader 'the wholeness of this living globe', grasp the 'inner spiritual unity of Nature', and remind us of our limited understanding of Earth's dynamic ecology.[1] Hughes's poetry since the mid-1960s has been intimately concerned with viewing Nature from an ecological perspective.

Environmental deterioration has, over the past twenty years, spurred ecologists, moralists, theologians and feminists to re-evaluate the position of humans in the planetary ecosystem. The intellectual historian Roderick Nash, in *The Rights of Nature*, offers a detailed and fully documented summary of how hundreds of British and American scientists and scholars have engaged in interdisciplinary work to consider extending ethical rights to animals, plants, rocks, and the entire planetary environment. Nash considers the development of environmental ethics to be 'arguably the most dramatic expansion of morality in the course of human thought.'[2]

Nearly twenty years ago Alvarez credited Hughes with having 'a fine, racing-mechanic's ear' for the literary market-place,[3] but with 1990s hindsight one can survey the achievement of thirty-five years and remark at how completely Hughes's work meshed with the vanguard of this fusion of ecology with environmental ethics. Hughes's poetry shares a basic premise with ecologists and environmentalists: the only way to save this planet is to change the perceptions of its human inhabitants about Nature.

Most of those engaged in recent scholarship concerning environmental ethics share the general perception that anthropocentric thinking has caused our ecological crisis by creating an 'I–it' rather

160

than an 'I–Thou' relationship with Nature.[4] The 'I–it' relationship invites the purely utilitarian use of planetary resources that has severely damaged the dynamic yet delicate balances within major planetary ecosystems, especially renewable and non-renewable components of the hydrological cycle and the intricate balances in Earth's atmosphere and soil.

'The Historical Roots of our Ecologic Crisis', a 1967 essay written by the medieval historian Lynn White, Jr, fostered much debate and re-evaluation of our Western Christian attitudes towards the environment. White boldly argued that 'everywhere today, whether in Japan or in Nigeria, successful technology is Western' and based upon the medieval Christian concept of the mastery and exploitation of Nature that has its roots in the Bible. Because in the Genesis account humans alone are made in God's image, it followed that all Creation was made expressly for the benefit and use of humans. According to White, once Christianity vanquished the animistic beliefs of tribal cultures, Christians could 'exploit Nature in a mood of indifference to the feelings of natural objects'.[5] Feminist historians of science such as Carolyn Merchant and moralists such as Elizabeth Dodson Gray consider this anthropocentric, hierarchical domination of Nature to be typical of patriarchal thinking.[6]

The ecologist Barry Commoner, in his latest work, *Making Peace with the Planet*, asserted that we can adapt existing production technologies to ensure environmental quality. What we need is to base *legislation* upon *social* rather than free-enterprise ideology. Pollution-prevention and global environmental consciousness must be the concepts that drive our legislation, not corporate profit-maximising and the inviolability of private ownership. Commoner believes we must develop grass-roots consumer awareness and generate consumer pressure to change the perceptions of legislators and executives.[7]

Although Commoner nowhere states this in this book, it is not difficult to extrapolate that if environmental change depends upon transforming individual perception, then poetry can play a significant role, for poetry can both question and transform the perceptions of its readers. Hughes, in his Nicholson review, stated that an optimistic view of Nature could help effect a change in our perceptions towards the environment. According to Hughes, a contemporary artist need not be limited to creating a vision of the 'nightmare of mental disintegration and spiritual emptiness' that is our cultural present. He may instead choose to fashion an alternative vision of a 'real Eden', the 'sacred' interdependence of each cell, the 'soul-state of the new world'. As we shall see, most of Hughes's poetry since *Crow* offers this positive ecological vision.

According to Nash's exhaustive research, the great majority of scientists and scholars who desired to end the 'I–it' attitude towards Nature also argued for a shift in perception away from anthropocentrism and towards a biocentric view that recognises the intrinsic value of all components of Earth's ecosystems and treats humans as but one of the millions of organisms interacting to ensure planetary survival. White also advocated a biocentric change in perception in his 1967 essay – a return to the Christian humility and the democratic brotherhood of all Creation as practised by St Francis of Assisi. To promote a similar change in perception among the faithful, many theologians re-examined Scripture to suggest emphasising passages that are less anthropocentric and more in keeping with ecological interrelatedness. The theologian Richard A. Baer, Jr, suggested an emphasis upon the intrinsic worth of all Creation contained in Genesis 1: 31, where God saw that everything He had made was good. Others emphasised the stewardship implied by God's directive in Genesis 2: 15 to till the ground of Eden and preserve it.[8]

Many scientists and scholars concerned about the environment responded to the need for a drastic transformation of perception by desiring to replace the dominant Western concept of egocentric individuality with concepts involving the intrinsic interrelatedness of self and environment. The theologians John Cobb, Jr, Mary Daly, Marjorie Suchocki, and Jay McDaniel emphasised the thought process of Whitehead as offering an ecologically sound alternative to Western dualism. By considering the actual subjective experience of the self as a unique example of Nature's own process of becoming, one can experience connectedness, a solidarity of self and environment, for each self according to McDaniel 'enfolds the entire universe into its own Nature...from a particular point of view that is unique to the self'.[9] Merchant, Gray, and Carol Gilligan echoed the thoughts of many feminists by stating that women's self-concept is less rigidly egocentric and closed; it is more concerned with giving, sharing, and webs of relationship that resemble ecological relatedness.[10]

Other ecologists and environmentalists advocated biocentric views where humans perceive themselves not as masters of Nature but as only one species among millions of equal organisms dynamically interacting within ecosystems. Dozens of nineteenth- and twentieth-century naturalists emphasised the kinship of humans with animals, and the importance of each and every element in God's Creation.[11] When the British ecologist Arthur G. Tansley coined the term 'ecosystem' in 1935, he was thinking as a biologist about how energy transfers – especially in climate and food – tended towards the creation of equilibrated, homeostatic systems among organisms; contemporary quantitative ecologists such as Eugene Odum discussed interdependence in terms of cybernetic energy transfers among organic communities.[12] James Lovelock's evidence suggests that the planet Earth is a sentient, self-sustaining, self-regulating biocentric whole – the Gaia hypothesis.[13]

'Deep ecologists' Arne Naess, Bill Devall, George Sessions and others advocated a more radical restructuring of human perception to emphasise the intrinsic right of all things in the biosphere to live and reach fulfilment.[14] The phrase 'biotic community' echoed throughout Aldo Leopold's famous 1949 'Land Ethic' essay. Here he emphasised the co-operative 'biotic interactions between people and land', conceived the land to be a sustained energy circuit, and stated his ecological precept that 'a thing is right when it tends to preserve the integrity, stability, and beauty of the biotic community. It is wrong when it is otherwise.'[15] Leopold seems to have been echoing the universal kinship philosophy of J. Howard Moore, who had written forty years earlier that 'the *Life Process is the End – not man.*'[16]

Others, including the contemporary American poet Gary Snyder,[17] expand the biocentric view of ecology on to the plane of a mystical reverence for all life as a sacred, interconnected whole. Theodore Roszak advocated the shamanistic world-view of American Indians because it restored a moral relationship between humans and Nature conceived as sacred.[18] The Catholic cultural historian Thomas Berry asserted in *The Dream of the Earth* that 'the ultimate lesson in physics, biology, and all the sciences, as it is the ultimate wisdom of tribal peoples', concerns acquiring the sensitivity to grasp the 'cooperative understanding' that operates within the 'total system'. To acquire this sensitivity we must respond sympathetically to the 'psychic energies deep in the very structure of reality itself.'[19] This is one of the most rarefied applications of ecology since Albert Schweitzer's mystical 'reverence for life' early in this century.[20]

Hughes has followed environmentalist literature since having read Rachel Carson's *Silent Spring* in 1962. His Yorkshire nurture and his Cambridge education in anthropology – especially his study of tribal societies and Oriental philosophy – combined to develop a sensitivity towards the energies in Nature and the reverence for life that Berry and Schweitzer advocate. As Hughes stated in his Nicholson review, ecology was one of the most basic intuitions of tribal societies: 'the idea of Nature as a single organism is not new. It was man's first great thought, the basic intuition of most primitive theologies.'

With uncanny consistency, Hughes's thematic development throughout his career has paralleled the development of major issues in the recent bonding of ecology with environmental ethics. One can see in his early poetry an emphasis upon kinship with animals and a longing to fuse with Nature's vital energy, in *Wodwo* a questioning of anthropocentrism, in *Crow* a comprehensive critique of anthropocentrism, and from *Gaudete* through *Wolfwatching* a gradual development of a biocentric vision that often incorporates a mystical grasp of the 'inner spiritual unity of Nature' that he admired in Nicholson. What some critics consider to be Hughes's bleakness is more correctly the result of a shift away from the anthropocentrism that dominates most poetry. Hughes does not expect moments of joy and exaltation always to relate to *human* goals and aspirations; he often presents such moments biocentrically, as part of the intrinsic worth of the elements of Nature themselves, quite apart from human designs. Many poems are indeed cheerless from a human perspective, for they celebrate the biocentric process while implicitly accepting the death of the individual as final and inevitable.

Hughes admired Nicholson's ability to 'write from an imagination constructed out of the actualities of the earth's life'. Similarly, Hughes's early poetry accentuates the actualities of survival struggles as well as the energies shared by humans and animals. In the title-poem of *The Hawk in the Rain* (1957), the hawk's will-power and awareness of Nature become ideals for the doggedly persistent persona mired in the mud of mutability. The fierce fire of jaguars and macaws, the unerring stealth of foxes, the instantaneous plunge of a hawk into a dovecote and the slavering competition of wolves are linked in the poems to kindred abilities in the human psyche. A quick, incisive grasp of essentials is shared both by Mozart and thrushes in *Lupercal* (1960). The survival lessons learned from animals in Hughes's early poetry are at least as important as those learned from human ancestors; both promote 'The live brain's' ability to 'master and last' ('Historian').[21] In all cases 'the brute's quick', as in the title-poem of *Lupercal*, can become the tinder to ignite energies in humans, to 'touch this frozen one'.

The early animal poems of the confident young adult are nevertheless anthropocentric, and to some extent concerned with exerting patriarchal control. The male in *The Hawk in the Rain* appears able to master Nature, to ride 'the morning mist/With a big-eyed hawk on his fist' (p. 23). The phallic strength of 'The Bull Moses' is as overpowering as the 'ammoniac reek of his litter'. Occasionally, moments of bravado combine with an emulation of ancient heroes.

The anthropocentrism of the early poetry vanishes abruptly in *Wodwo* (1967). After the central persona divests himself of his Western ego in the shamanistic death and rebirth adventure, he begins to become whimsically critical of his own anthropocentric thinking. Wolves must feed their own fur (p. 178), the sheep are 'undeterred' by Zen Buddhist meditations, and the landscape offers no reliable 'anchor' for human thinking (p. 173). One of the messages of 'Pibroch' is that the landscape has its own integrity apart from human value and perceptions, however visionary. Though 'aeon after aeon,/Nothing lets up or develops', this landscape is indisputably *there*; it existed long before humans trod the earth. Though the Wodwo of the title poem is free to choose his own world orientation, he is the 'exact centre' only of his own microcosmic universe. He is curious about the natural world, but prefers to surround himself with questions that check any attempt at anthropocentric mastery.

Meanwhile the most positive poems of Part III of *Wodwo* rejoice unselfconsciously and biocentrically in the free expenditure of energy in gnats and skylarks, and the unhurried plenitude of Nature embodied in full moons and cows, ripe for milking, methodically returning homeward. The skylarks and gnats of *Wodwo* offer the reader the first instances of what becomes a current of biocentric mysticism in Hughes, the longing for an ecstatic, dervish-like participation in the transfer of energy that one finds in later poems such as 'Riverwatcher' in *River* and 'Saint's Island' in *Flowers and Insects*. These poems celebrate a non-anthropocentric energy-flow from an ecological point of view that Tansley and Odum could appreciate.

Just as Hughes knew that ecology was really the 'first great thought' of tribal societies, so he need not have read Tansley to comprehend the ecology of energy transfer. The basic principle was known to ancient cultures. In a 1964 review Hughes wrote about 'the wild Heraclitean/Buddhist notion that the entire universe is basically made of fire.'[22] In 'Gnat-Psalm' Hughes presents the gnats, low life to humans, with their own integrity, their own intrinsic worth, their own obscure purposes, and their own microcosmic furnace of solar energy: 'they are their own sun/Their own brimming over/At large in the nothing'. Wired to the sun's energy, and at each moment 'giving their bodies to be burned', the energy passes indiscriminately among them – 'Everybody everybody else's yoyo'. The larks of 'Skylarks' similarly dance in a circuit of shared energy, 'flailing flames' as they lift from 'the fling of a bonfire'. They cavort until 'they're burned out/And the sun's sucked them empty'. The epigraph to 'Gnat-Psalm', a Hebrew proverb, signals a change from anthropocentrism to biocentrism in Hughes's thinking: 'The Gnat is of more ancient lineage than man.'

Crow (1970) presents a comprehensive indictment of the heavily anthropocentric thinking of Western science and religion. Hughes was familiar with the modern critique of the New Science, the Industrial Revolution, and the Protestant Reformation, from reading any of a number of sources, including at least Robert Graves, Max Weber and Friedrich Nietzsche. The ecological focus Nicholson gives this critique in Chapter Eleven of *The Environmental Revolution* may have spurred Hughes's indictment of Western science and religion in his review – a succinct ecological critique similar to that of Lynn White, Jr. Because the Bible, according to Hughes, reduces the Earth to a soulless 'heap of raw materials given to man by God for his exclusive profit and use', Western man has exiled himself 'from both inner and outer Nature' and is engaged in a 'desperate search for mechanical and rational and symbolic securities, which will substitute for the spirit-confidence of the Nature he has lost'.

These statements function admirably as a revealing thematic gloss on *Crow*'s anthropocentric escapades and their ecological consequences. Crow, like his trickster forebears, always tries to appropriate Nature for self-serving purposes. In 'Crow and Mama' he recapitulates Western science's domination of Nature through technology as a fearful flight into the pseudo-security of machines. His analytic distance at every turn alienates him from Nature and from his own Nature, which steadily becomes more aggressively that of a Black Beast (p. 28) at war with the cosmos in 'Crow and Stone'. Even when confronted by Nature in its sacred aspect, the Great Serpent, Crow merely 'beat the hell out of it, and ate it' (p. 45). The Protestant

Reformation God of this universe does not instruct Crow in the stewardship of Nature; God transforms consciousness and language into utilitarian tools, creating what Nicholson calls 'the techno sphere' as He demonstrates how to turn Eden's apples into cider (*Crow*, p. 78).

Hughes, in his Nicholson review, characterised Nature in traditionally feminine ways. In the master plan of the *Crow* sequence, Crow was to win Nature as his bride. But the poems where Crow achieves an ecological perspective and wins his bride have yet to be written. Because Crow in the 1970–2 trade volumes cannot comprehend the defects of his anthropocentric thinking, whenever he tries to commune with his vision of woman he conjures up a polluted landscape where 'this tank had been parked on his voice' while 'Manhattan weighed on his eyelid' and 'his tongue moved like a poisoned estuary' (p. 46).

Crow's attempt to recover Nature, his intended bride, began a movement towards biocentrism in Hughes's work that continued in major works of the mid-1970s, *Gaudete* (1977) and *Cave Birds* (1978). Carolyn Merchant argued that the replacement of animistic and organic attitudes towards Nature by mechanical models was for world ecology ' the most significant and far-reaching effect of the Scientific Revolution'.[23] For Merchant the Western attempt to dominate Nature as a utilitarian resource was indissolubly connected with the growth of male domination of women, and she hailed the new ecological awareness of today as working hand in hand with the feminist programme to see women as equals in human relationships that promote a holistic bond with society and Nature. *Gaudete* and *Cave Birds* paralleled the social and ecological goals of feminists, for in each case the culprit was the male rejection of Nature, and the resolutions concerned adopting a more biocentric vision that incorporated sexual equality and interdependence with Nature.

The voluntary celibacy of the Reverend Nicholas Lumb in *Gaudete* amounts to a refusal to grow, and his hallucinations of dead corpses and fertility rituals in the 'Prologue' presage his psyche's attempt to heal him in the central narrative, a surrealistic dream-world where his changeling double experiences erotic release and dissolution. The 'Epilogue' poems that follow, written by the newly-healed prelate, present a growth in awareness, a gradual process of reconciliation to a goddess of Nature that ends in an acceptance of her death-and-rebirth cycle and a mystical vision of worship. This goddess, familiar to those who have read the studies of Graves and

Neumann, is the animating principle of all of Nature and controls its organic cycles. The poems often achieve a deep humility in their own spare, quietly meditative way, a sense of subordination to the goddess that occasionally rises to an intense longing in 'Let your home/Be my home' (Poem XXVI).

The Lumb of the 'Epilogue' knows that he himself is the problem, and that he must 'rend to pieces' (Poem XVII) his own perceptions. He who perceives a 'useful-looking world' (Poem IV) with the analytic, anthropocentric ego is only 'half a man' (Poem I). He learns that his saviour is a she (Poem XXX) and that the axle of the cart that moves him is her 'needle/Through [his] brains' (Poem XXV). Unlike the conceptions of Nature as a passive, subordinate female that Merchant compiles from Western patriarchal culture, Lumb views his goddess as a combination of a powerful lioness (like the Hindu Devi) and a sky goddess (like the Egyptian Nut) that gives him a thumb or a dug to suck (Poem XXIII). In Poem XXXVI Lumb's sense of the primacy and superiority of this feminine goddess is so strong that he presents here in imagery that humanises and reverses the gender of the aloof Vishnu in the *Rig-Veda*, who created the world in three steps from the dust of his heel.[24] Lumb's goddess is definitely not an anthropocentric extension of male design or dominance. Here humans do not 'own' the Earth or the cycles of Nature; they are just one species among the myriad elements of a biocentric universe sustained by a nurturing female. The 'us' of the poem includes trees, river, flowers, sun, and humans *as equal* elements of the goddess's handiwork, and the humble persona recognises that these elements are 'nothing/But the fleeting warm pressure' of the goddess's 'footfall'.

Cave Birds, though a more introspective psychological drama, also progresses towards a biocentric vision. In her survey of how Western treatments of Nature through the ages have revealed links between conceptions of women and ecological practice, Merchant found that alchemical writings constituted one of the few sources where males and females achieved equal power on an earth conceived as a nurturing organic whole.[25] The callous, aloof male persona of *Cave Birds* embarks upon an alchemical journey to repair a crime against the feminine in Nature, as the substance of 'The plaintiff' and Hughes's BBC introductory comments revealed.[26] In 'The risen', at the end of the sequence, the alchemical transformation results in the emergence of a whole creature, acutely aware of the nourishing 'shell of earth' and conscious about how the 'dirt becomes God' as 'Each atom engraves' messages on his lens.

Hughes's subtitle for the Baskin drawing that accompanies 'The accused' indicated that his persona was a 'Tumbled Socratic Cock'. Nietzsche considered Socrates to be the forerunner of the scientific mind because of his confidence in rational analysis;[27] Hughes in other *Cave Birds* poems suggested that such confidence in abstractions promoted an egocentric insensitivity towards human suffering, the opposite of ecological interrelatedness. His BBC introductory comments also revealed that the persona's anxiety to understand his crime rationally, to restrict it to cause and effect, and to demonstrate his 'imbecile innocence' with grandiose concepts like 'Civilisation' and 'Sanity', are part of the problem.

A shamanistic journey to a psychic underworld in *Cave Birds* parallels an alchemical transformation where masculine and feminine elements within the protagonist – the *sponsus* and *sponsa* of alchemy – fuse into an androgynous whole in marriage. The narrator's court, judge and jury, as well as the healing feminine elements, a Jungian anima among them, are entirely within the self. The poems convey a belief that the psyche potentially has its own system of renewal and regulation that can foster a dynamic integration of self and world.

Throughout the poems the feminine helper appears in a receptive, nurturing aspect, even when depicted as an inquisitor who discovers the true problem. She is 'the one creature/Who never harmed any living thing' (p. 14) and always appears cloaked in the simple imagery of unadorned, organic Nature. When the persona surrenders his analytic ego willingly, 'He has conquered in earth's name' (p. 28), and when reborn he is delivered not to master Nature but to be nurtured by the equal brother-and-sisterhood of natural elements, a 'changed, unchangeable world/Of wind and of sun, of rock and water' (p. 44).

When *sponsus* and *sponsa* become an androgynous whole, the natural life-process resumes its movement. Where once the persona's world had died, renewal brings a sense of the ecological interrelatedness of microcosm and macrocosm where the persona experiences the Earth 'Rushing through the vast astonishment' (p. 52). 'Bride and groom lie hidden for three days', arguably the finest love poem Hughes has written, presents a true equality for the sexes as each cleanses and refurbishes the other's bodily organs.

Moortown Elegies (1978), *Remains of Elmet* (1979), and *River* (1983) are thoroughly biocentric sequences. The italicised line '*only birth matters'* near the end of 'Salmon Eggs', the concluding poem of *River*, aptly characterises the vision of all three works. In each the human persona is not the major focus of attention; he assists at more important and more central biocentric processes presented with a sacred reverence that in *Remains of Elmet* and *River* often achieves the paradoxically calm ecstasy of mysticism. Those who espouse a mystic reverence for Nature – Schweitzer, Berry and Snyder, among others – would find a kindred vision here. The substance of all three volumes is cognate with Aldo Leopold's belief that the integrity of the biotic community is paramount, and with J. Howard Moore's statement that in ecology *'the Life Process is the End – not man'*.[28]

Moortown Elegies relates Hughes's experiences as a farmhand on his Devon cattle-farm Moortown, purchased in 1972 and managed by his father-in-law Jack Orchard until his death in 1976. In the 1970s the farm contained about thirty beefcows and their calves, and one hundred and forty sheep. Here animals are no longer seen as analogues for the psychic energies in humans, but maintain their alien difference and integrity. When the persona does try to think anthropocentrically, events defeat the pretence, as in 'Roe-deer'. By deliberately restricting his poetic gaze to the limits of the actual encounter, Hughes refused poetic adornments that would have formalised the experiences into anthropocentric design and diluted their freshness.

Care and stewardship define the actions of the farmhands. If the cows want to muddy their field in the rain, so be it. If the ewes don't appreciate being herded into an iron-roofed shed in a snowstorm, the farm-hand presents their perspective without condescension. If he must force-feed dying calves and ewes for days, even if some obviously do not have the will to live, he does his task to the limit of his abilities. And if he must endure the exhausting tussle of dehorning, or slide his hand up a cow's hot birth tunnel, or even slice the throat of a lamb immovably trapped in the birth canal to save the ewe, he does what he can to save what life he can. The prime directive, always implied but never actually stated, is to act as fully in accord with the cycles of Nature as possible.

No sentimentality obscures the Darwinian necessities of the food-chain; without question the cattle are husbanded for human consumption. While it is true that world hunger could disappear if humans ate two meatless dinners per week (because it takes ten pounds of grain to produce one pound of beef), it is also true that the great majority of humans have been carnivores for hundreds of thousands of years, and will not suddenly become vegetarians. What matters ecologically is that wasteful habits are not condoned.

The distinction between necessity and waste contains an important corrective for anyone who assumes that Hughes's biocentric vision necessitates giving worms and vermin absolute equality. Hughes's position seems similar to that of Schweitzer, who handles disparities between his reverence for life and the obvious necessities of the food-chain by developing exactly this distinction between necessity and waste – a distinction that most tribal folklore within Hughes's reading also supports. Using animals as food sources is fine for Schweitzer and for Hughes as long as cultural values support a basic reverence for life and help develop sufficient moral conscience in humans to make careful distinctions concerning where necessity ends and waste begins. Vivisection is acceptable under humane conditions when the clear purpose of the research is to enhance life for all; in life-threatening circumstances of course humans have priority over animals, insects, and plants.[29] Hughes's biocentrism promotes a relative interspecies equality that functions most importantly as a corrective to the arrogant anthropocentrism that has placed global ecology in peril.

In *Remains of Elmet* the ecology of the Pennines, not the human observer, is the protagonist. A main theme concerns the hope that the decomposition cycle in the ecosystem will one day turn all evidence of the Industrial Revolution and its penurious culture into fertile soil for future renewal. One of the truths residing in what the ecologist Charles Elton dubbed the 'food-chain' is that the least sophisticated but most ubiquitous life forms are the most important for sustaining the pyramid. The food-chain would collapse without the bacteria and fungi that decompose waste and dead matter. In *Remains of Elmet* Hughes expresses the hope that the strong base of Nature's pyramid can outlast the ecologically unsound myths that direct contemporary Western culture.

Hughes wrote the *Elmet* poems after having seen the Fay Godwin photographs of his West Yorkshire childhood haunts that are included in the volume. Elmet, an old Celtic title for a large geographical area of West Yorkshire, became in Hughes's imagination a live ecological system that imprinted its landscape and weather upon all inhabitants. Hughes called Elmet 'a naturally-evolved local organism, like a giant protozoa, which is made up of all the earlier deposits and histories, animated in a single glance, an attitude, an inflection of speech'. The poems vividly realise Hughes's perception that

> The Calder Valley's eruption into modern history when it earned such titles as cradle of the industrial revolution in textiles, and cradle of the Chartist movement, and even, according to some, the cradle of the splitting of the atom, is now over. Geology and climate are reclaiming the primaeval gorge.[30]

Many *Elmet* poems emphasise the work of decomposers as the Earth reclaims and renews the spent labour of the Industrial Revolution. Here 'brave dreams and their mortgaged walls are let rot in the rain' and 'Heirloom bones are dumped into wet holes'. The receptive, nurturing Earth must process its spent creations: 'Before these chimneys can flower again/They must fall into the only future, into earth' (p. 14). The bodies of farmers and factory workers 'went into the enclosures/Like manure' (p. 33), while the purplish rays of moor light are 'swabbing the human shape from the freed stones' (p. 103).

The anthropocentric utilitarianism of Industrial Revolution culture caused an ecological disaster so severe that it is likened to the effects of a barbarian invasion (pp. 34, 90). The machine culture entrapped workers into lifetimes of somnambulistic machine-tending (p. 37). It spawned the 'railway station/That bled this valley to death' (p. 34), blackened stones with soot, and led to the aggressive repetition–compulsion behaviour that precipitated the First World War (pp. 13, 34). Long before 1914 this culture exhausted the physical and spiritual effort of many generations and sentenced hundreds of thousands to empty lifetimes and early graves. The workers could not appreciate Nature; even the Sunday release of football became a headache of anxiety as each moment 'collapsed that bit deeper/Towards Monday' and the return to soul-draining, repetitious labour.

Conversely, poems written from the perspective of the persona reveal an ability to appreciate the otherness of the moors, plants, rocks and trees in the landscape. Rocks testify to the endurance, the strong spine of the land. Even when Hughes uses the pathetic fallacy, it is to create a mode where he consents, like the Deep Ecologists, to the intrinsic worth of the elements. Outcrop rock becomes a cantor or 'a soft animal of peace' (pp. 44, 114). 'Heather' is not conscripted to human designs; it waits 'for the star-drift/Of the returning ice'. The high 'Moors', oblivious to human aspirations, 'are a stage for the performance of heaven./Any audience is incidental'. For Hughes the high moors always conveyed a feminine release and elation, a liberation from the constricting valley and its machine culture.[31] And trout, because they live free in an 'unspoiled, sacred world',[32] convey a magical sense of the pristine, mysterious otherness of Nature.

The environmentalist Paul Shepard maintained that to develop an ecological awareness in their readers, writers must convey 'a deep sense of engagement with the landscape, with profound connections to surroundings and to natural processes central to all life'. In such literature one experiences the self as 'constantly drawing on and influencing the surroundings, whose skin and behavior are soft zones contacting the world instead of excluding it'.[33] In Hughes's pellucid gaze, the ethereal lightness of his poetic line, and the simple and graceful, free-flowing imagery that is always busy linking humans to animals, landscape and skyscape, the great majority of *Elmet* poems convey exactly this sense of connectedness and deep participation in Nature. Nowhere is this more apparent than in 'Bridestones'. To experience Nature from the outcrop rock called 'Bridestones' is to experience how Nature encloses humans in a sacred marriage with its protective and nourishing second skin. The reader leaves touched by the sun and crowned with the wreath of weather, hills and stars.

In few works of Western literature is the reader so graced with a sense of the sacred in Nature as in *River*. Each poem glistens with what Berry and Schweitzer would call a reverence for life. From the 'precarious obstetrics' of humanly-assisted salmon-egg and milt clottings in 'The Morning Before Christmas', the fisherman persona embarks upon a quest to learn the ways of the coveted salmon, and gradually a spiritual dimension opens, culminating in a mystical consciousness of the oneness of Creation in 'Salmon Eggs', the final poem. The sequence celebrates ecological renewal in the hydrological cycle as well as the conservation and renewal of spiritual energy in the life-and-death cycle shared by all Nature. Nature is as alive and sentient as in Lovelock's Gaia hypothesis.

Each poem in *River* contains images of unspoiled Nature as delicate and riveting as the fox's 'touch-melted and refrozen dot-prints' in the opening poem. Instead of commandeering Nature to anthropocentric designs, the persona's gaze typically moves outward towards appreciating a biocentric life-process that is quite beyond

the comprehension of any individual. Many poems capture
Nature's energy so vividly that they approximate the animistic
beliefs of tribal societies, and this energy operates in ways that allow
each individual species of animal, bird or insect its own integrity.
The sea-trout's mystical absorption, the kingfisher's instantaneous
dive, the cormorant's singleness of purpose, the mink's inexhaust-
ible energy, the dartings of cock minnows, the eel's inwardness, the
damselfly's mating, the salmon's September leap, the otter's
stealthy departure – all are unique manifestations of a shared but
mysterious life-process, sparks of Nature's energy.

The persona observes that the sea-trout 'inhale unending. I share
it a little' (p. 94). Nature orchestrates an unending cycle of sustenance and energy transference – from the sun through the river to
the land and all dependent creatures. The persona most often functions as witness to mysterious biocentric events that forever draw
him out of his mean selfhood to merge with a process that is not
necessarily being performed for his express benefit. He is drawn by
the river-fetch into a state of absorbed curiosity and reverence for a
cosmic drama the scale and intracacy of which is often beyond
human comprehension, but endlessly fascinating. As the reader
vicariously feels the persona's absorption, he or she becomes
involved in the subjective process through which one experiences
deeply and intensely a connectedness between self and external
world, as in the process philosophy of Whitehead.

Conversely, when the persona self-consciously tries to anthropo-
morphise events into human terms, the result is usually an ironic
awkwardness or a reverse scrutiny from animals and landscape that
puts into question the entire analytic process, as in 'Whiteness' or
'Low Water.' The Earth is 'heedless' of human desires (p. 24);
humans are usually interlopers in a cosmic drama performed for the
general enhancement of life, but not for any particular private audience. The persona learns to conform to this view, with very biocentric consequences: the body of any individual of any species is
finally understood as simply an 'armature of energy' (p. 112), a
locus of forces shared by all species but ultimately inscrutable.

The fisherman persona stalks the salmon not for trophies, but to
learn their ways and what wisdom they may have to impart about
the cycle of life and death. He admires their loyalty to Nature and
their heroic, selfless patience. He also comes to know what the
salmon intuitively sense: that all must conform selflessly to cosmic
cycles that have never legitimised the arrogance of Western indi-

viduality. The salmon are loyal to a cosmic principle described in feminine terms as a nourishing, tireless river, a suprahuman force that has 'not once tasted death' (p. 118). Her power descends from the sun and through her hydrological cycle she 'will return stainless/For the delivery of this world' (p. 74). The fisherman throughout his quest displays a humility similar to Lynn White, Jr's description of St Francis, and a reverence for Nature akin to that of Native Americans, whose folklore echoes in poems such as 'The Merry Mink' and 'Creation of Fishes'.

Hughes articulates the core of his deeply biocentric vision in 'That Morning' and 'Go Fishing', poems that suggest Shepard's 'deep sense of engagement' with Nature and landscape. The title 'That Morning' obliquely alludes to Mircea Eliade's *illud tempore*, his favourite expression for the world-wide psychological drive of tribal cultures to erase profane history and connect with a paradisal Source inhabiting Creation. The poem recounts an experience on a 1980 Alaskan fishing trip when Hughes and his son Nicholas waded into a stream so crammed with salmon that they lost their 'doubting thought' and became so at-one with Nature that bears swam nearby and leisurely ate salmon from their talons. One manifestation of Eliade's *illud tempore* experience is the return to the paradisial unity with animals and with all creation that tribal humans believed existed before exile into profane historical time.[34]

'Go Fishing' is one of the most exquisite capturings of the psychological process through which one can become very deeply absorbed in Nature's ecological cycles. It suggests that by at least temporarily divesting oneself of the mean ego and opening the self to the river's cleansing action, one can let the mud and river-water dissolve and then heal the self. Here the individual becomes one with the water, 'as if this flow were all plasm healing'. This prepares the reader for a mystical moment of unity with the life-process in the final poem, 'Salmon Eggs', where the persona's 'eyes forget me' – the limited 'me' of selfhood – and a moment of spiritual enlargement follows, a consciousness that '*Only birth matters*'.

Since Hughes became Poet Laureate in 1984, his writing time has been compromised by personal appearances and an increased volume of mail. Yet in recent collections his biocentric vision remains strong and unwavering. The poems of *Flowers and Insects* (1986), for instance, do not relegate Nature to a function of human perception, as in Part I of *Wodwo*. Instead the humble inquiry into the survival struggles of Nature's non-human species continues. The poems express intimate connections between human personae and non-human species, most often to reveal a community of joy, suffering and mortality without condescension or sentimentality.

'Tern', 'Nightjar' and 'Saint's Island' present the intimate symbiosis of bird or insect with the ecology of its environment. The tern's environment has so fine-tuned his survival expertise that one might consider this bird the ocean's utterance. The tern is a 'blood-tipped harpoon' for capturing sand-eel; the ocean breakers have ground this harpoon sharp and the shore winds have honed and polished it to perfection. The owl in 'Nightjar' is so inseparable from his night-time environment that he all but vanishes when the moon wanes, at which time he 'yawns dawn/And sleeps bark'.

The mayflies' ten-billion-year-old vision of ecstatic participation in the sun's energy receives its yearly one-day satisfaction in 'Saint's Island'. Their vision of union with the sun's energy both 'nourishes' and 'consumes' them, for once they erupt from the mud they do not feed. They become dervishes 'Drunk with God', and they accept the one-day term of their spiritual fulfilment without evasion. After developing in mud for a year they do their jig and reel for one day and die. In visionary abandon they 'soar out of themselves' and 'fall through themselves'. Though the fisherman persona who views the mayflies' weird intensity initially wonders what worthwhile purpose this grotesque yearly display can possibly fulfil, by the end of the poem he feels that the mayflies' intense absorption in their brief moment of life outfaces the stares of their human observers. Biocentrism displaces anthropocentrism, and the poem ends with the persona wondering 'What are we doing on earth?' As the wind carries the mayflies towards the ocean, the persona reflects upon the pecking order in the food-chain: the trout wait for the mayflies, and the humans wait for the trout. But the mayflies do not wait; drunk with the sun's energy, their total absorption in their dance seems superior to the passive observation of humans.

Wolfwatching (1989) is structured to reveal defects in anthropocentric assumptions concerning animals and the environment. The phrase 'no man's land' appears twice in the volume (pp. 4, 23) and its meaning is less concerned with warfare than with an atrophy of perception, an inability to connect with the environment that is the result of the psychological massage of Industrial Revolution culture. *Elmet*-type poems displaying an ecological no-man's land alternate with poems where animals are so instinctively rooted to the environment and comfortable in it that they often appear superior to humans. As Hughes carefully juxtaposes these two themes through-out *Wolfwatching*, he reverses the optimism of *Remains of Elmet* and indicts Western culture as a disease that is ruining planetary ecology.

The *Elmet*-type poems of *Wolfwatching* offer painful personal glimpses of Hughes interacting with parents and relatives who have been spiritually immobilised by the legacy of their violent culture. Hughes's father William lives in a perpetual coma of silent forget-fulness, his brain so anaesthetised by the First World War and his spirit so broken that he is unwilling to discuss his wartime experi-ences with his son. Hughes's mother breaks unprovoked into sud-den and silent sobs in her sewing room (p. 17). Her vision has been so tainted that even local folklore becomes contaminated by the detritus of Industrial Revolution culture. The 'Leaf Mould' that in *Remains of Elmet* conveyed the hope for a better future generates folklore in *Wolfwatching*, where on family hikes every ant's egg becomes a weaver's shuttle, every pine needle a thread-end for a sewing machine (p. 33). Hughes's uncle Walter rehearses the war endlessly as an evil curse that he cannot transcend. Living in his dotage on tranquillisers and Madeira, his vision does not 'connect' at all with his environment: 'Nothing will connect' (p. 40) in this no-man's land. Walt's helpless and hopeless 'aye' masks his incompre-hension. Though a successful garment-factory owner, he is so obsessed by how truncated and unfulfilled his life has been since the war that he is eyeless in his environment.

Wolfwatching begins, however, with a sparrow-hawk and ends with a dove. These natural symbols of precise vision and hope retain their import in the design of Hughes's biocentric universe. In 'A Sparrow Hawk', the opening poem, the hawk's eyes are 'wired direct/To the nuclear core' of the sun's energy. The sun, the most important element in any ecosystem and the most prominent sym-bol in Hughes's poetry since the *Gaudete* 'Epilogue', infuses its energy to activate a kindred energy in all creatures: it 'whets the eyebeam' of humans with its power before 'your first thought' occurs.

'Little Whale Song' offers a model of ecological integration with the environment that parallels the thinking of environmentalists and feminists. In their quests for a less anthropocentric world, the feminists Joan McIntyre and Elizabeth Dodson Gray point to the brain-size and intellectual powers of cetaceans as evidence that humans are superior not by virtue of their intellectual capacity, but only because of their agile, opposable thumbs – devices most suited for a questionable technological grasp and ownership of Nature. Gray assembles material from McIntyre's collection of cetacean scholarship, *Mind in the Waters*, towards this end. She reprints, for instance, Carl Sagan's observation that half-hour whale songs, repeated virtually exactly, contain as many information bits as Homer's *Odyssey*. Gray also reprints evidence compiled by McIntyre from studies by scientists such as Paul Sprong and John Lily about cetacean sonar and echo location, the size and complexity of their brains, as well as evidence of their cooperative communal bonding and sanguine dispositions, to suggest that anthropocentric values and human language offer very narrow and problematic ways of comprehending life on our planet.[35]

Hughes's 'Little Whale Song' covers just as much ground with a radiant simplicity and economy. The poem celebrates the ability of whales to be 'perfectly tuned receivers and perceivers' of their environment. Because they enfold the environment into themselves with each tail-stroke, whales seem to exemplify definitions of the self as a subjective synthesiser of Whiteheadian process. Their contentment, joy and peace make them fitting models of ecologically responsible behaviour and examples that question the anthropocentric biases of Western individualism. Hughes also builds into the poem an element of environmental activism by alluding obliquely to the slaughter of cetaceans through the concluding tragic metaphor of whales as a Royal House experiencing 'The most terrible fall'.

'The Black Rhino' is the most ecologically activist poem in *Wolfwatching* – not because of the end-note about the facts of the slaughter of rhinos for Oriental medicine and aphrodisiacs or for the macho virility rites of Yemenite males, but because of the terrifying statement in the poem that the rhino has 'blundered somehow into man's phantasmagoria, and cannot get out'. A central insight of Bill McKibben's *The End of Nature* is that where Nature once existed independently of humans, our ability to change Nature through acid rain, global warming and genetic engineering has made Nature a 'subset of human activity'. We have become God's rival in our ability to influence climate and genetic development, and in our capacity to destroy creation. Though 'The Black Rhino' does not discuss these specific subjects, Hughes concurs with McKibben to the extent that humans, with their technological powers, have become in some ways stronger than Nature.[36] Whatever in the environment captures the desire of humans, or blunders into the 'phantasma-goria' of human consciousness, becomes infected, diseased – victim-ised by the 'lethal whim' and anthropocentric 'delusions of man'. Hughes packs a powerful moral punch in the rhino's statement that humans are the crime.

McKibben, writing in 1989, the same year as Nash, suggests in his conclusion a similar solution: we must change our way of thinking and adopt a more biocentric view before we destroy the entire planet. Hughes in his poetry has been suggesting such a change for the past twenty years. Reverence for the nurturing powers of organic Nature and respect for the intrinsic worth of all of Nature's creations have led Hughes to adopt a biocentric vision. Although the wolf in the title poem of *Wolfwatching* is as victimised as the rhino by 'man's phantasmagoria', the concluding poem, 'A Dove', indicates that Hughes continues to hope that humans will develop an ecological perspective. True to the hint in his Nicholson review, Hughes is still articulating his vision of the 'sacred' interdependence of every cell and the 'soul-state of the new world'. His poetry, a beacon directing us towards ecological and spiritual renewal, is vitally important for the survival of our planet.

Notes

1.   Hughes, Ted, 'The Environmental Revolution', review of *The Environmental Revolution* by Max Nicholson, *Your Environment* 3 (Summer 1970), pp. 81–3. A shorter version appeared in *The Spectator*, 21 March 1970, pp. 378–9. Nicholson was Director-General of the British Nature Conservancy from 1952 to 1966.

2.   Nash, Roderick Frazier, *The Rights of Nature: A History of Environmental Ethics* (University of Wisconsin Press, Madison, 1989), p. 7. See Paul R. Ehrlich and Anne H. Ehrlich, *The Population Explosion* (Simon and Schuster, New York, 1990), for exhaustive statistical data on the present environmental crisis compiled by a reputable ecologist.

3.   Alvarez, A. *The Savage God* (Random House, New York 1971), p. 29.

4.   Nash, p. 90 ff.

5.   White, Lynn Jr, 'The Historical Roots of Our Ecologic Crisis', *Science* 155 (March 1967), pp. 1203–7. Of course Christianity is not the only religion to have contributed to environmental degradation, nor are Christians the only humans whose fallibility leads to greed and ambition. For a solid response to White, see Robert H. Ayers, 'Christian Realism and Environmental Ethics', in Eugene C. Hargrove (ed.), *Religion and Environmental Crisis* (University of Georgia Press, Athens, 1986), pp. 154–71.

6. Merchant, Carolyn, *The Death of Nature: Women, Ecology, and the Scientific Revolution* (Harper & Row, New York, 1980), pp. 73–4, 155, 164–73; Gray, Elizabeth Dodson, *Why the Green Nigger?* (Roundtable Press, Wellesley, Massachusetts, 1979), pp. 3ff.

7. Commoner, Barry, *Making Peace with the Planet* (Pantheon, New York, 1990), pp. 211–43.

8. See discussion in Nash, pp. 95–108.

9. McDaniel, Jay, 'Christianity and the Need for New Vision', *Religion and Environmental Crisis*, pp. 188–212, esp. 207.

10. Merchant, pp. 2–8. See also Gray, Elizabeth Dodson, *Patriarchy as a Conceptual Trap* (Roundtable Press, Wellesley, Massachusetts, 1982), pp. 52–6; Gilligan, Carol, *In a Different Voice: Psychological Theory and Woman's Development* (Harvard University Press, Cambridge, Massachusetts, 1982), pp. 8–9, 79, 105; Cheney, Jim, 'Eco-Feminism and Deep Ecology', *Environmental Ethics*, 9 (Summer 1987), pp. 115–45.

11. This lengthy list begins with late-eighteenth-century writers such as Linnaeus, Gilbert White and Jeremy Bentham, and includes Darwin, Thoreau, Henry S. Salt, Aldo Leopold, and a host of others that culminate in Rachel Carson and Tom Regan. Yet Donald Worster reminds us that before 1920 the assumptions of a progressive yet entirely anthropocentric utilitarianism guided most animal rights thinking. See Worster, Donald, *Nature's Economy: the Roots of Ecology* (Anchor, New York, 1979), p. 256.

12. Tansley, Arthur G., 'The Use and Abuse of Vegetal Concepts and Terms', *Ecology*, 16, No. 3 (July 1935), pp. 284–307; Odum, Eugene P., 'Environmental Ethic and the Attitude Revolution', in Wm T. Blackstone (ed.) *Philosophy and Environmental Crisis*, (University of Georgia Press, Athens, 1974), pp. 10 -15.

13. Lovelock, James E., *Gaia* (Oxford University Press, New York, 1979); *The Ages of Gaia* (W. W. Norton, New York, 1988).

14. See Naess, Arne, *Ecology, Community and Lifestyle* (Cambridge University Press, Cambridge, 1987); Bill Devall and George Sessions (eds), *Deep Ecology* (G. M. Smith, Salt Lake City, Utah, 1985).

15. Leopold, Aldo, *A Sand County Almanac* (Oxford University Press, New York, 1949), pp. 201–26.

16. Moore, John Howard, *The Universal Kinship* (Bell & Sons, London, 1906), p. 324.

17. See Snyder, Gary, *Earth House Hold* (New Directions, New York, 1969); *Turtle Island* (New Directions, New York, 1974).

18. Roszak, Theodore, *The Making of a Counter Culture* (Doubleday, New York, 1969), pp. 239–68.

19. Berry, Thomas, *The Dream of the Earth* (Sierra Club, San Francisco, 1988), pp. 48–9.

20. Schweitzer, Albert, *Reverence for Life*, trans. Reginald H. Fuller (Harper & Row, New York, 1969), pp. 108–17. See also note 35.

21. Quotations from the poetry of Ted Hughes derive from the British Faber and Faber first editions, except for *Crow*, where I follow the more complete second Faber edition (1972). Page numbers in parenthesis are added when poem titles are omitted.

22. Hughes, Ted, 'Superstitions,' review of *Astrology* by Louis MacNiece and *Ghost and Divining Rod*, by T. C. Lethbridge, in *New Statesman*, 2 October 1964, p. 500.

23. Merchant, p. 125.

24. For the *Rig-Veda* verses see Wilkins, W. J., *Hindu Mythology: Vedic and Puranic*, 2nd edn (1900; repr. Curzon Press, London, 1973), p. 125.

25. Merchant, pp. 19–20.

26. Hughes, Ted, 'Cave Birds', BBC Radio 3, 23 June 1975, produced by George MacBeth.

27. Nietzsche, Friedrich, *The Birth of Tragedy and the Genealogy of Morals*, trans. Francis Golffing (Doubleday, New York, 1956), pp. 93–4. For a complete list of Hughes's titles to Leonard Baskin's *Cave Birds* drawings, see Sagar, Keith, *The Art of Ted Hughes*, 2nd edn (Cambridge University Press, Cambridge, 1978), pp. 243–4.

28. See note 16.

29. Schweitzer, A., *Out of My Life and Thought: An Autobiography*, trans. C. T. Campion (1933; rev. Holt, Rinehart and Winston, New York, 1949), pp. 158–61, 233–4; *The Philosophy of Civilisation*, trans. C. T. Campion (1949; rpt University Presses of Florida, Tallahassee, 1981), p. 318.

30. Hughes, Ted, 'Elmet', BBC Radio 3, 3 May 1980, produced by Frazer Steel.

31. Hughes, 'The Rock', BBC Home Service, 11 September 1963.

32. See note 30.

33. Shepard, Paul, 'Introduction: Ecology and Man – A Viewpoint', in Shepard and Daniel McKinley (eds), *The Subversive Science* (Houghton Mifflin, Boston, 1969), p. 5.

34. Eliade, Mircea, *Shamanism*, trans. Willard R. Trask (Princeton University Press, Princeton, 1964), pp. 89–98. Hughes reviewed this book: see Hughes, Ted, 'Secret Ecstasies', in *The Listener*, 29 October 1964, pp. 677–8.

35. Gray, *Why the Green Nigger?*, pp. 9–20. See also Joan McIntyre (ed.), *Mind in the Waters: A Book to Celebrate the Consciousness of Whales and Dolphins* (Charles Scribner's Sons, New York, 1974).

36. McKibben, Bill, *The End of Nature* (Random House, New York, 1989), pp. 58, 77–8, 89.

Select Bibliography

WORKS BY TED HUGHES

Poetry

(Unless otherwise stated all titles are published by Faber and Faber,
London, and Harper and Row, New York)

The Hawk in the Rain (1957)
Lupercal (1960)
Recklings (Turret Press, London) (1966)
Wodwo (1967)
Crow (1970)
Season Songs (US edn Viking, New York) (1976)
Gaudete (1977)
Cave Birds (1978)
Orts (Rainbow Press) (1978)
Remains of Elmet (1979)
Moortown (1979)
Under the North Star (US edn Viking, New York) (1981)
Selected Poems (1982)
River (1983)
What is the Truth? (1984)
Flowers and Insects (US edn Knopf, New York) (1986)

See also the thirty uncollected poems in Sagar's *The Achievement of Ted
Hughes* (below).

Prose

'Context', in *London Magazine*, February 1962.
'The Rock', in *Writers on Themselves* (BBC, London, 1964).
'Secret Ecstasies' (review of Eliade's *Shamanism*), in *The Listener*, 29 October
1964.
Poetry in the Making (Faber & Faber, London, 1967).
Selected Poems of Keith Douglas (Faber & Faber, London, 1968).
A Choice of Emily Dickinson's Verse (Faber & Faber, London, 1968).

Introduction to *Vasko Popa: Selected Poems* (Penguin, Harmondsworth, 1969); extended in *Vasko Popa: Collected Poems* (Carcanet, Manchester, 1978).
'Myth and Education I' in *Children's Literature in Education* (1970).
'The Environmental Revolution' in *Your Environment* I (Summer 1970).
A Choice Of Shakespeare's Verse (Faber & Faber, London, 1971)
'Myth and Education II' in Fox, (ed.) *Writers, Critics and Children* (Heinemann, Oxford, 1976).
Selected Poems of Janos Pilinszky (Carcanet, Manchester, 1976); reprinted with minor revisions as the *The Desert of Love* (Anvil, London, 1989)
Foreword to Fairfax and Moat, *The Way To Write* (Elm Tree Books, London, 1981).
'The Hanged Man and the Dragonfly' in *The Complete Prints of Leonard Baskin* (Little, Brown and Co., London, 1984)
Introduction to *Keith Douglas: The Complete Poems* (Oxford University Press, Oxford, 1987).

See also the two interviews and excerpts from Hughes's critical writings collected in Faas (below).

BIBLIOGRAPHY

Sagar, Keith and Tabor, Stephen, *Ted Hughes: A Bibliography 1946–1980* (Mansell, London, 1983).

CRITICAL STUDIES

Bishop, Nicholas, *Re-making Poetry: Ted Hughes and a New Critical Psychology* (Harvester Wheatsheaf, Hemel Hempstead, 1991).
Faas, Ekbert, *Ted Hughes: The Unaccommodated Universe* (Black Sparrow Press, Santa Barbara, 1980).
Gifford, Terry, and Roberts, Neil, *Ted Hughes: A Critical Study* (Faber & Faber, London, 1981).
Hirschberg, Stuart, *Myth in the Poetry of Ted Hughes* (Barnes and Noble, 1981).
Robinson, *Ted Hughes as Shepherd of Being* (Macmillan, London, 1989).
Sagar, Keith, *The Art of Ted Hughes* (Cambridge University Press, Cambridge, 1975; extended edn 1978).
Sagar, Keith, (ed.), *The Achievement of Ted Hughes* (Manchester University Press, Manchester, 1983).
Scigaj, Leonard M., *The Poetry of Ted Hughes* (University of Iowa Press, Iowa, 1986).
Scicaj, Leonard M., *Ted Hughes* (Twayne, Boston, 1991).
Scicaj, Leonard M. (ed.), *Critical Essays on Ted Hughes* (G. K. Hall, New York, 1992).
West, Thomas, *Ted Hughes* (Methuen, London, 1985).

Index of Works by Ted Hughes

General Index